Business Protocol:

Contemporary American Practice

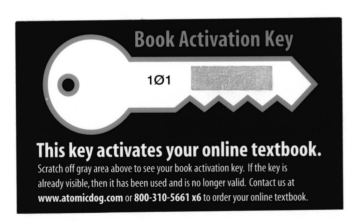

Book Activation Key

1Ø1

This key activates your online textbook.

Scratch off gray area above to see your book activation key. If the key is already visible, then it has been used and is no longer valid. Contact us at **www.atomicdog.com** or **800-310-5661 x6** to order your online textbook.

Business Protocol:

Contemporary American Practice

David Robinson
University of California, Berkeley

Cincinnati, OH
www.atomicdog.com

The body type in this book is set in Minion.
The display heads are set in Frutiger.

ISBN 1-931442-91-6

Library of Congress Control Number: 2002094845

Printed in the United States of America by Atomic Dog Publishing, 1203 Main Street, Third Floor, Cincinnati, OH 45202.

10 9 8 7 6 5 4 3 2 1

Contents

Chapter 1

Chapter 2

Chapter 3

Phone, Voice Mail, and Phone Conferencing   29

Chapter 4

Understanding e-mail   45

Chapter 5

Letters, Memos, and Reports   59

Chapter 6

Effective Presentations   81

Chapter 7

Rules for Group Presentations 107

Chapter 8

Business Dining 117

Chapter 9

Social Customs 133

Chapter 10

Bodily Fluids and Functions   153

Chapter 11

Looking the Part: What to Wear   163

Chapter 12

Recruiting   177

Chapter 13

Interviewing and the Hiring Process 197

Chapter 14

On the Job   221

Welcome

Protocol means more than reviewing honor guards

Business Success Depends on Understanding Protocol

Imagine a scene in the cafeteria of a large company. The firm's newest recruit catches the eye of someone he recognizes from the firm's brochures as the CEO. There's a long pause—an awkward moment. The CEO isn't sure whether this person is a visitor, an applicant, or an employee. The new recruit doesn't quite know what to say. At this moment, both people have the same duty—and that is to make the other person's job easy. If both the CEO and the recruit have a basic knowledge of business protocol, the chance meeting can be pleasant for both.

What Is the Meaning of "Protocol"?

When you think about the word "protocol," you may have an image of uniformed ambassadors bowing and using flowery language to address an ancient potentate. But protocol doesn't apply just to the diplomatic corps in long-ago times. In every business situation in every country in the world, there are unspoken rules of conduct that determine how people expect one another to behave. Just as Woody Allen said that time is Nature's way of keeping everything from happening at once, you could say that protocol is the way we limit an infinite range of human activities to some reasonably predictable set of behaviors.

In this book, we use the words "business protocol" to include some aspects of business communication and the parts of etiquette that relate to professional life. It's easy to scoff at etiquette as a prissy set of rules that apply to society matrons (is it permissible to send a thank-you note by e-mail?). However, as Judith Martin (who writes wonderfully entertaining and insightful columns under the byline "Miss Manners") says, etiquette is just a set of rules that enable us to live together without killing one another. All of us have experienced a brief moment of rage at a co-worker, and the passing thought, "Why, I'd like to kill that . . ."—but we don't.

There is a dark side to protocol. Lapses in protocol often signal who is a stranger to a group. Such lapses served a useful function in prehistoric times when it might be helpful to know who really belonged to a tribe, but now that we don't operate a tribal society, making newcomers feel out of place can be a detriment to effective working relationships. Studying business protocol is frankly a good investment in your personal advancement.

In the new century, learning business protocol in the US is particularly difficult, not least because we see very rapid changes in acceptable behavior. For example, in just the last few years, even the most staid and traditional Wall Street firms have adopted "business casual" attire and no longer require employees to wear suits. But the precise meaning of "business casual" is hard to define and certainly varies from one firm to another. As a retailer of business suits says in TV commercials: "The rules have changed . . . but there are still rules."

Not "Stupid"—Just "Different"

Whenever you make a serious effort to study the culture or language of another society, you'll come up with a rule of protocol or grammar that strikes you as "stupid." Why do they do it that way—don't they know it's wrong? Soup is a good example. In Asian meals, soup is often one of the last courses served. But in European dining, it invariably comes at the beginning of the meal. There's no reason why either is right or wrong— the cultural habits are just different. So if you read about something in this book and wonder why it's done that way, you may have to accept that there's probably no good reason. Differences between cultures are rarely stupid—they are just different.

Business Life in the "Dominant Culture"

The United States, with less than 5 percent of the world's population, contributes almost a quarter of the world's economic output. Simply put, American firms are very good at what they do. People come from all over the world to study at American business schools and, perhaps more importantly, some of the brightest, best, most hard-working individuals in the world come to the US to work for American firms.

Many things about American culture seem ugly to people arriving from other countries: Public spaces are often dirty, advertising signs are garish, and there seem to be more beggars on the streets of the cities than in the poorest countries in the world. And when American business people go abroad, they are often seen as impatient and demanding, and they are often spectacularly ignorant of other countries' cultures and customs. In this book, we approach American business culture from a humanist point of view, rather than a rule-bound authoritarian system. The goal is to help people work well together (see Box W-1).

Despite all these misgivings, there is an admiration for the American approach to business. It's energetic, practical, and pragmatic. Decisions are made according to the profit motive, not family ties. Promotion is according to merit, not social class or longevity. US corporations have a notoriously "flat" hierarchy with little bureaucracy and few "layers of government," so new ideas are rapidly embraced. Sometimes Americans traveling abroad are seen as "pushy," but they are more often highly regarded for their interpersonal warmth, enthusiasm, and openness. Although we can't say that corruption is non-existent, when it's discovered, it's severely punished and the incidents are relatively rare. Strangers do business with one another with full trust, and businesspeople interact with many government agencies with the expectation that the rule of law will be followed and administrators' decisions will be fair, equitable, and just.

To an outsider coming from another county, US business appears to have no structure, and it's hard to see how companies can function in an apparent state of anarchy. Chief executive officers (CEOs) of large corporations—some of the richest people in the world—routinely give interviews humbly dressed in a T-shirt and jeans. People don't seem to stand on ceremony, and it appears as if there is no code of behavior at all. The lowliest summer intern can greet the company president in the firm's cafeteria with a cheerful, "Hi, Larry!" and the president is likely to reply, "Let's go jogging some time!"

Box W-1

The Fundamental Rule of Etiquette

I n business you have but one job: to make it easy for other people to do their jobs. You can do this by putting yourself into their shoes. If you are at a business lunch, and your waiter comes out of the kitchen with a tray loaded with dinners for another table, it's not a good time to say, "I need more water here!"

But effective etiquette means more than the "Golden Rule" (treat others as you would wish to be treated yourself). Suppose you are taking a business trip that involves a connection between two flights. Your first flight is delayed and you miss the second flight. The Golden Rule would teach you that you shouldn't approach the desk clerk with a tirade like this: "I don't know how you people can be running an airline—you're *always* late." After all, it's not the agent's fault the first flight was late, and at this point, there's not much she can do about that. But she can work hard to find you a seat on the next flight out to your destination. Applying the fundamental rule of etiquette, imagine how the clerk will help you. She'll have to pull up your record on the computer and then look at alternative flights to try to find you a seat. With that in mind, you approach the desk with your ticket out and folded to show your name and original flights. "Good morning, my name is Abraham Sizer, and I need your help. I just came in on Flight 1472, and it was too late to make my connection. I need to get to Cincinnati. Can you re-book me?" This is how some people get upgraded to first class on the next flight out when others have to wait for hours for a coach class seat. Etiquette isn't just being nice— it helps get business done.

Like all rules, the Fundamental Rule has a corollary: When someone else shows a lapse of etiquette, apply generous amounts of forgiveness. Suppose you're at a business meeting and you join a conversation involving one of your subordinates. If your colleague fails to introduce you to the other person, you can introduce yourself. Helping other people overcome their lapses involves two parts: First, you must take responsibility yourself for making the situation work smoothly. Second, forgiveness implies forgetting. Don't brood on other people's lack of courtesy— show them by example how to do things better.

For all the apparent casualness, however, US business does indeed have its own protocol, its own unspoken rules.

A Practical Approach to Business Protocol

This book is written for people who are new to business in the United States—either because they are young and are in business school or college, or because they have recently arrived in the US. As you gain practical experience about business protocol in the US, you may observe substantial regional variations—it's a big country! But this book aims for a "middle American" approach. That is to say, the chapters don't try to define the routines of business in the American heartland of Kansas and Missouri, but rather this book sets out the customs and behaviors that would most likely be seen as "acceptable" in most business settings across the US.

Protocol makes life easier. Mastering the rules or protocol will put you at ease in any business setting and enhance your professional success.

Please note: we don't want you getting lost as you move between the Web and print formats, so we numbered the primary heads and subheads in each chapter the same. For example, the first primary head in Chapter 9 is labeled 9-1, the second primary head in this chapter is labeled 9-2, and so on. The subheads build from the designation of their corresponding primary head: 9-1a, 9-1b, etc.

The numbering system is designed to make moving between the online and print versions as seamless as possible. So if your instructor tells you to read the material in 2-3 and 2-4 for tomorrow's assignment, you'll know that the information appears in Chapter 2 of both the Web and print versions of the text, and you can then choose the best way for you to complete the assignment.

Finally, next to a number of figures and tables in the print version of the text, you will see an icon similar to the ones on the left. These icons indicate that this figure or table in the online version of the text is interactive in a way that applies, illustrates, or reinforces the concept.

About the Author

David Robinson is Lecturer in Marketing at the University of California, Berkeley, and has taught at Stanford University, the University of San Francisco, and Santa Clara University.

Every year more that 1,000 students take his Principles of Business class at UC–Berkeley, and running the class is a good opportunity for him to practice his interest in service operations.

Each summer Dr. Robinson takes a group of students on a Travel Study to the People's Republic of China. Observing intercultural differences in behavior led him to write about American practices that people take for granted.

Acknowledgments

Donny Chia first suggested the need for a book to bridge etiquette and business communication, and I'm grateful to him for the suggestion. Readers who are familiar with the writings of Edward P. Bailey, Jr., will see that I'm indebted to his work on Plain English. Over the years, I've learned most about etiquette from the commonsense approach of Judith Martin (who writes under the name "Miss Manners").

Jill Steinbruegge and Victoria Whetstone read and commented on drafts of the manuscript. I'm grateful to Kendra Leonard, my most thoughtful editor.

Finally, I'd like to express my gratitude to my students at the University of California, Berkeley, who have asked good questions, challenged my thinking, and kept me up-to-date.

David Robinson

Chapter 1

Introductions

Key Terms

Cultural norms	Non-verbal communication	Suffix

O u t l i n e

Confident introductions demonstrate your maturity

Two job candidates sit nervously in an outer office, waiting for an interview. A smartly dressed young woman enters the room, and the candidates aren't sure whether the new person is a secretary, another candidate, or the executive who will be the decision-maker for the job. One candidate stands up, makes eye contact with the newcomer, and extends his right hand.

"Hi. I'm Harry Smith, and I'm here for a 3 o'clock with Leslie Stein."

"Good! I'm Leslie. I'll be interviewing you. Nice to meet you."

Trivially simple, right? But the other candidate has just lost the critical opportunity to make a positive first impression.

So why do so many people overlook the chance to introduce themselves? We would all agree that there's a sense of awkwardness when we're in a business situation and we don't know exactly who's who. And yet we often hold back.

Perhaps this reserve comes from a very formal (and outdated) type of English etiquette in which it was considered brash and impolite to ever introduce oneself.

1-1 The First Rule

You can never introduce yourself too often.

Some people's reluctance to introduce themselves comes from shyness. But often people hold back because they're worried about seeming pushy. Or perhaps announcing your name signals that you think the other person isn't expecting you or has forgotten you. But there's no harm in a gentle reminder. A great example worth watching is actor Tim Robbins playing Griffin Mill in the movie *The Player*. Robbins plays the part of a Hollywood movie studio executive, and in each scene he always introduces himself (using first and last name) to all the famous actors who come across his path.

When you've met someone before, an immediate, simple restatement of your name—"Hi, Tom Studebaker"— could never cause offense. And if you miss that first moment, reminding the other party of your name becomes increasingly more difficult.

If you get stuck in a conversation in which you missed that first opportunity, though, and it becomes increasingly obvious that the other person is searching for your name, it's polite to help him or her out. Saying

> "I should've told you; I'm Margaret Thatcher."

puts the other person on the spot and implies that he or she made an error in not remembering you. The nice way out of this situation is to imply that the person probably does remember part of your name but—for good reason—doesn't remember the other part. For example,

> "Oh, I should've told you; my name's Margaret *Thatcher*, since I married Dennis."

Or, using the context of a mutual colleague:

> "I'm not sure Harry gave you my first name when he said I'd be working on your account. . . . I'm *Dennis* Thatcher."

Or perhaps an e-mail or phone identification:

> "My e-mail is the same: dennis.thatcher@conservative.org."

> "Just ask for Dennis Thatcher at the front desk."

1-2 Cultural Norms

Americans are friendly, outgoing people. Although they respect hierarchies and give deference to superiors, they usually choose a decidedly casual level of formality in most business interactions. The chief executive officer (CEO) of a large corporation will most likely greet a lowly salesman with "Call me Bill."

Of course, this type of behavior isn't true all over the world. Every society has its own **cultural norms.** An exaggerated stereotype of the rule for introductions in English upper class society is that one could never introduce oneself. That is why characters in Victorian novels are always begging their hostess at a social function to make an introduction. There is an old joke that, in England, it is *occasionally* permitted to introduce yourself, say if you're stuck in an elevator for more than 24 hours. At the end of the second day, you stiffly extend your hand, with these words: "Permit me to introduce myself. My name is Johnson." (Note, not "Tom" or even "Tom Johnson.")

But Americans like action and are very egalitarian. Successful businesspeople are comfortable introducing themselves. The following rules show how to make introductions correctly:

1. If you're expected for an appointment, always announce yourself by name: "My name is Jaime Pineda, and I'm here to meet Ms. Lee in purchasing." It's impolite to ask for the other party without giving your name too.

2. Never refer to yourself by a title ("Mr.," "Mrs.," or "Ms."). Because "Mr." is an *honorific,* other people can use it about you, but you shouldn't say, "I'm Mr. Pineda." "I'm Jaime Pineda" and "My name is Pineda" (for example, on arriving at a rental car counter) are acceptable forms.

3. Whenever possible, repeat your name in a way that helps people with unusual pronunciations or spellings:

   "I'm Celia Johnston—that's John*ston* with a 't.'"

   "I'm Tom 'Shevorsky'—that's spelled 'Przeworsky.'"

4. Speak almost artificially slowly and distinctly. Your name is very familiar to you but may be hard for someone from a different ethnic or cultural background to understand at first hearing.

1-3 Non-Verbal Communication

Although we think about spoken and written words when we use the term "communication," we form a lot of impressions of other people in social contexts from "**non-verbal communication.**" This means how people stand and sit, how they use gestures, and whether they touch one another. In US business situations most people begin and end a meeting by extending their right hands for a handshake. The handshake is immediate, firm, and brief. It's never wrong to extend your hand first (see Figure 1-1).

There's a range of style in handshakes. Some people routinely use the left hand to also grab your right shoulder or upper arm while shaking hands. Although this style of handshake may be uncomfortable for

Figure 1-1 Most American businesspeople are accustomed to being greeted by a handshake, rather than a kiss. Americans expect an easy smile and good eye contact upon meeting someone.
AP/WIDE WORLD PHOTOS

you, not much is meant by it; the other person is just attempting to be friendly.

Americans never avoid making eye contact and, even when greeting a superior, look the other person straight in the eyes. An easy smile (Ronald Reagan in his presidential years is a good role model here) is expected and does not signal a lack of serious purpose, as it might in other parts of the world.

In general, Europeans (especially Swiss and Germans) are more likely to shake hands, and to do this more often, than Americans. European women often shake hands (for example, two lady friends ending lunch in Geneva might well expect to shake hands). Some American women don't expect to shake hands, but this is generational—younger women in business expect to be taken seriously and routinely offer to shake the hands of either women or men with whom they are about to do business.

Americans almost never bow to one another (unless they are very experienced with Asian business and have traveled in Asia[1]). But in some

---

1. An excellent book that details the differences in non-verbal communication is *Kiss, Bow or Shake Hands* by T. Morrison, W. Conaway, and G. Borden, Adams Media, 1994.

industries (the movie business in Hollywood, for example) hugs and "air kisses" are the norm. An air kiss means placing right cheeks together and miming a kiss. Men almost never hug or kiss other men (except at moments of extreme joy, such as when a soccer team scores a winning goal), and the French or European style of fraternal kisses (right cheek, left cheek, right cheek) is extremely uncomfortable for most Americans— no matter how well-intentioned the gesture. So it's best to stick with handshakes unless you are sure that you have correctly observed the behavior of other people in a particular business situation.

1-4 How Many Names Do You Have?

Most people have a number of different forms of their name, which range in use from the most formal to the most casual. At the formal end, it's important to be clear about your "full legal name." So former US President Bill Clinton's name would be shown as follows:

> William Jefferson Clinton

At the informal end of the scale, everyone knows that this man preferred to be addressed and introduced by the diminutive form of his name: "Bill Clinton." Interestingly, the White House web page for President Clinton showed his name as William J. Clinton. This form— personal name, initial, family name—is the form most used in written documents in the US, and many forms will ask for "middle initial" rather than both given forenames.

US government officials and business people will expect your family name to come at the end: If the family name is Jian, you introduce yourself as follows:

> Zeming Jian, not Jian Zeming

An exception to this is printed lists of names (such as directories) that are alphabetized first by the last name and then the first name:

> Jian, Freddy
>
> Jian, Zeming
>
> Kim, Sean

In this example, the last person would introduce himself as "I'm Sean Kim."

The "family name first" rule is common in Asia and in Hungary:

> You'll recognize "Liszt Ferencz" as "Franz Liszt," the composer.

In addition to their full, legal name, most people have two or more familiar forms of their name that they prefer to be called (for example, "Bill Clinton"). Although some people have a childhood name ("Billy" or "Buddy," for example), which is used only within their family, many Americans use familiar, diminutive forms of their names at work (for example, "Libby Dole," for "Elizabeth Dole"). Using such names is consistent with American friendliness and informality, and it is almost never wrong to use the familiar form of the name after you notice other people in your workgroup using it. Finally, many American's have a so-called nickname, a name that is based on a personal characteristic and that has no relation to the formal name—for example, "Tipper Gore."

1-5 Be Thoughtful about Your Own Name

In business, you can choose how you are addressed. If your name is Robert, but you prefer to be called "Bob," you can gently correct people:

> "Good to see you, Robert...."

> "Please, call me Bob."

Or, if your have to repeat the correction, you can be firmer:

> "Well, Dick . . ."

> "Actually, I prefer to go by 'Rick.'"

Think about the consistency of your name, however, and don't set people up to make a mistake. If you really prefer to be called "Kristy," rather than "Kristen," consider having "Kristy Wells" printed on your business card so that you don't have to constantly correct people. Some people have a nickname in quotation marks on their card and on their signature line for letters:

> B. J. "Bugsy" Littlejohn

In some parts of the US (particularly in the Southern states), naming first-born sons after their fathers and grandfathers is a family tradition. These people then need a **suffix** (such as "Senior") to their legal names so that property and legal communications go to the right person. The form is

> Rhett Butler, Senior (the grandfather)

> Rhett Butler, Junior (the son)

> Rhett Butler, III ("Rhett Butler, the third" for the grandson)

T A B L E **1-1** Tips for Making a Good Introduction

Did you remember to . . .	announce yourself by name?
	never refer to yourself by a title?
	repeat your name in a way that helps people with unusual pronunciations or spellings?
	speak almost artificially slowly and distinctly?

The form "II" as in "Rhett Butler II" is used when a son is named not for his father, but for another relative such as an uncle.

In business, most suffixes aren't needed. Indeed, someone who has

Alex Proudfoot, IV

on his business card probably doesn't make a good impression; Americans rejected royalty when they overthrew King George III. Some exceptions are when two people with the same name work in the same firm or when customers want to know whether they should be asking for Albert Gore, Junior, or Albert Gore, Senior, when they call. Table 1-1 provides a summary of some things to think about to make a good introduction.

1-6 When You've Forgotten Someone's Name

A situation that everyone dreads in both business and in social contexts occurs when you run into someone you know—perhaps quite well—and you just can't remember his or her name. If the other person doesn't make a quick self-introduction, you can easily become stuck in a conversation, desperately trying to search for the name. As hard as you try, you can remember all kinds of details about this person, *except* his or her name.

Meeting this challenge straight on is best:

"I'm terribly sorry [shaking head, with eyes scrunched]. I just blanked out here. Please remind me of your name."

"I remember we met at the convention last year . . . and I'm remembering everything about you, but—forgive me—I just can't come up with your name."

In many business situations you can work around this situation by saying

"I wonder, do you have a copy of your (business) card?"

1-7 Introducing Other People

Learning how to make gracious introductions between business acquaintances will get you ahead in US business. Because people are often not very good about introducing themselves, your efforts will be gratefully received. Introductions put everyone at ease and facilitate business. Learning how to make courteous and confident introductions will make you look good.

The rule for introducing people is simple. You always introduce the lowest-ranked person *to* the highest-ranked person:

> "Mr. Gates (president of the firm), may I introduce Tina Jones? Tina is a summer intern from University of Washington, working in our marketing department."

Note that part of the introduction is to give a context and to make a reason to repeat the name. As with your own name, if it's a little unusual, link the name to something familiar:

> "This is Orly Katzoff. Orly—that's like the airport in Paris—is working with us in testing this summer."

The form "May I introduce …" is quite formal and appropriate when you're talking to a superior, but in many contexts, the form "This is Sheila Wong . . ." is perfectly appropriate.

After introducing the junior person *to* the senior person, you then reverse the process, but without stating the obvious (in this case, "Mr. Gates is head of the firm"). Again you should give some context, as illustrated in Figure 1-2:

> "Tina, as you know this is Bill Gates. He was just on campus last week, speaking to the Board of Governors."

Unless the context is a reception line for very senior executives, dismissing yourself after making the introduction is quite appropriate:

> "And, if you'll excuse me, I have to talk with some people in Production."

Most Americans refer to one another simply as "first name, last name" (for example "Bill Gates") even if someone is quite senior. The form "Chairman Gates," which is common in Asian countries, is never used, but the form "Mr. Gates" would not be wrong under circumstances of considerable formality (for example, a job interview as opposed to a party). When you're addressing and referring to women, you'll have to make a

Figure 1-2 When you're introducing a lower-level worker to an upper-level one, always introduce the lowest-ranked person to the highest-ranked person.
©Stockbyte/PictureQuest

decision as to whether to use "Ms.," "Mrs.," or "Miss." "Ms." is never wrong and is increasingly used in business to the exclusion of the two forms that indicate whether someone is married. However, if you know that the person prefers to be called "Mrs.," you should try to use that form in speech. For example, former US Secretary of State, Madeleine Albright, was usually mentioned in the press as "Mrs. Albright," although—with a doctorate from Columbia University—she could have been introduced as "Dr. Albright," as her predecessor Henry Kissinger was often referred to as "Dr. Kissinger."

1-8 The Key Is Practice

No matter how much you may feel uncomfortable and how much you "hate" introductions, learning the correct protocol and practicing at every possible opportunity will increase your self-confidence and your professional image. And, of course, once you've gained confidence, you won't hate introductions.

Put This Chapter into Practice

1. Decide on the form of your name you are going to use in business and use it consistently for self-introductions. Think about whether any unusual parts of your name need explanation, repetition, or tying to something more familiar.

2. Use social opportunities to practice making semi-formal introductions of people to one another.

Effective Communication

2

Key Terms

Active voice

Business context

Channel of communication

Gender-neutral

Level of formality

Medium, media

Passive voice

Plain English

Tone

Outline

Plain English makes sense

Choose the channel of communication with care

Suppose you receive the following message:

> **Be advised that there is a mandatory meeting on Wednesday next at 11:00 A.M. pertaining to the new budgetary cycle.**

This message sounds like the sort of thing that people in business write, I suppose. But if you just arrived from another country to work in the US, or if this was your first job, it would be difficult for me to explain to you what "be advised" means, and you would notice that no one uses "pertaining to" in daily conversation in the office.

Now, consider this alternative:

> **There is a meeting at 11 o'clock next Wednesday morning to discuss planning for next year's budget. It's important that we have input from all members of the team, so please make sure to attend.**

The meaning of the message is clear, and the tone is more friendly and inviting.

Plain English (www.plainenglish.co.uk) is an international movement to eliminate bureaucratic language that is unnecessarily complex and misleading.[1] It's not difficult to write in Plain English, and the approach can be expressed in three main rules: use simple, direct sentences; avoid the passive voice; and use commonly occurring words in preference to obscure words. Let's look at these rules in detail.

---

1. Tom McArthur, ed., *The Oxford Companion to the English Language*, New York, Oxford, 1992, p. 785.

2-1 Use Simple, Direct Sentences

Many concepts in business are quite complex (for example, selling a "put" on a stock cannot be readily explained in one sentence), and most business transactions have important consequences. For example, your firm agrees to sell parts to a manufacturer who depends on them arriving on time. What penalty will you face for late delivery?

With the reasonable goal of being completely clear about the terms of transactions, many business documents have grown extremely long. Look at the next car rental contract you sign: On the back of the form you'll be agreeing to "terms and conditions" that are printed in microscopic type and that few people who are not trained lawyers can actually understand.

There is no reason why even the most complex ideas cannot be expressed in simple sentences:

> If you don't bring back the car when you agree, we will begin charging you a late fee.

The Plain English movement has demonstrated that even complex legal documents, such as life insurance policies, can be re-written in terms that are legally binding but are perfectly clear for a non-expert to read.

2-2 Avoid the Passive Voice

The **passive voice** is a construction of language in which the object becomes the subject of the sentence:

> Tom hit the ball.

In the passive voice this sentence becomes

> The ball was hit by Tom.

From a literary standpoint, the second sentence focuses attention on the ball, and what happens to it, rather than on Tom. In contemporary American English, the passive voice is arcane, and in a country where many people speak English as their second (or third or fourth) language, it's a sentence structure that can be very hard to follow.

With some effort, you can re-write almost all passive sentences into the **active voice.** For example:

> Travel vouchers are to be submitted within seven days of your return to your regular place of employment.

You can restate this sentence in Plain English as follows:

> When you return to your office, submit your travel voucher within seven days.

Many times, when you edit out the passive voice, you'll have other opportunities to improve the wording to make a sentence better Plain English. For example, consider this sentence:

> Enclosed is a brochure of your new health benefits.

In Plain English, you would say

> With this letter I am sending a brochure that explains your health insurance in detail.

2-3 Avoid Obscure Vocabulary

The first step in avoiding obscure, bureaucratic language is to stop and ask why people would want to use such words and phrases as "pertaining to," "herewith," and "please find enclosed." Writers who use these terms are probably aiming to appear formal and serious—they are signaling that this is not a chatty note from a friend, and perhaps that's a reasonable purpose. But more often, the hidden text is that the writer wants to appear well-educated and erudite. Indeed, the worst bureaucratic language comes from low-level government officials who have *not* had a good education, and the best Plain English comes from some Nobel Laureates (look at the editorials and opinion pieces in *Business Week* and the *New York Times*, for example).

The test for bureaucratic vocabulary is simple: If you cannot imagine yourself walking into a colleague's office and beginning a conversation with "Pertaining to . . . ," then don't use it! (In this example, the conversation would begin with "I need to talk with you about. . . .")

Now that's not to say that we write as we speak. In daily conversation we often use sentence fragments, and most speakers interrupt themselves to revise or amplify a point they are making. In written language we avoid slang and most colloquial expressions that may be acceptable in spoken dialog.

Of course, if you're writing a technical document such as the instruction manual for a heart defibrillator, you will use some terms that you wouldn't use in everyday speech. Edward Bailey[2] has defined these two simple rules for word choice:

- Use technical terms only when you need them (and make sure they are well defined).
- Use rare words *rarely.*

2. Edward P. Bailey, Jr., *The Plain English Approach to Business Writing,* New York, Oxford, 1990.

Box 2-1

Using Gender-Neutral and Non-Sexist Language

An important part of contemporary Plain English usage is to avoid referring to anyone in business documents by nouns or pronouns that indicate only one gender. The reason for this is that it is considered "sexist" (that is, diminishing the rights of women in most instances) to refer to employees as "work*men*" when some of them are likely to be women. The right approach is to choose a **gender-neutral** noun, such as "worker," "customer," or "employee." In some cases, new words have been created to provide a gender-neutral alternative: "Congressperson" and "chairperson" are examples. Although these words were criticized by conservative individuals when they first came out, they've reached broad acceptance, and you'll demonstrate sophistication by learning to use them naturally.

When it comes to pronouns, we don't have a good gender-neutral form. If you write "Each worker will report to his manager," this statement implies that all workers are male. Some writers add footnotes saying, "Whenever this document says 'he,' 'she' will also be included," but that seems awkward. Similarly, going through an entire document and writing "he or she" and "his or her" will make your prose difficult to read. Many businesspeople use the words "they" and "their" as if they were gender-neutral singular forms (although from a grammatical point of view, they are plurals). You'll find increasing use of the form "Each worker will report to their manager" as the preferred gender-neutral pronoun. You may encounter some people who think this use is ungrammatical, but you might ask them what gender-neutral term they prefer. You can accept the "they, their, them" use in the singular as an almost mainstream practice and one that is likely to be more common in the next few years.

In informal speech, you'll often hear people referring to a group of themselves and co-workers as "guys." Technically, this word implies male gender, but in the form "The guys are going to work late and then go out together," it's inoffensive, even if some members of the group are women. A problem occurs when you look for the parallel form to refer to a group of women. The feminine of "guys" is "girls" (or "gals" in slang). But "girls" is also the parallel form of the diminutive "boys." So if you refer to a group of female colleagues as "girls"—even in a complement such as "The girls have been working very hard on this project"—you may find some colleagues who'll take offense. Carefully avoiding the term is a much better approach. You can say "the women" or "the ladies" (although that language might be considered a little pretentious).

Finally, although you may often hear adult men referring positively to a group as "the boys," as in "The boys will all be going skiing next weekend to celebrate the end-of-quarter," be careful that it's a diminutive which you should almost always avoid in the singular. The term "boy" was common in a master-servant relationship and has unpleasant connotations of slave owning, and it should never be used. For example, even if you are being served by a waiter in an informal setting at the side of a pool at a country club, getting attention by calling out "Boy!" would be a big mistake in US culture.

2-4 Limitations of Plain English

No one would claim that careful adherence to the rules of Plain English leads to great literature. Indeed, Plain English documents are probably fairly boring to read if they are long. A Plain English editor would doubtless re-write the opening of Charles Dickens's *Tale of Two Cities* "It was the best of times, the worst of times" as "There was a great deal of political and social uncertainty in Paris at the end of the eighteenth century." True, but not nearly as eloquent. Plain English has its place in business, but it is not a campaign to constrain the richness of the English language in other contexts.

2-5 An Objective Is a Golden Rule for Any Communication

In his best-selling book, *The Seven Habits of Highly Successful People,* Stephen Covey articulates the rule "Begin with the end in mind." Use this rule for every letter, memo, or e-mail you write and for every phone call, speech, and presentation you make. Although your boss may tell you "I guess you better write to their legal people . . . ," a letter to the attorneys in another firm is not an end in itself. You should stop and think: "If this letter is successful, what result do I want to see for the firm?"

In the recruiting process, a job candidate may often be uncertain where he or she stands with a firm. Have offers been given to other candidates? Have I been rejected? Am I still under consideration? Has the opening been eliminated? A voice-mail message such as "I'm just calling to follow up" is not wrong, but "I'm calling to check that you've received my resume and to ask about coming in for an interview" clearly has the next step in mind. The "end" of this phone call (its goal) is to get an interview—and it's better to say so.

In advertising, it's generally agreed that the purpose of any promotional message is to *inform, persuade, or remind.* I would add to this that successful promotional messages can do only one of these things at a time. That is, an ad that is good at reminding existing customers about a brand is unlikely to work if it also includes wording aimed at encouraging non-users to try the company's products. The same rule applies to all business communications. They work better if you can first answer this question: "Is this communication designed to inform, persuade, or remind?"

Going back to the example that opened this chapter, consider an e-mail sent on Tuesday:

> Just a heads-up that the budget meeting is tomorrow, Wednesday, at 11 A.M. in conference room C.

This e-mail is clearly a "reminder." If some members of the work-group consider meetings a waste of time and aren't planning to attend, this e-mail would hardly convince them. For that, we would have used an intermediate e-mail, after the first announcement (inform) to *persuade:*

> A number of people have asked whether they really have to be at the budget meeting on Wednesday. The answer is: Yes!
>
> If we don't have input from everyone, we won't be able to achieve consensus on our capital spending priorities for next year. So please arrange your workday to be sure to attend.

Most business communications have a clearly stated purpose: Send us information, here is a check, and so on. However, they almost always have a sub-text too. For example, if we write to a major customer indicating that we can't fill an order for a particular product, the sub-text is: But we *do* hope you'll buy more of the things that we *can* supply. When a firm turns down a candidate for a summer internship, the sub-text is often: But we *do* hope you'll apply for permanent hire when you graduate.

Your business communications will be most effective if you can clearly articulate the goals of the communication before you begin to write. The purpose and the sub-text become clear if you ask yourself these questions:

> "What result do I want to achieve?"
> "If I don't do it correctly, what's the worst that can happen here?"

2-6 Level of Formality

People who teach English grammar like to define absolute rules, such as "You should never begin a sentence with a conjunction." But in practice, even sophisticated English speakers will find good reasons to break the "rules." (The last sentence began with the conjunction "but," and you handled it well.) Most well-educated speakers of English know that the possessive form of a word that ends in "s" still takes "apostrophe-s" like all other words. For example, a car belonging to Prince Charles is correctly referred to as "Prince Charles's car." But in practice (and certainly in everyday speech), most English speakers would say and write "Prince Charles' car."

If the rules can be defined but well-spoken people violate the rules, does this mean that the language is being corrupted and even well-educated people are becoming careless users of language? Absolutely not! Expert speakers of English naturally adjust the **level of formality** to the context in which they are speaking or writing. For example, "Yeah, we'd better check with their rep" is appropriate for office conversation although it has a low level of formality. "Please contact their sales representative and confirm their production schedule" means the same and would be appropriate in a letter—a context where most businesspeople would naturally expect a higher level of formality.

Informal speech uses abbreviations, contractions, and colloquialisms. Personal pronouns are common. There is a continuum of formality, and at the highly formal end of the scale, language has no contractions and writers avoid the use of personal pronouns. Certain vocabulary words also signal the level of formality: "Hope" is more informal than "expectation," for example.

Consider the following successive entries from the *Oxford American Dictionary:*

> *Onus*   A Latin word, and a rare vocabulary word—signaling high formality
>
> *Onward*   Everyday speech, mid-level formality
>
> *Onwards*   A more formal version of "onward"
>
> *Onyx*   Translucent quartz—in Plain English this would be used only as a technical term, and hence in high-formality situations
>
> *Oodles*   Meaning "lots of"; perfectly acceptable in casual conversation, but not in more formal contexts
>
> *Ooh*   An outcry; again, unlikely to be part of a public speech or other formal presentations
>
> *Oomph*   Clearly slang, and hence only in low-formality contexts
>
> *Ooze*   A relatively rare vocabulary word, but expressive and might be used in low-formality contexts

You can see how some words would be perfectly acceptable in a social context (standing in line waiting for a movie, chatting with a friend) but wouldn't be acceptable if you were making a presentation to the board of directors of your firm.

2-7 Matching Level of Formality to the Business Context

Most well-educated native speakers of English—or indeed any other language—naturally determine the appropriate level of formality from the social context in which they're communicating. It's important to know that the **business context** is not a univalent environment for which a single level of formality is appropriate. Some business situations are almost entirely social, such as a company party or celebration, and they

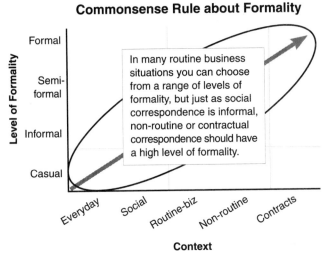

Commonsense Rule about Formality

In many routine business situations you can choose from a range of levels of formality, but just as social correspondence is informal, non-routine or contractual correspondence should have a high level of formality.

Figure 2-1 The middle of the chart indicates a range of acceptable levels of formality.

demand a low level of formality. Greeting a co-worker with "To whom were you speaking at the drinks table?" is grammatically correct but would seem strange, because it's too formal. At the other end of the context continuum, many business documents are either contracts or serve a contractual purpose—job "offer letters" are an example. No matter how relaxed and casual a work environment the firm aims for, no one should write a letter that uses the imprecisions and colloquialisms of social speech: "We have great perks" doesn't mean the same as "You will be covered by health insurance after your first 90 days on the job."

The social context determines the level of formality in a manner best expressed by a diagonal region between the two scales, as in Figure 2-1.

Note that at the lower and upper end of the scale in Figure 2-1, the context determines a very narrow range of acceptable choices: Contracts are always written in formal language, and office chitchat always uses very casual language structure. But in the middle of the range, the oval is broad, and this matches a range of acceptable levels of formality. Routine business transactions include letters ordering materials and thanking customers. Non-routine contexts include being unable to fulfill a previous agreement and sending warning letters and demand letters for non-payment. So in many business situations you have some flexibility between the "informal side of semi-formal" and the "quite formal side of semi-formal." You are constrained, however: You can't use informal language and refer to a customer as a "chump," nor should you use highly stilted formal language, such as "Under the terms of an agreement entered into on. . . ."

Choosing the right level of formality is not difficult if you think about the communication objective. For example, an e-mail to a small group of co-workers would normally be considered routine and would demand a low level of formality. But if the purpose of the e-mail is to convince your colleagues that you are very concerned that no one is following an agreed plan to shut off office equipment at the end of the day to save energy, then a slightly more formal tone would show that you are serious.

2-8 Choosing the Right Tone

In addition to level of formality, both spoken and written messages differ in their **tone.** For example, given the business task of writing to a customer about an unpaid bill, it's possible to adopt a tone that is anything from a friendly reminder to a hostile demand. You can think of "tone" as the third dimension in a cube where the other two dimensions are context and level of formality:

Hostile Officious Cool Businesslike Pleasant Warm Friendly
————————————————————————————————————→

Beyond the ends of the continuum, there is "Attacking" on the left and "Seductive" on the right. But you won't have much use for such tones in business.

You choose the appropriate tone by thinking through the desired "end." If you want the customer to pay up and never do business with you again, (in this example) a frostily "Cool" tone may well be your choice. On the other hand, if you equally want to get paid but see the strategic importance of keeping the customer, you might choose a tone that is downright "Friendly."

Whenever you receive a letter or e-mail that irritates you, it probably violates some of the commonsense rules about matching formality and context and about choosing an appropriate tone.

2-9 Choosing the Right Channel of Communication

In business, when you need to get in touch with someone, you have a choice of several different **channels of communication.** The channel of communication is the **medium** (plural: **media**) through which a message is sent, such as writing or oral communication. Suppose, for example, you are in charge of arranging a routine lunch where your firm will be hosting some executives from an existing customer of your firm. You are in the Marketing department, and your team has agreed that it would probably be a good idea to invite some people from the Product Engineering group. There's no specific agenda, but you want to show the client the range of professional expertise at your firm, and during informal conversation, you may get some good ideas for new product development. Your team has decided that the best engineer to invite would be a colleague, roughly the same standing as yourself, Heidi Liu.

To invite the colleague, you are faced with several choices for how to enlist her help with the meeting. You might pick up the phone and call her. This will get you a direct answer, and you could do some negotiation: "Next Tuesday, well, I could do that . . . but only if it's early and I'm absolutely out of there by one o'clock." But Heidi might be a little grumpy and terse with you. Have you imposed? Does she dislike working with your group, or has she had a bad experience with this customer? The answer may be simple: Heidi was working on a complicated calculation, and your phone call interrupted her. Although the business lunch is important to you, important to the firm, and so, at the limit, important to Heidi's team, making the arrangements are not time-sensitive from Heidi's point of view. There was no reason to interrupt.

This situation suggests that e-mail would be the best medium here. Heidi can reply to you when she's taking a break from calculations, and on the day of the meeting, she can readily check the copy of the e-mail to confirm the time and location. If she can't oblige you, she can write back: "Sorry, I have to be in Houston that week. See if Tommy can go instead." Although the message is brief, you probably wouldn't experience the answer as curt if you and Heidi already had a good working relationship.

Would you ever issue the invitation in person? Well, let's assume that Heidi works at the same general location as you, but in an adjacent build-ing. Walking over to her group and inviting her in person would take some time out of your workday. But on some occasions you would take the extra effort. Suppose you knew that Heidi had bad work experience with this customer in the past—the client insisted on many last-minute design changes. You might want to influence and encourage her to set the previous events aside and try to develop a better working relationship with the client. At the least, you would want to let her know that you understood that the meeting might be difficult for her. Don't be tempted to add that sort of "spin" (side comments) to an e-mail: "Heidi, I know the people from Acme Co. are a pain, but could you see your way. . . ." Why? You never want to put a negative comment about another firm or person in an e-mail (see Chapter 4, "Understanding e-mail").

TABLE **2-1** Advantages and Disadvantages of Using Media

Medium	Advantages	Disadvantages	Best used for
Face-to-face meeting	Promotes trust Easy to adjust content and level of formality while the meeting is in progress Disagreements can be negotiated	Expensive Time consuming	Recruiting Team building Brainstorming Developing new business Confidential and sensitive personnel issues
Phone call	Immediacy: No waiting for an answer Opportunity to restate or clarify if the recipient doesn't understand	Interrupts work flow Tend to go on too long Hard to judge emotional component No permanent record	Quick "fact checking" and scheduling Social interaction
Video conference	Can be a "milestone" event— the day and time by which work groups report progress Relatively inexpensive, compared with in-person meetings	Interactions are likely to be stilted Takes substantial organization to get all participants available at the same time (especially across time zones) Limited possibility for "breakthrough" success if participants haven't previously met face-to-face	Routinely scheduled team meetings where team members are in different geographical locations

Common sense suggests that a written invitation is probably way too formal in this circumstance. You wouldn't write a formal letter to a colleague at the same firm, and a memo implies that you take Heidi's acceptance of the invitation for granted, and you are almost ordering her to attend. Even when you and Heidi are at different levels of the admittedly collapsed hierarchy of US companies (imagine that you are the Vice President for Marketing and one of the founders of the company, and Heidi is a new-hire entry-level engineer who has been with your firm for only a few months), a memo would appear to be ordering someone around in an officious manner. Because American firms operate on informality and direct contact, you would still probably use e-mail and write directly, or perhaps have an assistant make arrangements with people you suggested.

Medium	Advantages	Disadvantages	Best used for
e-mail	Quick Easy to copy several people at once Can be saved or printed Time-shifting does not interrupt recipient	Lacks emotional cues so may lead to misinterpretation	Normal communication between co-workers
Memo		Quasi-formal	Routine announcements of uncontroversial procedures
Letter	High formality indicates seriousness Can be the basis of a formal contract Permits sober reflection and analysis of proposals	One-sided communication—does not permit adaptation or negotiation Time consuming to prepare well Delay before response	Documenting items agreed on at a face-to-face meeting Statement of terms and conditions of a business deal Formal introductions (of yourself or your firm) Formal warnings (to suppliers, people who owe the firm money, and to employees)

Table 2-1 presents a summary of the merits and problems with different types of communication, and they are treated in more detail in later chapters.

2-10 Firms (and People) Have Their Preferred Method of Communication

When you join a new firm, you'll find that the company as a whole, or perhaps just your workgroup, has a definite preference for the medium of communication. For example, in the big strategy consulting firms, although all partners have access to e-mail, they often travel away from their own offices. They carry laptop computers, but "replicating" (downloading e-mails from the firm's server) often takes time, and consultants may check their e-mail only once a day, in the evening—perhaps less often if they are out of the country. But they can check voice mail relatively easily, from airports while waiting for flights or even from a client's office between meetings. So consultants have a strong preference for voice mail. Note that you almost always get the consultant's voice mail and not the individual in person.

In the example described in section 2-9, Heidi could have avoided the interruption to her calculations by ignoring her ringing phone and letting your message go to voice mail. In some firms, this is acceptable. But in many firms a ringing phone is an indication of urgency and not answering the phone (as a matter of routine) could be a cause for considerable disapproval from your superiors and other members of your workgroup. So it's important to get a general idea of what the group norm is in your workplace.

Within each firm, people always have their own preferences. For example, some older executives readily admit to being "not very good" with e-mail. They rely on their assistants to handle it, and some even have each message printed out. If you know this is true about someone you have to work with, you can adapt and use the phone or in-person visits. Similarly, some individuals strongly prefer face-to-face conversations to making phone calls within the firm. Again, once you understand a colleague's personal style, you can probably make a good adaptation.

2-11 Why Face-to-Face Meetings Still Matter

Business trips are expensive. When you add the cost of airfare, hotel, taxi, and meals, the total comes to several thousand dollars, before you add in the lost productivity caused when one member of a firm is away from the office. But despite the advent of the telephone, e-mail, and video conferencing, most businesspeople still rely heavily on face-to-face meetings (as illustrated in Figure 2-2).

Executives are paid to make decisions, and as we like to say in business school, to make decisions in the face of uncertainty. We have to plan for our firm not knowing for sure whether the economy will boom or be depressed next year, whether our competitor will launch a rival product or abandon the field entirely, and so on. Making decisions involves two parts. First, an executive has to gather enough information. Note that the word is "enough"—often there won't be sufficient time or resources to gather all possible information. Then the executive has to make a choice such as

Figure 2-2 Sometimes a face-to-face meeting is better than sending e-mail or calling, even within an office.

Photo: comstock.com

choosing between competing investments, whether to extend a customer credit, and so on.

Businesspeople expend money on face-to-face meetings because both the quantity of information is greater, and the quality of information is richer. For example, potential suppliers may describe themselves as "very sophisticated," but site visits to their factories may reveal broken-down equipment and little evidence of research and development activity. A retailer may indeed have 25 stores, but an in-person visit will reveal whether the parking lots are empty or whether eager customers are lined up at the cash registers.

A great deal of business depends on trust, and this is where business-people make a qualitative assessment. If customers keep you waiting, you begin to wonder how prompt they'll be about paying their bills. If a supplier goes out of his or her way to drop you at the airport so you can take an earlier flight home, you have a good sense that he or she will work hard to deliver the right goods on time.

So, although success in business depends on careful calculation and rational decision-making, an emotional element always comes into play. Consciously or not, executives make a judgment about how they feel about their business partners, and to date, no one has come up with technology that can supplant the experience of a face-to-face meeting.

Put This Chapter into Practice

1. Take a letter you've received that doesn't seem quite right. Analyze it for formality and tone in light of its context and apparent purpose. Try to edit it to overcome problems and so that it conforms to Plain English.

2. Identify people in your workgroup who prefer different styles of communication, such as "give it to me in writing, and I'll look at it."

Chapter 3

Phone, Voice Mail, and Phone Conferencing

Key Terms

Conference call   Mute button   Video conferencing

Outline

Often a phone call is the first opportunity to demonstrate your professionalism

You already know that the telephone is useful for getting immediate answers, but it can also be seen as an irritating interruption to most executives' workdays. A few years ago, phone systems reflected a strict hierarchy: You would call a firm's main switchboard, and if you asked for an executive by name, your call would be transferred to an assistant who would greet you with: "Dale Patel's office; may I help you?" You would then have to make a case for why your call should be taken, and you might eventually be switched through to the person you were calling.

These days, few executives have old-fashioned "secretaries," and team assistants are likely to be busy with their own work. Many times when business associates give you phone numbers, they are quite likely to be direct lines that will ring directly on their desks. For this reason, you should be careful about giving out numbers that people have given you in confidence, and you should know that almost all companies consider their internal phone lists to be confidential (see Box 3-1).

3-1 Answering Your Business Phone

Unless you've been specifically trained during your firm's orientation to answer the phone with a standard phrase and a particular order of items, such as "Good morning, Megacorp. Trading Division, Tracy Kim speaking," you should answer the phone with your name: "This is Tracy Kim" is fine. You don't need to say "speaking"—the caller knows what you're doing. Unless you are answering for someone else, don't use the word "office"—it's wrong to say, "Tracy Kim's office," if you are Tracy. You use

Box 3-1

Guard the Privacy of Phone Lists

Companies' internal phone lists are the crock of gold at the end of the rainbow for headhunters, people who are trying to sell to your firm, competitors, and, sometimes, even criminals. If you innocently give a photocopy of your firm's phone directory to someone outside the firm, you at least expose everyone on the list to annoying sales calls. Many of the extensions may be "unpublished" and not shown on managers' business cards (their published numbers may go to voice mail or to assistants first.) So be careful when someone outside the firm asks you for a copy of the list. You're undoubtedly violating your firm's work rules, and you may get yourself into a lot of trouble.

that form only if you are answering someone else's phone: "Mike Wong's office; this is Tracy Kim."

Answering with just "Hello" is definitely wrong. This leads to wasted time and various iterations of "Is Tracy Kim there?" "This *is* Tracy Kim" and so on. Your callers will feel awkward at the start of the call if they don't know whom they are speaking to. You can see that this violates the fundamental rule of protocol: You should help other people to do their jobs as easily as possible.

Why do many Americans just answer the phone with a mumbled, " . . . ullo?" If you ask them, they'll tell you that they were instructed to do this by their parents. Because many Americans grew up as "latch-key kids" (that is, home alone without adult supervision after school), parents feared that child molesters and potential robbers would be spurred on if they knew that little Timmy was home alone. They believed that answering the phone with any information ("Hello! This is Timmy") would let bad guys know that junior was home alone. Just saying "Hello" probably wasn't effective at hiding the fact that an 11-year-old was home alone, but rightly or wrongly, that's where this habit came from.

3-2 Taking a Phone Call

If you absolutely have a deadline due (for example, you have to finish a spreadsheet in time for a 2 o'clock meeting), it's reasonable within most workgroups to just let all phone messages go to your voice mail. If team members need to see you on the same urgent project, presumably they will walk into your office.

If you decide to take a call, you can enhance your professional effectiveness by training your callers to be concise. If someone wants to ramble and tell stories, it's reasonable to interrupt and ask, "So, how can I help you today? I'm in the middle of something here." It's often helpful to restate the caller's concerns in your words: "So, if I have this right, you've seen the invoices for May and July, but you still haven't received the June invoice and our accounting department is giving you the run-around?" Then take the concern to a reasonable action step: "I can make you a copy and send it to you. Can you give me a fax number?"

Many people confuse what is *important* with what is *urgent*. Because the telephone is a device that permits other people to interrupt you at their convenience, you should be comfortable imposing your own time-table: "I can get you a copy of that tape—but it won't be until next week. Is that all right?" Of course, you should have a reliable method for managing your pending tasks (many e-mail systems such as Microsoft Outlook have a "task manager," so you can note pending tasks on your personal computer).

A related difficulty is tactfully ending a phone call—no matter how pleasant it has been for you—when the caller seems to want to talk forever. When two people meet face-to-face, many non-verbal signals (stance, moving toward the door, and so on) signal that one party wishes to end the conversation. But those cues are absent on the phone. Linguists who study human speech patterns note that toward the end of phone conversations, people tend to use shorter sentences, and indeed, short words. You can adopt those ideas, and also get into the habit of restating the purpose of a call:

> "So, let's re-cap here: You are still interested in our technology, but you still have three other vendors to see. You won't be able to make a decision until the beginning of next year. So I'll plan to call you back then."

3-3 Managing Your Own Voice Mail

Voice mail is usually part of your firm's phone system. It is a way to digitally record messages, and it allows "random access" so you can skip, delete, save, and forward messages. Voice mail can be one of your most important business tools. Using it effectively allows you to time-shift (you take your calls only when it's convenient for you) and place-shift (you can check your messages while you are away from your desk).

You should make sure that your voice-mail greeting sounds cheerful and fully identifies you, especially if there is any likelihood that a caller may have been looking for another employee with the same last name:

> "You've reached Lesley Schultz in the technology group at Purchasing. Please leave me a message at the beep."

This is a good model. Note that it does *not* include a ritual apology ("I'm sorry that I'm not here to take your call right now") or a promise to return the call (which is self-evident). Your callers will appreciate a short message.

In many workgroups there's an option for a caller to "escape" from voice mail and reach a real person. The form for the message then would be

> "You've reached Lesley Schultz in Purchasing. If you need to talk with someone immediately, please press 03 to transfer to my assistant Ronnie Shaw. Or leave me a message at the beep. Thank you."

When you listen to your voice mail, your system will allow you to save or delete messages. It's worth investing some time to learn additional features such as how to listen to only new messages, how to skip forward or back, and how to forward or delegate a message to someone else. In most firms, the standard for acting on voice mail (or at least voice mail that does not indicate a panic situation requiring your immediate attention) is to respond within 24 hours. In some industries (television news reporting would be one example), a 24-hour delay would be too long. So be sure to learn the accepted standard in your workgroup. If you have a pending item, it's worth making a quick response to let the caller know that you are not ignoring the message:

> "Terry, just to let you know I got your call . . . I'm at a sales meeting in Orlando, and I'll be happy to get you those figures next Monday when I'm back in the office."

Some firms encourage all their employees to change their phone message every day:

> "Hi, this is Scott, and today, Monday, I'll be in the office most of the day, except for a meeting from 11 to noon. I'm probably on another call. Please leave me a message, and I'll get right back to you."

A message like this certainly conveys energy and immediacy, which is why this technique is popular with firms that are selling something, such as real estate agents. Updating your welcome message every day takes time, and more importantly, discipline. There's nothing worse for your professional image than a message that refers to ". . . today, Monday," on Wednesday.

You should certainly change your voice-mail message when you're going to be away for a day or more, such as when you're on vacation. Many voice-mail systems allow you to record an "alternate greeting," such as the following:

> "This is Tommy Chiang in Direct Sales. I'll be traveling away from the office until the week after Labor Day and may not be able to respond to your message until Tuesday, September 9th. If you need immediate assistance, please contact Ahmed Zabolly at 555-6789."

Using the alternate greeting allows you to save your routine message and return to it when you are back at your desk.

3-4 Leaving a Voice-Mail Message

Whenever you phone someone else, you should anticipate ahead of time that you may reach voice mail. No one wants to plough through a message like this:

> "Wow, Sheila, I was hoping to reach you . . . I guess you're not there. Well I just wanted to go over some things with you . . . um, one was, do you know when the quarterlies will be ready? I need your figures to complete the budget planning for next fiscal year. I should've said . . . this is Pat in the Treasurer's office ... I think we met at the off-site last year . . . anyway, I don't need the exact income, but I do need revenue. And there was something else I had to ask you, but I guess I'll have to call back."

The keys for voice messages that you leave are

- Brevity
- Clarity
- Action step

The way to achieve such a message is with a moment or two of planning before you make the call (perhaps even making a few notes). Here's the revised example:

> "Sheila, this is Pat Chiang in the Treasurer's office. I'm working on the budget for next year, and I need two figures from you from last quarter: Revenue and head-count. If you could call me back with those, my number is 555-1621, or you could e-mail me at "pchiang"—that's chiang with an 'i.' Thank you."

Note that this caller gives advance notice that a phone number is coming (". . . my number is"), and giving the e-mail is a way to repeat who's calling. Another way is to repeat the name and phone number at the end. If the caller heard you correctly the first time, he or she can skip the rest of the message.

When you're leaving your own phone number, remember that a number that is *very* familiar to you may be unfamiliar to your caller. Always pause before the number and speak quite slowly and very distinctly. Some numbers are easily confused. "Nine" and "five" can sound close, so if your phone number includes those digits, say "nine" with a heavy emphasis on the end so that it sounds closer to "niner" and say "five" short and close to "fife." For the same reason, emphasize the end of "one" and say "zero" instead of "oh." You should always leave your number. There's nothing more frustrating than a message like "Hi, it's me! Call me back—you know the number." The person you are calling may usually contact you from his or her desk, where your number is entered into the phone's speed-dial memory, but just this once, your colleague may be trying to return the call from an airport and doesn't have a phone directory along.

Finally, make sure your message has an action step. Do you really need the other person to call you back? If so, with what information? Or were you just calling to leave information? In that case, it would be polite to say, "No need to call me back, I just wanted to let you know. . . ." This should lead you to the conclusion that phone messages shouldn't be one-sided discussions, and you should avoid complicated "if, and, but" constructions. If you are unsure what to do about a situation, you'll need to schedule a meeting or a person-to-person phone call. In that case the message should be something like this:

> "As you can see, it's a complicated situation, and I'm not sure how to proceed. Please, could you call me back, and if you get *my* voice mail, perhaps you could suggest a couple of times when I could reach you in person."

On some occasions in business, a voice message simply won't fulfill your needs, and you'll want to reach a live person (see Box 3-2).

3-5 When You Reach a Person and Not Voice Mail

Especially if you're recruiting, you are more likely than not to reach voice mail or an assistant. But you should be prepared for what to say if you

Box 3-2

Avoiding "Voice-Mail Jail"

Well-designed voice-mail systems are wonderful—you can leave a message for one specific person, or if you have a question that anyone can answer, you can choose an option that switches you to a live person. But some companies seem determined to prevent you from ever reaching anything other than voice mail. All lines lead to what is jokingly called "Voice-Mail Jail." No matter what you do, you can't seem to reach anything other than a recording.

There are some tricks that you can try to get around this problem. Even if the recorded message doesn't offer you the option to "press zero to talk to my assistant," you can try that, or 03 or the # key (different systems have different transfer options). Then, if you are trying to reach an executive and you get an assistant, it's fair to ask when is a good time to reach the manager in person, or if you can schedule a specific time for a phone conference.

If you are recruiting, an old trick is to call at the very beginning or end of the workday (see Figure 3-1). Many managers are still at their desks at 5:45 P.M., for example. Their assistants have left for the day, and the only calls they are expecting are from family members. If you try this ruse, understand that you'll catch the person on the other end a little off guard, so be extra polite—and brief.

---

reach a "real person." It doesn't make a good first impression to say, "Oh, wow! It's actually you! I thought I'd be getting voice mail!" And don't waste time with extensive apologies and fatuous recitations about how busy the other person must be.

All this means that, just as for voice mail, you should have your call outlined beforehand—three bullet points and an action step would be typical. Be sure to introduce yourself fully and carefully without mumbling. State the purpose of your call and aim to be both brief and strategic. The best definition of "strategic" is this: If this call is successful, what will result? Suppose you know that you are but one of several hundred applicants for a great job, and you've managed to find out the name and phone number of the decision-maker. You'll want to get across "three reasons why" you should be hired, and your goal is to make sure that you are offered an interview. If you are trying to land a new account for your business, clearly state what your firm has to offer and ask for a brief appointment to make a presentation. If you are professional and concise, few people will say "No."

Figure 3-1 One way to avoid "voice-mail jail" is to call at the beginning or end of the business day, when the phone will most likely ring through to the person you're trying to reach.

Don't forget to end with polite thanks to the person on the other end, but, again, no great effusive outpourings of gratitude are needed: Saying "Thank you for taking my call. I'll be sure to contact your assistant tomorrow to schedule an appointment. Goodbye." is enough.

3-6 Cell Phones

Mobile phones (cellular phones or "cell" phones) produce vehement reactions: People either love them or hate them. On the positive side, they've changed communication from place-to-place to person-to-person. You no longer need to remember a list of different numbers to reach one person, and you don't have to call around and ask if someone is there. In addition, it's easy to get voice-mail service with a cell phone, so many busy professionals rely on their cell phone as their primary phone number.

However, the rapid adoption of cell phones (more than 100 million are in use in the US—almost half the population has one) has caused a great disruption to civilized society because conventional rules of etiquette didn't anticipate a situation in which you could break off a conversation to talk to someone who is not present. We can make a commonsense approach to this problem by breaking it down into two parts:

First, using a cell phone in a public place often means that you are ignoring the people whom you are with—never a good idea. Second, cell phones can be noisy and disruptive: The ringing is distracting in public places, and the majority of users speak much more loudly on the phone than they would to someone right next to them.

With those problems in mind, we can easily derive some common-sense rules for good manners when using cell phones. If you were in a casual conversation with a friend walking down the street and you saw a business colleague nearby, would you say "Hi"? Of course. But if you were sitting having coffee with a friend, would you turn your back to the table and begin a long conversation with the waiter about sports scores? I hope not. So, if the setting is informal, then it's generally considered reasonable to answer a cell phone and take a brief message—but a long conversation would definitely be rude. In a semi-formal meeting, you might be able to respond to a ringing cell phone by saying, "If you'll excuse me, let me just take this . . ." and then making it clear to the caller that you are otherwise occupied and will call back later. But as the level of formality of the meeting increases, taking a call is unacceptable. In any formal business meeting, even the intrusion of a ringing cell phone that is not answered would be considered a discourtesy. At the highest level of formality—say a job interview—even having a cell phone visible tends to signal a lack of wholehearted commitment to the meeting at hand. So, although it's certainly useful to take a cell phone with you on job interviews (to check directions or to call if you are unavoidably delayed), you should always make sure that it is turned off and put away in your briefcase or purse before your meetings begin. Most formal restaurants (defined by a place with waiters and tablecloths) consider it very bad manners to use a phone at the table.

In informal settings, you should exercise some judgment about how you use the phone. In bars and cafés people routinely use their phones briefly, even at the table. But most people would find you rude if you engage in a long conversation or speak above a normal volume. If you have an important business matter, and the connection is not good, you should excuse yourself and leave the table. You can take the call in a corridor or use a phone both. Be sensitive to the concern that speaking on the phone means that you will be ignoring the people whom you're with. So your absence should be limited.

Many cell phones have a "silent" mode that replaces the ringer with a vibration, and of course, all cell phones can be turned off. You should be very careful to turn off your phone in movies, theaters, and concerts, and you should put the ringer on "silent" in most social settings. However, be aware that the vibration from a silent cell phone incoming call can be disruptive itself, if you interrupt a conversation for no apparent reason to answer your phone.

Most cell phones come with "Caller ID" so that you can recognize who is calling by looking at the phone. For that reason, most cell phone users answer the phone without identification, by just saying "Hello," or by greeting the caller when they recognize the name. That behavior is acceptable for informal social use, but in business (for example, if you are a salesperson who gives out a cell phone number to customers), it's still much better to give a full greeting when answering the phone. This principle also applies if you are in a recruiting situation: If a recruiter is calling you, just answering with a grunt doesn't get the conversation off to a good start.

One unfortunate corollary of the ability to reach anyone anywhere at anytime is that all plans become tentative: "Well, we're going out to get something to eat, but we probably will go to a movie later. I'll give you a call. . . ." Although a certain amount of spontaneity is expected in social situations, you should work hard to avoid multiple to-and-fro call-backs in business. Try to think through a situation and offer a reasonable plan; then call back only if circumstances unexpectedly change.

3-7 Conference Calls

A **conference call** is a system that allows many participants to join in the same conversation. It's used commonly in certain industries, such as financial services. There are two types of conference calls. One is essentially one-way closed-circuit radio: Using your phone, you "tune in" and hear an announcement of something such as a firm's quarterly reports. Conference calls like this can be used to connect literally thousands of people.

The second type of conference call is interactive—it's like a group meeting, where a dozen or more people can be on the same conference call. In this case, you can talk as well as listen (see Figure 3-2). These types of conference calls are useful for updating progress in long-duration projects where team members are far distant from one another. They are more likely to work well in routine situations and when the team members have previously met and know one another well. Another good use is for a workgroup that comes together intermittently, such as to plan a new staff orientation program once a year. Again, conference calls work best when there is a foundation of previous face-to-face contact. Of course, the advantage of the conference call system is that you can stay at your own location and avoid having to invest perhaps a couple of days of travel to complete just one meeting.

Figure 3-2 A conference call is a system that allows many participants to join in the same conversation. The advantage of the conference call is that you can stay at your own location and avoid having to invest perhaps a couple of days to travel to complete one meeting.
©Keith Brofsky?PhotoDisc/PictureQuest

For both types of conference calls, the system usually requires that you dial an 800 number and punch in an access code. You'll have to clear your schedule and make sure that you are not interrupted (including putting up a sign on your door if necessary). It's important to avoid distracting noises (such as background office conversations or shuffling papers), so many people use speaker phones for conference calls and use the **mute button** to silence the microphone on their phones, unless they are actually making a contribution.

Conference calls are most successful when a printed (or e-mailed) agenda is shared by the participants before the call starts. The agenda should show the name and affiliation of all the people on the call and should have an estimated time for each part of the meeting. Participants usually greet one another by identifying themselves and saying, "I'm on." One person acts as the moderator, watching the timing and moving the conference along by carefully summarizing discussion. The moderator should state consensus, or what he or she believes to be consensus, and then "poll" the participants to see whether everyone is in agreement. For example:

"So, most people think the harbor cruise wasn't worth the extra expense, and we should just book an additional dinner at the hotel?"

The moderator should encourage input from everyone by referring to a list of participants. If you act as moderator and find that you are being sidetracked in a debate about which there appears to be no clear agreement, it's sometimes helpful just to state that and move on: "OK, so we have lots of opinions about the Friday night entertainment, and no clear plan at this point. So, we'll have to get back to you with some specific bids for the alternatives. We can send them out in writing before the next call."

The moderator should try to clarify wishes and hopes ("We need a better cost estimate") and develop them into action steps with deadlines that are assigned to specific group members.

Many people find that the most difficult part of conference calls is sustaining attention (because the call may last more than an hour). You may find that you need to take a break for a few minutes and then re-join the conversation. Taking notes may help keep you focused on the discussion.

3-8 Video Conferencing

Video conferencing has been heavily promoted as a way for firms to save on travel costs. Although many different systems have been introduced and you'll see many firms proudly show off their video-conferencing facilities, you probably won't find that many are used. Video conferencing has not fulfilled its promise to eliminate business travel. Why not? Well, there are many reasons. Most people don't feel comfortable being on camera. In a (voice) conference call, you can scratch yourself or move around in your chair without wondering what this looks like to other people. Looking into a camera and talking may feel pretty idiotic at first. Just seeing a picture of a colleague doesn't give the richness of non-verbal communication that is part of a face-to-face meeting, and if the video transmission has distortion, jitteriness, or delays, the whole experience is like watching an ancient Charlie Chaplin movie—pretty laughable. In theory, a video conference allows participants to share visual information, such as charts and schematics. However, much the same result can be achieved with fax or the Internet exchange of documents and then a (voice) conference call.

Like conference calls, video conferences work best when the participants have some history of a face-to-face working relationship, when there is a pre-announced agenda, and when one person acts as the chairperson or moderator. It's highly unlikely that, even with a great deal of pre-planning, a video conference could substitute for a face-to-face

Figure 3-3 A video conference, which can be conducted on-line or
through traditional camera feeds, allows participants to
share visual information, such as charts and schematics.
©Digital Vision/PictureQuest

meeting when you are proposing new business with people you haven't
met before. Because there is an element of theater about video conferencing (see Figure 3-3), you'll have to think about whether you should have
some graphics made to make a particular point (such as the growth in
sales of your product).

Video conferencing has a few requirements that differ from voice-
conference calls. You'll probably be required to attend a specially equipped
conference room that has the correct lighting and a plain background.
The conventional wisdom is that you should avoid wearing distracting
patterns, and you probably should not wear the medium-bright blue
called "French blue" for a shirt or blouse. Some systems use the TV
production device called "blue screen" to overlap images, and it depends
on the bright blue being used only for a background. If your firm uses
video conferencing with any regularity, the company's audio-visual
specialists will undoubtedly manage the equipment. You should take some
time to get their advice on how to make your appearance professional, and
they will be able to arrange some practice sessions too.

Put This Chapter into Practice

1. Ask your professional colleagues and talk to someone who has experience with video conferencing.

2. Practice leaving short, concise voice-mail messages and clearly articulating your call-back number.

Understanding e-mail

4

Key Terms

Alias   Flame   Spam

O u t l i n e

e-mail is not just a letter that you can send quickly

Several times each week, I receive an e-mail with a vague subject line, such as "I have a question for you. . . ." I'm always tempted to say, "And I have an answer for you!" as I hit the Delete key. Like many professional people, I receive several dozen e-mails a day and have to choose which ones get my full attention. Coming up with a good title for your e-mail is just one of many practical rules for making your use of e-mail efficient and professional.

e-mail is a cross between a phone call and a written memo. In part, it's like a phone call because the style is usually quite brief and informal. But the communication is not as rich as a phone call because it's only a one-way communication, not a discussion. e-mail has some advantages over the phone: It doesn't interrupt the recipient, and it can be used to make a permanent record (other people can save a copy of what you wrote or can print it out). The good part of this semi-permanence is that it can be used to announce a policy that co-workers can check back with in the future. The bad part is that e-mail can be a "smoking gun" if someone sues you or your firm.

e-mail comes in two flavors: text-based (called "plain") and HTML-formatted[1] (called "styled"). Although most people read e-mail from the Internet and can see formatted text, if your recipients use a text-based program such as PINE, they won't be able to read your message if you send in HTML. The workaround is to send your message as "plain and styled"

---

1. "HTML" stands for "Hyper Text Markup Language."

(this is an option on your outbound e-mail program). Remember that people who receive a text-only message won't see formatting the same way you do on your screen, so e-mail protocol includes some conventions about punctuation (see section 4-5 for more details). An advantage of HTML-formatted text is that you can include URL[2] and "mailto" hyper-links that the receivers can activate with a simple mouse click.

"Instant messaging," which is popular among friends, is simply an e-mail system that keeps track of who is—and who is not—logged on to a system at any one time. So it's great for former high school friends who are away at college. You can break up the boredom of writing a term paper by seeing who's hanging out online. But for just that reason, you should probably avoid instant messaging at work. "Chatting" through e-mail can be a huge waste of time—you don't want to give the impression that you don't have your full attention on your work. And quickly replying to an instant message carries a big risk that you'll disclose company secrets or write using slang that is inappropriate at work.

The e-mail system at work belongs to your company, and the firm has fairly broad rights to examine and copy what you write. In practice, most professionals do a reasonable amount of social communication through their company e-mail. For example, using the company e-mail to arrange a purely social lunch meeting is likely to be considered a *de minimis* use (that is, so small that it doesn't matter) of a firm's e-mail system. However, your firm may have policies against using e-mail extensively; for example, managing an after-work sports league on the firm's e-mail could get you into trouble. Certainly, you should never, ever use company e-mail to set up a private business or to look for a new job. For that reason, many people have a work account and a personal account (see section 4-2 for more details). From the firm's point of view, allowing a certain amount of personal use of an e-mail system probably means that business messages are more likely to be read outside office hours, which is why companies tacitly encourage employees to use the firm's e-mail for social purposes.

Sections 4-1 through 4-6 provide some basic rules for outgoing mail—mail that you send.

4-1 Your e-mail Account Name

Choose your e-mail name with care: Although your friends from summer camp all understand why your name is *stinky@hotmail.com,* it doesn't look good on your resume. Cute nicknames don't look professional.

---

2. "URL" stands for "Uniform Resource Locator."

e-mail names with numbers are easy to mistype. For example, you can tell at once that there's a typo in *haryrpotter@mail.com,* but it's more difficult to catch that *harry878@mail.com* was supposed to be *harry787@mail.com.*

e-mail names that contain underscores, such as

>   charles_windsor@royalty.com

may be difficult for correspondents to enter correctly. The underscore character "_" requires the writer to use the Shift key and hunt around the keyboard. Moreover, the underscore can become obscured if an e-mail name is automatically underlined in a web document. So it's best to avoid this character, if you can. Some e-mail systems permit the use of a period within the name, as in

>   ronald.reagan@government.gov

Many firms choose e-mail names for you, but that approach may not be helpful. If everyone calls you "Jimmy Carter," but the e-mail administrator assigns you *jamesecarter@bigco.com,* you may have to live with something you don't like, and which colleagues don't recognize. So it's worth anticipating this problem, and when someone tells you that you're going to be given an e-mail account, you should try to have some input to the name that is assigned.

If you are assigned an e-mail name that you wouldn't have chosen for yourself, a good workaround is to use a carefully written signature file. A signature file is a tag line that your e-mail program automatically adds to every outbound message you send. You can use it for your exact name and affiliation (if that's not clear from your e-mail name) and your phone numbers (very handy if you hope to get a callback). However, don't use it to express your personal philosophy, such as "Life is hard . . . then you die." The touching quote, which changed your life, may not be quite as appealing to other people.

4-2 Multiple e-mail Accounts

Many people have one e-mail account at work and another for social and domestic use. The good part of having multiple accounts is that you won't be accused of using company resources for some personal activity such as organizing a class reunion. But be careful about multiple e-mail accounts. They can be very confusing if people don't know which one to use to reach you. You wouldn't give two street addresses to a friend who was going to come over to see you, and if someone asked for your address to mail a letter, you wouldn't say, "Well, you could mail it to the house or to my fish-ing cabin, which I sometimes use." When someone doesn't read an important e-mail, the excuse "I haven't checked that account for a while" is an unprofessional response. Business associates need one clear address through which they can always reliably reach you.

4-3 e-mail Manners

Only some subjects should be communicated by e-mail. On the one hand, e-mail is very good for practical issues: setting times and places of meetings, handling decisions that can be made without much discussion, and posting general "FYI" (for your information) topics that don't require a response. On the other hand, e-mail is terrible for anything that involves emotional content. A message such as "I really didn't feel that you were listening to my suggestions" definitely needs to be delivered in person. If someone upsets you in a face-to-face meeting, he or she can probably sense your distress and calm you down. But that kind of feedback doesn't occur with e-mail. Firing off an angry tirade is easy, and such e-mails have a special name: **flames.** You should delete all "flames" before you send them out. If you are seriously angry about something, schedule a discussion and talk about the issue face-to-face. Even a simple comment such as "That's *not* the way I wanted this handled!" could be very upsetting to a co-worker.

Jokes forwarded by friends enliven the workday. But there's a tremendous downside. Quite a few young professionals have been fired for forwarding jokes with racial or sexual content that violate their firm's policies. Although you may have had a chuckle at the first few lines of a forwarded joke, further down there might be something raunchy that you didn't see. Although this rule sounds puritanical, it's best not to send out or forward *any* jokes at all using your firm's e-mail.

Remember that e-mails can be stored, copied, and forwarded. So a simple, friendly "I guess we all know who had too much to drink at dinner last night!" can look pretty awful when it's forwarded to your boss.

Many programs keep copies of your outgoing mail, and (because your firm owns the e-mail system) courts have repeatedly held that you have no right to privacy of messages on the company's e-mail. So pretend that every message you write might be printed and posted on a bulletin board in the company cafeteria. "Can we meet after work on Friday?" is pretty innocent, but "Want to catch some action with a big guy?" (however much intended as a joke) probably fails the bulletin board test.

An e-mail sent is not necessarily an e-mail received. If you mistype a recipient's name (for example, *buhs@government.org* when you mean "bush"), the e-mail will eventually come back to you (it's called a "bounce-back") with a note from your e-mail system: Message Undeliverable. However, if you happened to type the name of another person in the organization (in this case, if someone had the name "John Buhs" and his e-mail was indeed *buhs@governnment.org*), your message would appear to be delivered. You can check on delivery by sending yourself a blind copy (when you get the copy, you at least know the e-mail has been sent). For important issues, don't be afraid to call and follow up: "I wanted to be sure you received my e-mail. . . ."

e-mail can be useful for documenting work that you have done. For example, if you are a junior member of a team, and you've asked nicely two times to reserve the conference room for your boss and no action has been taken, your "Sent" e-mail files prove that you have been making the request.

On the other hand, don't copy your boss on every little e-mail (this practice is called "copying up"). It gets tiresome, and it doesn't make you look good. There's a happy medium here: You reasonably should keep your superiors informed of what you are working on and when you will be gone from the office. On the other hand, you should resist merely showboating. Don't send up copies that merely show how clever you were at handling an issue (or how unreasonable your colleagues are being).

Most e-mail systems time-stamp the date and time you send an e-mail, and records clearly show when an inbound message was sent. Be careful to be truthful if you have overlooked something because e-mail is a clear documentation of just when you were informed.

4-4 Titles for Your e-mail

Put 90 percent of your effort into the title (see Figure 4-1). Microsoft Outlook and some other modern e-mail programs allow someone receiving your mail to preview about the first four lines of a message. However, on many e-mail systems, all your recipients can see at first is the title or "Subject" line. So your title should let the readers know the essence of your message: "Cannot meet next Tuesday" is much better (and more likely to get a meeting rescheduled) than a message titled "Hi from New York!"

Colons in titles can help to structure your ideas:

Re: Quarterly Results: Not due till Friday: Revenue available now

This example tells most of the story and makes your message clear.

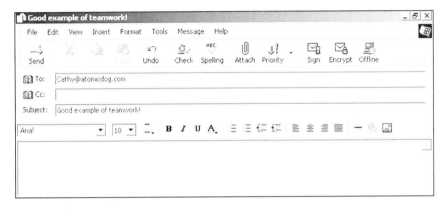

Figure 4-1 The title of your e-mail is the first thing a recipient sees and most important thing to think about when you're composing it.

4-5 e-mail Styles

Several short e-mail messages are better than one long message. When you send several messages, your recipients can reply to items one at a time. With the exception of routine information (summaries of committee reports are one example), you should aim for a message that can be read in one screen without scrolling. Many cell phones and pagers can now receive e-mail on the Short Message Service (SMS) protocol, so you should try to make your most important information come early in your message. Ask yourself, "How will this look if I could read only two lines of the text?"

There are many schools of thought about salutations (greetings) and closings. One argument is that because the recipients know who they are, they don't need a "Dear Bill" at the beginning, and it only wastes valuable screen "real estate." In general, you don't need a formal close, such as "Sincerely, Sarah Brown." But if your e-mail address is non-intuitive (*8822K@aol.com*), it's a good idea to say who you are, so you might introduce yourself quite early in the message:

"Hey, Sherry: This is Justin from your training class writing to ask. . . ."

A little bit of formatting can go a very long way. Unless you are a computer science propeller-head, use of the Shift key is always nice, and a few line breaks and paragraphs will add to the clarity of your communication:

> Tom,
>
> Do you have the Q3 figures? I need revenue estimates for the Sales Meeting at Noon today.
>
> Thank you, Maggie

The preceding example is much clearer (and friendlier!) than the following one:

> Send the Q3 figures ASAP. I need revenue estimates at once.

e-mail tends to use punctuation in a different way from ordinary letters and memos. Underline before and after a word like _this_ is read as *italic,* and an asterisk before and after like *this* signals **bold.** Used judiciously, these tricks can add variety to your writing and clarity to your message.

In letters, quotation marks usually signal either reported direct speech (He said that he was "highly impressed" with your work) or an unusual use of a word (He said he was "married" to his job). But in plain-text e-mail, they are useful for setting off words, so people use them much more frequently. Here's an example:

> I guess to get everyone to buy in on this, it's time to call a "meeting."

But you should AVOID ALL CAPITALS; this format is hard to read and looks like you're shouting.

No matter how close your relationship with someone, save swear words for face-to-face casual conversations. Obscenities look terrible when forwarded, printed, or even just read on someone else's screen. (Reason: The written word imposes a moderately high level of formality; even if you mean a casual comment, your lively language will look more serious when it appears in print or on the screen.)

A clear question can be a useful summary and conclusion to an e-mail. "So would you prefer to meet later in the day or postpone till next week?" increases the chances of a helpful (and fast) reply.

4-6 Sending e-mail to Many People at Once

"**Aliases**" and "distribution lists" allow you to send a message to many people at once. Your e-mail administrator may have set up an alias so that typing the word "marketing" in the "To:" line sends your e-mail to everyone working in the Marketing department. If you regularly write to a group of people, for whom an alias doesn't exist, creating a group name or distribution list on your own computer is worthwhile. (You must

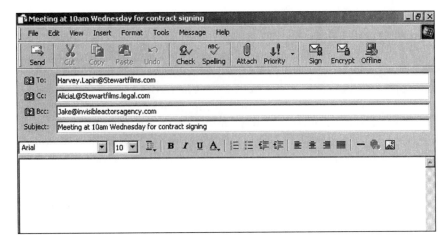

Figure 4-2   This e-mail is to Harvey.Lapin@Stewartfilms.com; Harvey can see that AliciaL@Stewartfilms.legal.com also gets a copy but doesn't see that Jake@invisibleactorsagency. com gets a copy too.

choose a name, and you'll need to select the recipients one time, but after that, you just use the group name.)

However, if you live by the alias, you can die by the alias. If you send out too many e-mail messages to more people than you need to address, you risk becoming an "autodelete." That is, people will be so accustomed to receiving irrelevant messages from you that whenever they see your name they'll delete your messages without reading them. So choose to address the smallest group that does the job (not everyone in a department).

In addition to the "To:" line for the original recipient, e-mail comes with two forms of copy: "Cc:" means a copy is sent to someone else, and "Bcc:" means a "blind copy" (see Figure 4-2). When you send an e-mail to Harvey with a blind copy to Jake, Jake gets a copy of the message but Harvey can't see that it's also been sent to Jake. Your e-mail program may—or may not—tell the recipient of a blind copy that it's a copy of a message. This can cause confusion if the person being copied thinks that the original message was for him or her.

Sending a copy of a message to yourself is sometimes useful, if you've logged on to a computer other than your own machine.

If you are sending an e-mail to a long list of people, for which you don't have an alias, a useful trick is to put their names into the "Bcc" field, having addressed the e-mail to yourself. Everyone gets the message, correctly addressed to them, without a header containing dozens of other names that fill the screen.

How many times should you remind people about an event? For most events, the advertising rule "inform, persuade, remind" translates into no more than three e-mail announcements: The first is a quick "heads up" so that people are aware of the event and can provisionally save the day and time; the second e-mail has more information so that people who are interested can make a decision whether to attend; and the last is a quick reminder in the 24 hours before an event to ensure good participation.

Remember that any e-mail you send can be instantly printed out or forwarded. An e-mail that begins "Just between you and me . . ." is an invitation to a recipient to "Fwd" the message to just the person you did *not* want to know your opinion.

4-7 Managing Incoming e-mail

Now let's look at some commonsense rules for in-bound e-mail.

You should be sure to always check your business e-mail account regularly. Unless you are on vacation or traveling away from your office, a *minimum* frequency would be to check your e-mail at the beginning, middle, and end of the workday. (The rule should be "morning, noon, and night.") Because business colleagues may use e-mail to update you overnight (in preference to waking you with a phone call), you should begin your workday with a quick review of your e-mail to see whether there have been any urgent changes in the day's planned activities.

4-8 Prioritizing Your e-mail

One good tip for handling a large group of e-mails after an absence is to answer the "most recent first." You'll encounter lost data that colleagues have suddenly found—"Sorry, I've got it! I realized it was in your previous e-mail!"—and "impossible" meetings that have been called off—"Sorry, I realized that next week won't work for you because you're at the sales meeting."

Answer selectively and by priority. Not every e-mail needs an answer with your opinion. Prioritize by who has sent the message—your boss and customers will appreciate getting your attention at once. Some e-mail programs allow you to highlight incoming mail from certain people in different colors.

Understand what turn-around time (response speed) is expected within your firm or workgroup. Some consulting firms understand that the partners may not be able to conveniently log on to e-mail more often than every other day if they're traveling. (For that reason, they may prefer voice mail.) On the other hand, in some financial services firms, a 45-minute wait for a reply during the trading day would seem like eternity.

Make sure you know how the "Bcc:" works. That is, you may not be the only person reading an e-mail that appears to be a private note to you.

4-9 Deleting, Filtering, and Saving e-mail

Never be afraid to delete: that's what the Delete key is for. Delete **spam**—the e-mail equivalent of junk mail, such as a message sent (without much thought) to a very large group of people, or a commercial message from a firm that has "captured" your e-mail name; jokes; and Fwd's (forwarded messages) from people you don't know. e-mail can contain viruses, and most of them are in files attached to original messages. Even someone you know may unwittingly forward you a file that contains a virus. Many professionals won't open an e-mail attachment unless it contains information that they've been expecting (so don't be surprised to get a phone call to confirm, before someone will open a file that you sent).

Messages can exist in (at least) two places: On the server—that is, the computer that handles e-mail for your firm—and also on the hard drive of your computer. Indeed, a message could be on both your laptop and desk machine. Keeping old messages poses a small security risk (other people could "spy" on your work if they gain access to your computer if you leave it running and unattended). But for most people, it's just too useful to keep old messages so that they can be referred to.

Understand whether the original versions of your messages are being left on the server—you may exceed a limit on file space. You can choose to routinely delete them from the server as you read them on to your machine, and you can have different preferences. For example, your e-mail program on your laptop is set *not* to delete. When you log on to your desktop, you can see both new messages and have a permanent copy of messages you already saw on your laptop.

The number of old messages can become large. Your e-mail program may routinely prompt you to "archive" old items (you move items received during certain dates to a separate file and reduce the space needed for your "inbox"). But a better solution is to learn to use folders to save messages. For example, you might have one folder labeled "Admin" for routine administrative announcements and another labeled "Project X" for a new product development. Sorting into folders makes retrieving relevant information much faster.

Investigate whether your e-mail program can "filter"—that is, automatically move spam into a separate folder. You can check the folder with less frequency than your regular messages. e-mail programs that have a "preview" allow you to look at the first few lines of a message without opening it. This feature can be a great time-saver because you can very quickly see what to delete.

You can try to "unsubscribe" to unwanted spam. The annoying message may include instructions to a web site where you can remove your name from the list. Or you can try replying to the spam with the word "unsubscribe" in both the title and the message. Some e-mail administration programs automatically search for the word and remove your name from a large alias. However, many experts warn that merely replying to a spam only confirms that your e-mail address is active, and will expose you to even more spam. It's probable that Congress will enact some restrictions on spamming, as many corporate mail systems are dealing with more spam than legitimate business messages.

Delete all "flames" that are sent to you. The person who sent such messages to you probably regretted sending them a few minutes later. Reading all the nasty things someone has to say about you will only ruin your day. If someone is really interested in working through some tough issues, talk face-to-face.

Remember, however, that many computer operating systems keep all deleted messages in a file called "Trash." This feature is helpful if you decide later you need something (you can "restore" it from Trash). But the downside is that a copy of sensitive material may be on your hard drive until you remember to "empty trash."

4-10 "Reply to All"

When you're replying to e-mails, be very careful of the "Reply to all" function. If you have any doubt that the system you're using too easily slips into "Reply to all," better to start a new message with the recipient's name typed in. For example, if your office administrator sends out an e-mail to everyone in your firm noting that there's been a change in your office supplies firm, you don't want 2,000 colleagues to get a copy of your message saying, "Thanks for telling me about the new office supplies firm. I forgot to tell you—I need a new stapler for my desk."

Put This Chapter into Practice

1. e-mail is probably one of the most important productivity tools in modern offices, but it comes with its own vices as well as virtues. If you learn to master your e-mail program, you'll greatly increase your professionalism and effectiveness on the job.

2. Take the worst e-mail you received recently and re-write it, putting 90 percent of your effort into the subject line.

Letters, Memos, and Reports

Outline

Most firms have a "house style" that you should follow carefully

A few years ago, a newspaper story noted that the cost of sending a business letter had risen to more than $15. This amount seems astounding—when you think about mailing a letter, probably only the cost of the stamp comes to mind, and that's not much. But when you add in the staff time to prepare the letter (and all the overhead on the worker such as health care costs and vacation time), the cost of printing, getting the letter into the mail, filing a copy, and so on, you can see how the $15 adds up.

So it's not surprising that in many instances you'll find that your firm discourages you from sending a letter. Many companies respond to simple letters of inquiry with phone calls or e-mail, and the amount of business conducted by regular mail is dropping. However, in certain circumstances you'll have to write a letter. Letters often form the basis of contracts such as in purchasing or in employment. For that reason, in business the content of your letters will require some thought, and you'll need some precision in choosing the right words.

No matter what level you are hired at, very few US companies will provide you with a secretary. You'll be positively laughed at if you write out a letter by hand and ask your team's assistant to type it for you. You will be expected to write letters yourself, directly using the computer on your desk (although you may well assign a junior colleague to deal with addressing envelopes, mailing, inserting brochures, and so on). If you are writing a letter on a complicated business topic with important consequences for your firm, it's certainly acceptable to ask a colleague to review the letter before you send it out (you can easily do so by e-mailing a file **attachment**) to make sure there are no ambiguities. For example, you should be confident about saying to a co-worker or to your supervisor: "I've written the letter to SupplierCo rejecting their bid and asking them to re-submit. Could you take a look at it before I mail it?"

Let's begin with the easy issues: formatting.

5-1 Layout for Business Letters

Before you send a letter on behalf of your firm, look around for copies of materials recently sent by members of your workgroup. Your firm will have one or more types of official stationery. For example, each division may have a separate "letterhead," or there may be a special letterhead for a product line or promotional campaign. Be careful never to use the company's letterhead or envelopes for personal correspondence. For instance, if you decided to write a letter to the editor of a business magazine commenting on a recent article, if you mistakenly use the firm's notepaper, your letter will be mistaken as an official pronouncement of your firm.

The firm may have a specific typeface and layout that you'll be expected to follow. Ideally, the firm will have a written style guide that can be brief but comprehensive—often one well-written page can improve the "public face" of a workgroup. However, it's quite possible that you'll be given no guidance, and you'll find inconsistencies in examples from your workgroup. As a default, you should follow these rules.

1. Whenever possible, try to make your letter no longer than one page. Most letters that are longer either need to be broken down into two separate communications (different people are likely to work on various issues) or "deconstructed" into a **letter of transmittal** (see Table 5-1, "Types of Business Letters" on page 71) and one or more attachments (an "attachment" is a term that refers to any report or document that is sent with a letter, although more often than not, it is not actually *attached* with a staple or clip). For example, if you are arranging a conference for several of your suppliers, you'll have a lot of information about transportation, lodging, participants, and the agenda. Each deserves a separate document, rather than being crammed into one letter, which can be confusing. Other overly long letters deserve to be broken into two or more separate communications.

2. Always center a letter on the page. If you're writing a short note of acknowledgment, having a paragraph scrunched at the top of the page, followed by a lot of blank space after your name, looks unprofessional.

3. Use a *serif* font (such as Garamond, Times Roman, or Book Antiqua), not a *sans serif* font such as Arial or Univers. Don't use a font size that is too small. Many printers default to 10 point, but 12 point will likely look better. Use single-spacing within paragraphs and double-spacing between.

4. Almost all firms use a "block" format with all the parts of a letter beginning at the left margin. One exception is that some firms still put the date on the far right ("right justified"). There's no virtue in this placement, and you can avoid it unless it is part of your firm's "house style." Using "full justification" (where the right margin is straight as well as the left) requires your word processing program to pack spaces between words in each line of text. This can make some unusual-looking spaces and make a block of words in a paragraph hard to read. A "ragged right" margin is easier to read.

5. When letters were written with typewriters, it was usual to indent (or "**tab**"[1]) one inch at the beginning of each paragraph. Because you'll be using a computer and you'll double-space between paragraphs, you don't need this indent.

5-2 Parts of a Letter

Businesspeople expect information in a letter to come in a particular order. There are some differences between the accepted style in Europe and the US, and you should know the standard form for American letters. The sections are as follows.

The date comes first. This is the date you write the letter—not the date that you meant to write the letter. If you try to backdate a letter—put a date on it from a day before the date of the day when you are actually writing—you could run into trouble if the letter is ever used in a court case against your firm; it gives the impression that you were attempting fraud.

The format for the date in US commerce is

September 15, 2003

You also may see this format: September 15th, 2003 (although that would be exceptional). Note that you don't use the day of the week, as in "Wednesday, September 15th . . . ," which might be used in a social letter between friends or family.

---

1. "Tab" is short for "tabulator," an invention that allowed the carriage of a typewriter to move over one inch or so, rather than one letter space—so-called because it allowed typists to set up *tables* of numbers.

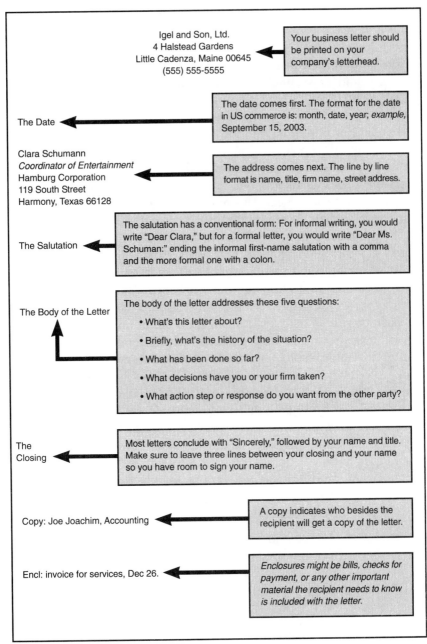

Figure 5-1   The parts of a business letter.

The format *Month, Day, Year* is uniquely American. (One suggestion is that it was a symbol of separation from Great Britain after the Declaration of Independence, but because the US national holiday is always referred to as "the Fourth of July," that explanation hardly makes sense.) In Europe and most other parts of the world, you'll see the following format:

>15 September 2003

This logical "small, medium, large" ordering is quite common among US computer companies, so you should feel free to follow it if it is acceptable to your firm.

The address comes next. The line-by-line format is Name, Title, Firm name, Street address, as in this example:

>Jan Schiewe, MD
>
>Medical Director
>
>Mid-town Hospital
>
>1234 Main Street
>
>Anytown, CA 12345-0100

Note that you usually don't use an **honorific**[2] on the address but do include a degree that is used professionally. Using the form "Attn.: Jan Schiewe" is old-fashioned. In most cases, the word "Attention" doesn't add any value. If a **recipient**—the person to whom you are sending the letter—says, "Mark it to my attention, or it'll never get to me," the format is

>Medical Staff Office: Attn.: Jan Schiewe, MD
>
>Mid-town Hospital
>
>1234 Main Street
>
>Anytown, CA 12345-0100

Never, ever put "Attention" and then a name on the last line of an address. Most mail is sorted automatically, and the sorting machines "look" for the last line of the address to machine-read the ZIP code. It's always best to look up the extended ZIP (ZIP + four) because it really does speed delivery. Use the two-letter post office designated abbreviation for the state, and in the US the city name is not in all capital letters as it is in parts of Europe.

You begin a letter with a salutation, which has a conventional form:

---

2. In full, "honorific title," meaning a formal style of address, such as "mister" or "doctor."

Dear Jan,

or

Dear Dr. Schiewe:

If you use the informal first name, end the greeting with a comma; if you use the formal title with honorific (in this example "Dr."), then the salutation ends with a colon. You'll see many letters addressed by first name only, even when the correspondent doesn't know the recipient. Such a greeting may seem jarring as it presumes a low level of formality. A reasonable rule would be to use the "Dear Tom," form only when you've met the recipient in person and would address him or her by a first name.

The form "Dear Dr. Jan Schiewe" is wrong and shouldn't be used. In general, for people whom you don't know, you should use the honorific "Mr." for all men. For women, use "Ms." unless you know specifically that the recipient prefers to be addressed as "Mrs." (For example, the former US Secretary of State was always referred to as "Mrs. Madeleine Albright.") You will have problems if you don't know whether the recipient is male or female. If the letter is important (for example, if you are applying for a job), you'll need to make a phone call. An executive with the name "Dana Leath" would be impressed that you called to say, "May I ask, is 'Dana Leath' Ms. Leath?" At the limit, in rare circumstances in which you are confronted with a name you cannot understand, it's probably better to begin a letter with "Dear Phat Quach" rather than "Dear Ms. Phat" when in fact Mr. Quach is male and is called "Phat" by his friends.

Many business letters have a subject line—you can see why. Some pairs of firms have hundreds of pieces of correspondence going between them every week, all on different topics. The form for a subject line is either two lines above the salutation, left justified (the most common American form), or centered and two lines after the greeting. The line is introduced with either the word "Subject:" or the word "Re:." ("Re" is a contraction of "in re," Latin for "in the matter of.")

Turning now to the body of your letter, you should quickly get to the point. (This is in contrast with communication in Japan, and some other countries, where beginning a letter—even a business letter—without some pleasantry about the weather or recent holidays is considered rude.) If you have chosen not to use a subject line, your first sentence should indicate your purpose:

"I am writing in reply to your request for a new quotation for insurance on your boat."

Box 5-1

To Whom it May Concern

Y ou may come across a letter written by someone else with the strange salutation "To whom it may concern." It was a form of address used when a letter was sent to a recipient that the writer could not identify by name. This is very old-fashioned. It was common for letters of reference given to departing household servants such as butlers and maids. They would carry this general recommendation with them as they looked for a new job. This anonymous salutation was also used when someone was writing to a company but did not know who would actually be handling the letter.

This salutation is an old-fashioned form that violates just about every rule of Plain English, so you should avoid it. The reaction of most modern business people is "Well, it doesn't concern *me!*" That is, your letter can easily be ignored. "To whom" is a very high level of formality, so it begins in a rather stiff manner—unlikely to engage the reader. And "may concern" implies some doubt—perhaps it concerns you, perhaps it doesn't.

These days, with cheap long-distance phone rates and universal access to the Internet, you should easily be able to find the correct name, spelling, address, and mail code of the person who will handle your request. But in some circumstances you'll have to write to a company when you have been unable to find a personal name. In that case, address the envelope and letter to the correct department, such as "Human Resource Department" or "Accounts Payable: Student Loans," with as much detail as possible so that your letter lands on the right desk. Then, for the salutation, invent a nice, slightly flattering title such as

> Dear Human Resource Professionals:

or

> Dear Student Loan Officer:

It pays to be as precise as possible. For example, if you write "We provide free shipping," a customer could claim in the future that this was a promise to always ship at your firm's expense. If you are offering free shipping for a limited time and only on orders more than a certain total value, then it's best to say precisely that.

If you're having difficulty in formulating a letter to address a complicated business situation, try this simple framework:

- What's this letter about?
- Briefly, what's the history of the situation?
- What has been done so far?

- What decisions have you or your firm made?
- What action step or response do you want from the other party?

Not all letters need to end with an action step. For example, if you are just giving people information that they requested, you might have nothing further to say. However, as a general rule, if you can't think what the action step should be, perhaps you needn't send a letter at all.

In some business disputes you may need to write a letter to document your side of the story. In that case using the words "to document" may be helpful. An experienced businessperson will read this as signaling that you are very serious and may move toward litigation (suing the other firm or person). You should never threaten, no matter how unreasonable the person to whom you are writing has been. If you think the situation may end up in court (for example, when your firm is owed money), you may need to foreshadow the possibility of legal action, but do so with regret: "I'm sure you'll agree that neither of us wants this dispute to result in litigation. . . ." If you are seriously considering a court action, then you should carefully consult with your firm's attorneys (who may be referred to as "counsel" or "the legal department") and have them review the wording of every letter.

The closing for a letter has a set form. Historically, letters written in English ended with profuse expressions of fealty, such as "I have the honor to remain your grace's most humble servant." This form was gradually contracted to "Yours sincerely," although most Americans now end with the single word "Sincerely," as in this example:

Sincerely,

Harriet J. Makepeace

Corporate Counsel

Some people still use "Yours sincerely," but note that because it is a sentence fragment, the "s" on "sincerely" is not capitalized. In countries that use British English, you'll see "Yours truly," from people who've not met each other, and "Yours faithfully," if a high level of formality is intended. In American English, "Sincerely," is the most formal term, followed by "Cordially," (a word that means both "sincerely" and "warmly") and "Best regards," or "Best wishes,". These forms in turn have been abbreviated by some writers to "Best," on its own—which seems meaningless. Be careful about ending with "Best personal regards," in business. This is certainly appropriate to use in social correspondence with a friend, but in business it might be misinterpreted as implying that you want a business relationship to develop into something more intimate.

There should be three or more lines between the closing word(s) and your name. You should use the same form of your name as written on your business card, although signing a more informal name is acceptable. For example, the printed words might be "Charles W. Ford," with "Chuck Ford" signed above. It's a good idea to sign letters (and contracts) in blue ink (or some other color if your firm has a distinctive color scheme to its printed material). The color signals that this is an original document. This is especially important in two circumstances: First, in contract negotiation it may matter which of a set of documents was an original (and who has the originals and who has copies). Second, when you are sending out a mass mailing (for example, sending resumes to many employers or sending a letter to many different customers), a blue-ink signature shows a more personal touch, whereas signing in black ink makes the letter look "generic."

After your name, you should indicate your job title, and either whom you work for or the title of your workgroup, as in these examples:

Condor Nell   Jack Lee

Assistant to Mr. Eisner   *Intern, Marketing Group*

If you're expecting a mail reply, and your company uses internal addresses or **mail codes,** you could mention that fact in the body of your letter ("If you'll mark your letter Mail Code 1900, it'll reach me directly"), or you could add this information under your name, as follows:

Leo Chan

Associate Director

Mail Code 1900, Millennial Building

Next, some firms indicate who will be getting copies. For example, if you are writing to a client and also sending a copy of the same letter to your Accounting department, you would indicate

Cc: Accounting

"Cc" is an abbreviation that derives from "carbon copy." Because no firm uses carbon paper anymore, it's probably better just to write

Copy: Accounting

but follow your firm's "house style."

Next, you can indicate any enclosures. If they are self-evident within the context of the letter, you will likely omit this line. For example, you don't need to add

Encl.: Resume

when you are writing a cover letter to apply to a job, and you would not need to add an "enclosure" line for a letter of transmittal sending a report or brochure. However, when someone else will complete the process of stuffing the envelope and mailing your materials, this is a very useful line, for example:

Encl.: Our check for $982.18

Copy of your invoice dated 15 May 2004

Finally, many firms still use initials to indicate who actually typed a letter. It's hard to see what purpose this served except, perhaps, when executives really did write out letters by hand and have them typed. If there was an error in the typing, the executive knew whom to talk to. But the form

DOR/jb

indicating that Jeanie Bell typed a letter for David Robinson doesn't seem to add much value and looks fussy; and because most people type their own work these days, the form "DOR/dor" looks positively ridiculous.

5-3 Writing and Signing for Other People

Often in business superiors will ask you to write on their behalf (see Figure 5-2). This may be a request that you prepare a draft of a letter and send it to your boss by e-mail for completion; or it may mean that you are to prepare a nearly final version of the letter, ready for your superior to sign; or finally, the leader's intention may be for you to write a letter and sign it yourself. So it follows that you should always respond to such requests by seeking clarification: "Do you want it to go out in my name— or would you prefer to sign it?" Don't worry about writing something that someone else signs—this isn't school homework and it's routine in business.

On occasion, your supervisor may instruct you: "Just sign the letter for me." For example, a busy CEO may wish to appear to have responded personally to a request for a company brochure but simply doesn't have time to sign all such letters. You can handle this situation in many ways.

Figure 5-2 There will be many instances in business when superiors ask you to write on their behalf.
©Steve Cole/PhotoDisc/PictureQuest

The best is if you are encouraged to send out letters with your own signature, while mentioning your boss, as in this form:

"Ms. Fiorina has asked me to reply to your request. . . ."

However, if you are really supposed to sign *for* the boss, you'll have to ask around your workgroup and try to determine the consensus of how people handle this situation. In some firms, you'll find people just write the boss's name in their own hand-writing (this doesn't seem to be a good idea, and implies fraud). Many firms use the form where the manager's name is written out by an assistant, who then adds his or her own initials: "Fred Smith/jk." You may also see this form: "Fred Smith by Jacqui Kennedy" (all written out).

5-4 Some Routine Types of Business Letters

There are hundreds of reasons why a company would send out a letter to a customer, supplier, or partner firm, and the wording preferred by your

T A B L E **5-1** Types of Business Letters

Type of letter	Purpose
Acknowledgment (Appendix 4a)	Lets people know that you have received material that they sent
Transmittal (Appendix 4b)	Accompanies something that you are sending; says to whom the material is directed, what's enclosed, and its purpose
Thanks (Appendix 4c)	Expresses gratitude to a business associate for special consideration or effort
Informational (Appendix 4d)	Gives the recipient news or instructions, such as a place to meet, directions to your firm, or details about a product
Contractual (Appendix 4e)	Forms the basis of a business agreement, such as bidding, ordering, or offering employment
Good news (Appendix 4f)	Tells the recipient something positive, such as a new product announcement or a price cut
Bad news (Appendix 4g)	Denies a request or announces something the recipient won't like, such as a product discontinuation or price increase

firm may have a set form that you are expected to follow. (You may even hear the term "**boilerplate.**" This term refers to certain blocks of text that are routinely added for legal protection—although no one expects people to read them in detail.) When you are new to a position, one good activity to orient yourself is to look through the files for some recent examples, and ask your boss or a friendly colleague about terms that are unfamiliar.

Aside from industry-specific letters, in general, business letters can be classified as one of the seven types described in Table 5-1.

Here are some details on the content that might be appropriate in each case. A letter of *acknowledgment* is often brief—even to the point of seeming curt. Your purpose is just to let someone know that you have received something without indicating what your firm's actions will be. In most cases, you'll avoid writing this type of letter and just respond with a phone call. However, you will encounter some situations in which you are expected to "document" that your firm received the material by providing a specific, written response.

A letter of *transmittal* accompanies one or more other documents such as a brochure, a bid, a contract, or a check. The form is simple. Say what you are sending and why, and carefully list the contents on the "Enclosure" line. A letter of transmittal might have a simple action step, such as "Please call me when you've had a chance to read this."

The purpose of the *letter of thanks* is self-evident. The protocol here is to write quickly to acknowledge assistance that someone has given you, especially when it is beyond the ordinary. Making reference to some specific aspect of the kindness will show that your letter is not "boilerplate."

In an *informational letter* make sure you provide all the information necessary (for example, instructions for a career fair might include information on parking as well as the location). It might be a good idea to give yourself some time to develop such a letter over a few days, making notes as you go along, and have the draft checked by interested colleagues to see whether you've left out anything. An informational letter should always end with contact information in case the recipient has needs that weren't covered in your letter.

The most important aspect of a *contractual* letter is to recognize when you are in a situation in which what you write will commit the firm. If you are unsure about such situations, check with your boss or if necessary the firm's legal department. Employment, bids, and counter-offers are common situations, but many others may be specific to your company and its industry. The language will be precise and quite formal. For example, writing "Harry, I *loved* the new bid!" could arguably read as an acceptance, but what you meant to say was "Harry, I wanted to acknowledge that we've received your carefully prepared bid. We are now in the process of giving all the bids careful review and hope to make a decision by early next week."

Pretty much all other business correspondence can be determined as either "good news" or "bad news." Being able to identify such situations is important, especially concerning the order of ideas.

In a *good news letter* you can choose to begin with your main point, such as "I have exciting news; we've just cut prices on our entire model line by 30 percent." Or you could lead in gradually and come with the good news as a "surprise" toward the end.

A conventional form for *bad news letters* has a particular order of ideas. If you start with the main news up front, your recipient may ignore the rest of what you have to say. If you bury your point at the end, the person reading the letter may never get to it. So the convention is as follows:

Begin with a "gentle lead" that acknowledges some positive aspect such as valued patronage. ("I was pleased that you've enjoyed more than 40 years of successful photography with your Photomatic-50.")

Next, clearly state the bad news in unequivocal terms with some reasonable justification or explanation. ("We cannot replace the switch on your camera as it's out of warranty.")

- Don't "catastrophize." ("I realize this means you are going to have to buy a whole new camera.") And don't over-explain. ("If we repaired all 1955 models for free, we'd be bankrupt.")
- Seek to ameliorate or sweeten in some reasonable way. ("I'm enclosing a packet of lens cleaners" or "The new models don't have this switch, so I'm sure you'll get long use out of a replacement.")
- Don't indulge in what's called "Doing and Undoing." ("We can't give you a new camera, but here's a check for $50.")

The good news about bad news letters is that in your particular line of business, common problems will come up (for example, Human Resource executives often have to tell candidates that they didn't get a job), so you'll develop both some expertise and some preferred phrases for handling most situations you encounter.

5-5 How Your Firm Handles Mail

At your home and in a small office, mail arrives each day in one pile. However, large corporations may have one address where mail is received for thousands of people. You'll soon get to know how your mailroom works.

To identify your specific location, you may be known by your office number, workgroup, or a code that will be called "mail code" or "mail drop." If you can give this specific code to people who are writing to you, you are likely to receive your incoming mail up to one day earlier than you would otherwise. Most of the mail received by large corporations is invitations, conference brochures, and magazines. Firms have established routines: Mailroom staff will probably sort code-address mail first and then during the workday try to identify first class or priority mail identified by name but not mail code. Lastly, as much as there's time available, they'll sort through the advertising material.

It's important to know your mailroom's routine for both incoming and outgoing mail. For material sent to you, your firm may schedule deliveries to your office twice or more per day. On the other hand, you may have a mail slot in a central mailroom where you are supposed to check regularly for your mail. You should know what happens to express (overnight) packages. Does the courier (for example, Federal Express) bring them to your desk? Are they received by the mailroom and brought to you at once? Will your mailroom or front desk call you when a package arrives? Or is it subject to the routine sorting and inter-office delivery schedule?

You can also increase your effectiveness by understanding your company's outgoing mail procedures. Letters you have written may be collected from your department and taken to a central mailroom for postage to be applied and then taken by van to a main post office sorting facility. On the other hand, your mail could be subject to one or two days of delay as your firm processes it, before it even leaves the building. If you know the routines and the time deadlines (for example, mail leaves your department at 3 P.M., but you can still make the same day's mailing if you take it by hand to the mailroom by 4 P.M.), you can achieve better results.

Because mailrooms are cluttered with advertising material and sometimes overwhelmed by the volume of incoming mail, the sorting and delivery process for regular mail imposes many delays. So a lot of business executives rely—indeed *over-rely*—on express (overnight) delivery such as FedEx or UPS. You may find that almost every document in your business seems to go out by an express courier. You should try to resist this temptation. First, avoiding such deliveries will show your boss that you are cost-conscious. Second, using express delivery for routine documents may give your customers or business associates the impression that you are a spendthrift or that you don't have good judgment.

Many busy executives rely on catalog or Internet shopping for personal items. Having packages delivered to your work is often convenient because you know that someone will always be there to accept delivery and sign for them, and you know that your goods will be safely kept. Some firms positively encourage this practice as a way to reward employees for working long hours. But other firms have found that the volume of personal packages has become too great and is a distraction to the main purpose of the firm, so they've instituted a strict ban on accepting personal packages.

Of course, you would never put a personal letter or bills into your company's mail system to attempt to get the company to pay postage. However, even if you are using your own stamps, you might want to find a mailbox on your lunch hour. Your personal mail will likely be delayed for one or two days if you use your company's mailroom.

Your firm is likely to have some system for internal mail. It may be rapid, secure, confidential, and sophisticated. Pick-ups may be twice a day, or more often. On the other hand, you may encounter a system that is prone to misdeliveries and that is treated as an afterthought, to be addressed when incoming US mail has been handled. So it pays to quietly evaluate the system and to understand whether that system is useful in your firm. You may well identify occasions when it's worth your while to deliver time-sensitive material to other departments in person.

5-6 Memorandums or "Memos"

A memorandum is usually a communication that is intended only to be used within one firm or organization. It's used to send out information that recipients are likely to refer to over a long period of time. For example, if a workgroup agrees on a schedule for vacations (so that there is always coverage for the office), the plan might be written up in a "memo." Memorandums are also used to provide a written record of a meeting, phone call, or conference, for a firm's internal records.

With these purposes, you can see that memos have largely been replaced by e-mail. (In the vacation schedule example, you send out an e-mail to all the members of a group—each member can keep a copy on his or her computer and refer to it in the future.) As written records, memos have serious limitations—the style tends to be bureaucratic and stilted, and there is no place to sign, so it's often unclear whether memos are "original" or indeed authentic.

The form for a memo is as follows. There is invariably a "Memorandum" heading at the top. This format comes from the memo's use in legal situations, and at least serves the purpose of indicating that it is a semiformal document, not just an odd piece of paper. A memo is always laid out "top justified," that is, beginning at the top of the page and using up only the amount of paper necessary. Unlike a letter, it's not centered on the page.

After the title "Memorandum," there are four or five lines of identifying information:

Date:	4 July 1776
Subject:	Draft Declaration of Independence
From:	Thomas Jefferson
To:	Ben Franklin
Copy:	Col. Washington

(The "Copy" or "Copies" line is optional.) Many different styles are acceptable. For example, the captions may be double-spaced or not, the "To" might come before the date and before or after the "From." However, you should always double-space after the heading before beginning the text of your memo, and notice that you should always tab over so that the specific names and dates line up in a block.

The text should be formatted the same as for a letter: single-spaced within paragraphs, double-spaced between; left justified with a ragged right margin, and using a serif font of about 12 points.

A memo has neither a salutation ("Dear Tom,") nor a closing ("Yours faithfully,"). This means that there is no place for the author to add a signature. Some memo writers write their initials next to their names. As you can see, someone else can fairly easily generate a fraudulent memo. For example, if you find a typed memo on your desk appearing to come from your boss and announcing that you are now eligible for 16 weeks' vacation each year, you would most likely think it is a prank from a co-worker. But an e-mail from your supervisor's e-mail account telling you that the firm is granting a pay raise to all employees might be more believable.

It's important to recognize that memos can be in a number of different formats, and before you write one, you should look around at examples in your workplace and try to follow the preferred style. If you detect inconsistencies, at least ask your supervisor which format is preferred.

5-7 Content of Memos

Memos tend to stay around for a long time and may be read by people outside your workgroup. So you should choose a moderately high level of formality and aim to be as concise as possible. For example, the following could look really unprofessional:

> After no end of fighting and backstabbing we all agreed to take the
> Friday after the Fourth of July off. Try not to drink too much!!

A better alternative would be this example:

> At the team meeting this week, the group members agreed that
> the office will be closed on 5 July, and we will all take this day as a
> vacation day.

5-8 Faxes

The advantage of a fax—short for "facsimile transmission"—is that it takes just moments to transmit. You can send a letter from Jacksonville to Jakarta in seconds, not in the days that even airmail would take. However, faxes have some limitations and disadvantages. Because the fax will likely be printed out in black and white, you'll lose the impression of formality provided by your firm's colored, headed notepaper. Many workgroups share a central fax machine, and it's very easy for your important document to be mistakenly included with someone else's material at the recipient's firm. Or your fax could be received and mislaid by someone who didn't know who was expecting it. Finally, although your fax machine may indicate correct transmission, a paper jam at the other end can mean that your document never printed out.

Make sure, then, that you know this rule:

> A fax sent is not necessarily a fax received.

To address the problems outlined in this section, you should make a "cover sheet" that clearly indicates the intended recipient (with details such as mail code or specific office location), the number of pages that follow, and the call-back number for any problems in transmission. Most businesspeople phone recipients to alert them that a fax is coming and ask for a confirming phone call that all pages have been received. In general, faxing very many pages at once (say more than a dozen) is not a good idea as this may exceed the capacity of the recipient's machine. An alternative is to send a long document by overnight delivery or perhaps as a file attached to an e-mail message.

The use of faxes varies considerably within industry. In some companies, it's a primary method of communicating. All the executives may have their own fax machines (sometimes referred to as "my desk fax" to indicate that your message won't be lost in a mail room), or they may be able to "read" faxes on their personal computers. In some circumstances a faxed signature will be treated as a legal binding contract, and in others only the signed original document is acceptable.

5-9 Reports

If your job requires you to write reports designed either for your own company or for publication outside the firm, there's no doubt that your firm will have a specific format that you are expected to follow. It's possible that most firms in your industry will use a specific order of sections— for example, for bids or for financial analyst reports.

To learn the house style, you can ask your supervisor if your firm has a Style Guide (or similar named document). If it doesn't, ask your boss to show you one or two good reports, and—if possible—one or more reports that he or she did *not* like. You can then analyze the documents and generate your own idea of an acceptable style.

Here are some things to look for:

1. How are graphics (tables and graphs) handled? Are they integrated with the text or placed at the end? If so, are they called "Exhibits," "Figures," or "Appendices"? Are they usually numbered or lettered?

2. Do good reports use the first person "I" and "we," or is a lot of effort taken to write reports in an impersonal style?
3. Does the house style use side headings (like Box 5-1) or headings written in a broad left margin?
4. How are references handled? By inclusion in brackets in the text (FDA Annual Report, 1997), by **footnotes** at the bottom of each page, by footnotes within graphs and tables, or by **endnotes** (at the end of the text).

The style that you will write in will be very different from the style expected for many liberal arts college papers, or indeed from the style you may have used for lab reports in engineering school. Again, try to find what people consider to be "good" and learn from it. The writing style of *Business Week* and *The Wall Street Journal* are good models to follow.

If you're working for a start-up firm or are writing a report for a team that has no good models for you to work from, word processing software programs, such as Microsoft WORD, contain good templates that can guide you through the sections and format for a generic report. You should be able to adapt them to your purpose.

5-10 Executive Summary

You may well find that all reports in your firm come with an "Executive Summary." This is different from an "abstract" that is found at the beginning of a scientific or academic paper. The Executive Summary may be quite long (two or more pages at the beginning of a long report), although it's always good to keep it to one page if you can. Unlike an abstract, it should repeat almost verbatim the specific recommendations from the end of your report.

The Executive Summary serves two functions. First, it serves in place of the main report for people (such as board members) who need to know about your process, options you considered, and your conclusions, but who don't have time to read your whole report. Second, for people who are going to read the whole report, your summary should lead them into the main body of the work and should foreshadow your main points. You are not writing great literature, and you won't be spoiling a surprise ending.

5-11 Editors and Graphic Artists

In a large firm, you may be surprised to find that, although you write the first draft of the words in a report, and it may indeed be printed with your name on it, many other people will work on the project. You may be assigned to a technical writer who will act as your editor. The editor may "tighten up" your prose and may ask you for clarification in places. Don't be afraid to stand up for yourself if you feel the editor is making you say something that you didn't mean. However, on the other hand, try not to be defensive, and don't experience editing as criticism. Remember, major writers from Charles Dickens to F. Scott Fitzgerald relied on professional editors at their publishers.

5-12 Writing as a Group

You may find yourself assigned to write up a report as a member of a team of several people who have been working on the same project. If you've ever tried this team approach, you may have found that it seems like an almost impossible task if you gather as a group and try to write sentence by sentence. Many groups try to solve this problem by breaking the task into parts and assembling them at the end ("You do the financials, and I'll write the introduction . . ."). The result invariably looks like Frankenstein's monster: stitched together and quite ugly as a whole.

The solution is to work from an agreed **outline.** You get the group to meet together and agree, in general terms, about what the report will say. Turn on the outliner in your word processing software. (In MS WORD, you open the Format menu, choose Bullets and Numbering, then choose the "Outline numbered" tab, select the style you want, and click OK.) Type in your main points first, for example:

1. Group met 3 times over 6 months
2. Three possibilities, only one is feasible
3. Need $100,000 budget to complete project

Then you can expand each main point by pressing the Tab key to successive levels of sub-detail and sub-sub-detail:

1. Group met 3 times over 6 months
    a. Team members from Marketing, Engineering, and Manufacturing
        i. Finance promised to send a rep, but no one attended
2. Three possibilities, only one is feasible
    a. Switch production to factory in Singapore
        i. Shipping would be too expensive
    b. Outsource production to supplier
        i. Quality control problems in the past
        ii. Their bid is very high
    c. Run our factory on overtime
        i. Feasible if we can start within the next month

3. Need $100,000 budget to complete project
   a. Covers the cost of overtime
   b. Project will be done by the end of the quarter

At this point you can have the group members review the outline. Perhaps you need to add some details, explanation, or additional justification. Or perhaps you can omit some minor points. Using an outliner on the computer, you can easily "promote" or "demote" sub-points to major points and vice versa, just by adding additional tabs.

Once the group members agree on the outline, it's best to acknowledge that because only one person's fingers can hit the keyboard at a time, the best use of group members' time is to have one person write the report, sticking closely to the outline. If the outline has been well prepared, the report will almost write itself, with each line of the outline becoming a complete sentence. It's a good idea to have another team member act as editor, and on a long, complicated report, other team members can be working on appendices and exhibits.

Put This Chapter into Practice

1. Find an example of a letter that is too long. See how it could be re-worked as a short letter with attachments.

2. Ask colleagues to show you some reports that they like and one or more that they don't like. Try to identify the differences between the two.

Chapter 6

Effective Presentations

Key Terms

Audience heterogeneity
Catastrophizing
Inform, persuade, or remind
Placeholder
Prop

Q&A
Rate of speech
Stance
Visual aid

Outline

You can't say, "I'm no good at public speaking"

Sooner than you think, you'll be asked to make a formal presentation as part of your job. You can't work in American business and hide behind, "I'm just no good at public speaking." Whether you're good at it or not, you'll be required to do it. But effective public speaking is much easier than you may think.

First, with the exception of CEOs addressing shareholder meetings or sales conferences, very few people have to give formal speeches to large groups of many thousands of people. You'll most likely be facing a friendly audience of at most a few dozen colleagues or customers who are interested in what you have to say. Second, if you are well prepared and follow some simple rules, you'll be successful. There are many different styles of effective public speaking. Yes, some people are charismatic, some people are highly amusing. You don't have to emulate a style that doesn't match your personality. Your goal should be that when you sit down, your boss will turn to you and say, "Thank you. That was thoroughly professional!"

6-1 Keep It Short

Only Fidel Castro gives speeches that are four hours in length. In contemporary US business, 45 minutes is a very long speech. Even when financial professionals are pitching a multi-billion dollar takeover, or when consultants are reporting the results of a six-month investigation, you may well see an initial presentation that's just 20 minutes long, followed by a period for questions and answers (**Q&A**). You'll note that you rarely see the president of the US giving long speeches using formal rhetoric.[1] Most often, you'll be aware of press conferences, where the president may make an opening announcement, often no more than 5 minutes long, followed by more than an hour of questions.

When you see that several hours are allotted to a particular topic, it's most likely that some of the time will be spent on a presentation, some on Q&A, and some on a general discussion. It's very unlikely that you will be expected to speak for hours at a time unless you are running a training session (for example, explaining a new software program that your company has adopted). Because the attention span of even well-rested, highly motivated adults is rarely more than 45 minutes, when you have a long training session, you should make an effort to break up the meeting into lectures, practice sessions, discussions, and so on. If you are presenting for part of a long meeting, and you notice audience members nodding off or beginning to talk among themselves, it's reasonable to say, "I think we're all getting a little tired here. Let's take an informal 5-minute break, stretch our legs, and get some fresh air. Then we can come back and give this our full attention."

6-2 Understand Your Purpose

In advertising, we like to say that the function of any marketing communication is one (and only one) of the following three possible purposes: **inform, persuade,** or **remind.** You can apply the same philosophy to any presentation you give, and, in fact it's even simpler: Because you can treat any "reminder" as just a special form of informative speech, you can categorize presentations as either "Informative Speech" or "Persuasive Speech." The distinction is not academic. The preparation for your presentation will be different, as will be the words that you use, depending on whether you are trying to persuade or if your goal is merely to inform. You may notice when you hear a speech that just doesn't seem to go well, you are often left wondering: "Was he just trying to tell me something, or was he really trying to change my mind and win me over?" You can be clear about your purpose by asking yourself whether a beginning such as "I'd like to tell you about . . ." or "I'd like to convince you that . . ." is most appropriate for the start of your talk. Only one of these choices should fit.

---

1. In general, the science of writing or speaking, but often used to mean a grand style of declamation.

6-3 Settings

Because you are unlikely to be addressing thousands at a sales convention, what should you expect? If you'll allow that the largest group that you'll address won't really be very large, we can define three categories of audience: small, medium, and large. Your approach will be a little different with each type.

To begin with presentations to *small audiences,* many presentations today are given to customers, or within a firm across a desk in an executive's office. One or two people may be listening to you, and you are likely to remain seated. However, it's a good idea to be specifically prepared, and to be clear in your mind about the transition from when you are just chatting pleasantly to when you have started your presentation. You could mark the shift by saying, "Well, let me get started with . . ." and announce your topic. Some in-office presentations use **visual aids** in the form of brochures, flip charts, or a PowerPoint® graphics presentation on a laptop computer. In this setting, you should aim for an informal style. That in no way precludes your being professional and authoritative; however, you should expect interruptions. In general, you should answer questions and give clarifications as you go along, but you can resist attempts to completely interrupt your speech. For example, if an executive says, "I just don't see where this is going, it all sounds like stuff I've seen before!" you are within your rights to say pleasantly, "Well, let's go through all of this, and then I'll be happy to take your questions."

The most common audience size is *medium*—that is, a group of from 6 to 24 people who gather to hear a report. The typical setting is in a conference room where your audience sits at a large table. You are likely to use some visual aids, although not necessarily projected media like PowerPoint®. Some type of handout is common in this situation. Although the audience will sit, you should always stand up (even if you are not at the head of the table) to indicate the beginning of your presentation. You should anticipate a few questions as you go along. In most business settings, the unwritten rule is that audience members can ask questions that require further definition or restatement of something that was unclear during your talk, but substantive questions can be left until the end of the talk. (Bear this point in mind when your role is to be "audience." Try to let the speaker get through the presentation before interrupting with questions.)

You can announce that you would prefer to take questions at the end (although it sounds a little defensive), but it's probably better to graciously answer a few questions briefly as they come up and deflect long, complicated questions until the end. "Perhaps you could hold that question until we're through?" is a polite way to phrase this.

We can call the third audience type *large*, although the most you will encounter in typical business situations will be from 24 to 70 people—still small enough for you to address in a well-designed small lecture hall without using a microphone, amplifier, and loudspeakers. There's a probability that you'll have some kind of visual aid, and you should be quite formal in making a clear start and a clear end to your talk. That is, don't chat to audience members in a way that makes it unclear that you've started your presentation. Most likely you'll indicate the end of your prepared remarks by calling for questions. If someone interrupts with a question as you are going along, you can answer if it's brief ("You're right—that was the *fiscal* year, not the calendar year . . ."), but you'll most likely defer most questions to the end. The reason for this is to give the best coherence to the logic of your speech.

6-4 Using Visual Aids

You may—or may not—use one or more visual aids with talks to all audience sizes, but the description of the three audience sizes and settings implies that some aids are more likely to be expected than others. The decision as to whether to use visual aids at all, and if so what to use, will depend on the nature of your talk, the equipment available, and your careful assessment of the good and bad side ("pros and cons") of each type of aid (see Table 6-1).

Perhaps the simplest form of illustration for your speech is to have a handout. It's cheap to prepare, and people can take notes as you are going along. Written handouts are essential when very many facts and figures are involved, especially when audience members will need something to take away with them. This is true for budget meetings, quarterly financial reports, and times when you are announcing new policies and procedures. However, if you hand out materials at the beginning or during your speech, there's inevitably some distraction in large meetings as materials are passed around from one row to another. In meetings of any size, there is always a tendency for audience members to look down at printed materials, rather than seeing the expression of your face and your gestures.

Simple **props** can be very effective for gaining attention. For example, in small meetings a photograph can lead into a compelling story. If you are describing a piece of miniature technology that is smaller than a dime,

TABLE **6-1**   The Types of Visual Aids
for Presentations

Type of Visual aid	Pros	Cons
Handouts	Useful, indeed essential, for presenting long lists of numbers such as financial reports and budgets. A permanent memorandum of your speech.	Most people stop listening to what you are saying and start to read as soon as they are given a handout. The "rustle factor" as people turn pages can be very annoying.
Props	Great for getting attention or making a compelling visual point.	If you pass something around so that everyone can see, the "stage business" of passing from one row to another can distract from your talk.
Overhead	Can be projected with the room lights on in most cases. Can show fine detail from photographs.	May be hard for people at the back of the room to see and the projector is invariably quite noisy.
PowerPoint®	Very flexible, permitting color and graphics. Gives a professional, polished look to any speech.	PowerPoint® special effects such as motion have a tendency to overwhelm your speech, and people always focus on the screen, not the speaker, so you lose the value of your expression and gesture. The room lights need to be at least dimmed, which can lead the audience to snooze if you are not careful.
Video	Highly attention getting. A short video clip is often the only way to show a product in use. Video clips are a good way to break up a speech that is getting too long.	The room lights have to be fully off. Making sure the equipment, especially the sound, works well adds anxiety to a presentation.
35 mm slides	Compelling color and detail.	Expensive to produce and impossible to change at the last minute if you discover a mistake. Slide projectors can be noisy and usually require an assistant to be operated well. Slides can jam.

holding up a coin as you make your closing can bring the point home. Props often work well when they are hidden (for example, in a bag or beneath a table), but you shouldn't delay too long, or your audience will feel that you are playing games with them. In all but the smallest meetings, don't rely on passing something around. For example, if you pass around two sample fabrics in a medium-sized meeting of just 12 people, 24 transactions will take place (plus some back and forth!) while you are speaking, and this can be very distracting.

Overhead transparencies once were the most common form of visual aid although they are increasingly replaced by projected computer-driven displays. When you use overheads, you almost never need to dim lights, and you can manage your own media. An overhead projector can be noisy, so it's best to turn it off whenever possible—and while it is on, speak up loudly. It's important to have the projector properly placed and focused before you begin. There's a trick to this, which avoids your giving away any possible surprise on your first slide. Place a pen or paper clip gently on the flat surface of the projector: When you have adjusted the projector so that the outline of your object is clear, turn off the projector and put on your first transparency (it goes "right way up" facing you) and when you turn on the projector, your slides will be shown in perfect focus. Overhead projectors have the advantage that you can read your own slides without turning back to the screen. They can show color, but the hues are somewhat washed out (especially compared with projected PowerPoint®), and you cannot show very fine detail on an overhead.

Projected computer-driven display using the program PowerPoint® has achieved overwhelming popularity. Almost anyone with a desktop computer or a laptop can create a presentation that just a few years ago would have cost thousands of dollars in graphic designer fees. The slides can be shown directly on a computer screen, or projected to make a large, bright image. PowerPoint® presentations can include graphs, spreadsheets, photos, and even sound and video clips. The elements of each slide can be animated, and slides and elements can change either on a mouse-click or automatically on a pre-set timer. However, the visual imagery is so compelling that audience members may not pay attention to the speaker. So that you can manage this possibility, it's best to begin with the projector turned off or the computer screen blanked,[2] introduce yourself and your topic, and then begin the presentation and the main part of your

---

2. In MS PowerPoint®, in the "Slide Show" view, press the "B" key on the keyboard to toggle a blank screen on and off.

talk. At the other end of your speech, turn off the projector again and adjust the lighting so that the audience is once again focused on you. Most people who use PowerPoint® make the room too dark. If your slides have been well designed, then you should only need to dim the lights (or shade windows in part on a sunny day). Lecturing to an audience in the dark is likely to send them to sleep—quickly! If one or two of your slides are dark, or have a lot of detail, you could lower the lights briefly while those particular slides are displayed.

There is no set number of slides that can be shown in a talk of a given length. However, in college lecturing, 12 to 20 slides (admittedly, with each explained in some detail) are enough for a 50-minute lecture. If you find that you are rushing slides during a run-through of your talk, you probably have too many. Consider reserving some as "back-up" to use during Q&A. It's a good idea to have a blank slide at the end of your presentation so that the screen goes dark (rather than reverting to an ugly "slide sorter" view in the program).

Whenever you are speaking with any type of equipment—and this is especially true with PowerPoint®—you have to ask yourself, "What could go wrong?" Travel with a second copy of your presentation on a different disk, and for "mission-critical" presentations (such as winning a big order), consider duplicate sets of computer and projection equipment so that you can quickly switch over if you are faced with an equipment failure. You should plan in advance what you will do if projection equipment fails: In a training session or course, you can probably move some material around. In this case, call for a discussion or break, and come back to the presentation later. But in most situations you'll have to decide whether to go ahead without your PowerPoint® or to abandon the meeting.

Video clips can be very compelling. They can tell a short story, conveniently demonstrate a product in action, or can show more detail than any amount of verbal description. You can expect to use either VHS (ordinary videotape) or, in some circumstances, video that runs on computer such as QuickTime. In most settings, you'll need the lights almost completely off for video, so you should plan for the lighting to be up both before and after the show.

Unless you work in an "artistic" environment, such as a museum or design firm, you are unlikely to encounter 35mm projected slides. The level of detail and the richness of color are compelling. But 35mm projectors are noisy and almost always need an "attendant" (at least to turn them on and off, if not to focus and to change slides). The room needs to be dark, and this makes it difficult to give a talk, and instead you are left to merely comment on the slides.

6-5 Knowing Your Audience

When you know the purpose of your talk, the setting, and the approximate size of the audience, you'll want to find out as much as you can about your audience. Consider a simple example where you have to give a routine quarterly report about a project. Who will be in the audience? Are these people familiar with the current status (because they've been working on aspects of the project, or because they've already seen written reports)? Will what you say have to come as a surprise? What functional areas (accounting, marketing, production, etc.) are the audience members from? What is their attitude toward this project?

You can get this information from a knowledgeable (and friendly!) insider. It helps to be forewarned when people are initially hostile to what you are going to say: "Finance opposed this project from Day 1, so they're going to have a field day when you tell them we're over budget and behind schedule." If you are appointed as an emissary from your firm to another firm (for example, if you are asked to go "talk to a supplier"), you should at least call to find out about the audience—and most likely it will pay you to take a preliminary meeting with the person whom you think can most help you. Who is likely to be invited to hear you? What are their backgrounds? What do you know about their level of interest?

You may feel as if you've been given an impossible task: Some of the people are engineers with graduate degrees who know more about the underlying science of your project than you do, and some of the people barely understand the nature of the project in its most general terms. Reassure yourself! You are dealing with a very common problem called "**audience heterogeneity.**" *All* audiences are "heterogeneous"—that is, they vary from member to member in terms of interest, expertise, and predetermined attitude toward your speech. Your task is to identify the range of each parameter and "preach" to the middle 75 percent. In general, then, you will choose the level of detail and how technical to be in a way to appeal to the middle part of the group. Then, from time to time, you should acknowledge the presence of others in your audience. For example, you might say

> "Now I know that a few of you don't have a background in biochemistry, so before I go into the reaction, let me just summarize that this is how we synthesize the new drug—you don't need to follow the details."

At the other end of the spectrum, you acknowledge the experts by saying something like this:

"Now, I know that many of you will realize that this description is going to be quite a simplification of the process. . . ."

6-6 Planning Your Presentation

You'll be much more likely to have a successful presentation if you think through what result you'd like to achieve. This is called "beginning with the end in mind." Suppose your firm has decided to phase out a long-standing product, and you have been assigned to break the news to a supplier who has made a good profit from your business and has come to rely on it as a mainstay. Is your goal to get the bad news out and leave as quickly as possible? Probably not. Your firm has interest in keeping the supplier on line during the phaseout, and no doubt in preserving the business relationship for possible future work. That is the "end" from your point of view.

Next, you would make your assessment of your audience. If you had heard the other firm proposing discounts for greatly increased volume, you could anticipate that your phaseout would come as a shock. You would plan your speech to begin gently, to emphasize the benefits and successes of the past working relationship and then move to some general comments about natural life cycles, before moving to the bad news. If you know that executives at the other firm have talked often about consolidation in your industry or new competing technologies, your approach would be different. You can begin with an acknowledgment of realities and move quickly to expressions of hope for different work in the future.

6-7 Structure of an Informative Speech

We'll begin by planning an informative speech, and then we'll show the modifications necessary for persuasion.

Your work should have a logical flow: from small examples to general conclusions, *or* from generalities to the specifics of your situation. In some circumstances *history* (first, we did this, then that happened, and so on) will guide your talk—but in many business situations history is considered "bunk" (worthless in the words of Henry Ford). You can have a structure of dealing with domestic issues first, and then moving to international business. But it's important that your talk should have a structure. You are more likely to achieve good structure if you write an outline first, before you begin to think through your talk sentence by sentence.

If you are planning a talk, make a list of all the ideas that you'd like to get across. You probably have more than a dozen written down. Now, think back to the last major speech, sermon, or presentation you heard— think of one that you thought at the time was really good. Now, write down what you think the speaker's main points were. Most likely, you found it hard to come up with more than three or four points. Yes, it's true. Whether you speak for 5 minutes or 45 minutes, attentive audience members will probably be able to grasp and remember only three or four main points.

With this information in mind, you can plan your speech. For an informative speech, you should anticipate making an introduction to your topic, making three or four points, and then coming to a conclusion.

At the very beginning of your speech, as you rise to begin, in all but the small in-office setting, you should start by identifying yourself. If the chairperson of a meeting says, "OK. Here's Nick with the financials," you would begin by saying, "Good morning. I'm Nicholas Chang, financial analyst with the advanced projects group." Although all the people in the room may be friendly faces, not everyone may be sure of your full name or role. It's professional to make a self-introduction in all cases when you haven't been fully introduced by someone else.

The introduction to your speech should accomplish two objectives. First, it should get the attention of people in the audience, and second it should foreshadow where you are going in your speech. You can get attention with a prop or with a short story. Many public speaking experts suggest you start with a joke to "break the ice." But the form of telling one or two irrelevant jokes and then saying, "Well, that has nothing to do with microprocessors!" is frankly old-fashioned, and most people would find it irritating. More to the point, it's hard to come up with jokes that don't depend on disrespecting some racial, ethnic, or religious group, or that don't have a sexual undertone. Any of these will get you into trouble, so it's not a good idea to start in that way.

"Foreshadowing" means that you give your audience an idea of the scope of your speech and what your main points will be. Within the talk, if it's of any length, you'll need to do some additional "signposting," as in "We've covered the financials, and before I go over the strategic impact of this idea, let me talk about the production issues."

There is an old line from the military that the key to success in public speaking is "Tell them what you are going to say, say it, and then tell 'em what you just said." Although this sounds trivial, it contains some truth: Although in written work we carefully avoid repetitions, in public speaking, some well-planned repetitions help the audience get the point.

Of course, your presentation would be quite boring if you said, "I'm here to tell you about the progress on the ABC Project. I'll be reporting our work so far, I'll overview the financials, I'll make one or two bland jokes about our boss, and then I'll call for questions." This would be very boring. You may have some little surprises in your talk. But you certainly should foreshadow where you are going: "I'm going to report that we've made an unexpected break-through on the cost of parts ordered from suppliers."

You've now come to the main body of your speech, and you are going to go through your points in the order that you planned. Carefully planning your transitions from one section to another can show expertise in public speaking. You briefly summarize one section and then move on:

> "So, to sum up, although we spent more on design work, we had some savings from open positions, so we're still pretty much on budget. I'd like to turn now to the planned work for the next quarter. In the second quarter, we plan to complete. . . ."

Note the subtle repetition at the end of the example. This approach is especially useful whenever you introduce a technical term: " . . . these workers experience Carpal Tunnel Syndrome. Now Carpal Tunnel Syndrome has been identified as a chief cause of Workmen's Compensation claims. . . ." When you move to a new section (especially when you have visual aids), don't just read a title. For example, a slide title might read "Second Quarter Work Plan," but you would still use the natural conversational form: "I'd like to turn to the work plan for the next quarter."

In your conclusion, you will briefly restate your main points. As best you can, try to paraphrase yourself, rather than use exactly the same words—it'll make your speech more interesting. An ideal conclusion nicely summarizes what you've said and also moves the discussion forward. For example, if you're giving a report on project status, in addition to summarizing the work done so far, you might draw some conclusions about how future projects should be tackled.

6-8 Structure of a Persuasive Speech

When your task is to persuade your audience, rather than just inform them, preparation will be more important than ever. In addition to knowing who will be in your audience and their background, you'll need to assess how much they disagree with the position you're going to present. At one extreme, if the audience is in total agreement (you are speaking to Disney executives about the need to produce wholesome family entertainment), there's really no need for a persuasive speech. At the other extreme, if your audience is in complete opposition to you (for example, you plan to speak to Microsoft employees about why the Justice Department antitrust prosecution has been good for the firm), then a persuasive speech of any length or form is unlikely to be of much use. In fact, when you are facing a major change in a firmly held belief, management experts would say that you need not one speech but a multi-faceted long-term campaign involving carefully planned steps to move opinion your way.

However, in most situations you will face in business, you will confront an audience with a range of opinions, and some audience members may already be close to agreement with what you have to say. For example, let's suppose you have to persuade a group of managers to cut back on travel expenses. Because many managers will likely own stock in your firm, there's likely to be at least unspoken support for cutting expenses. Perhaps the worst that you'll face is one or two people who like to travel, enjoy the prestige of traveling in Business Class, and think that the move to cost cutting is an over-reaction to temporary difficulties.

The approach for a persuasive speech is to begin by reaching out to your adversaries. In this instance, people in the audience will probably have a good idea of the topic before you start to speak (everyone in the firm knows there's a big push for cost containment). Moreover, people can likely anticipate what you are going to say (there's zero chance that you'd be there to say, "I want more of you to fly First Class instead of Economy"). So to persuade, you'll start by acknowledging the importance of face-to-face meetings and how Business Class travel reduces the stress of long inter-continental flights. This beginning might surprise those in the audience who are "with you" on the need for cost containment but will engage those who are set against you. You can then move into your persuasive thrust. You can show how one full-fare Business Class ticket costs more than four trips to the same destination bought as advanced purchase tickets. You could demonstrate that if each department in the firm could cut just one trip per quarter, the whole company would save $1 million in this fiscal year.

This example is an introduction to persuasive reasoning. You can make comparisons and analogies to help people grasp the size or the seriousness of what you're proposing. Use "round numbers" such as "less than $500" or "more than four times as much." If you give exact comparisons, such as "This alternative costs 3.52 times as much as . . . ," your audience will wonder whether they are to pay attention to the decimal places because another example will be 3.53 or 3.51. Careful selection of your words can make your speech powerful. For example, you can describe some travel as having "little if any direct contribution to the bottom line." However, you should be careful to avoid hyperbole (exaggeration or extreme wording), such as calling a proposal "ridiculous" or referring to an amount as "huge" or "enormous." A little understatement such as "will help us achieve substantial cost savings . . ." is a better style.

If you've done some research and have facts at your fingertips, you've just made a *rational* appeal. For thousands of years rhetoric experts have identified three common "appeals":

- Rational
- Emotional
- Moral

An emotional appeal encourages people to imagine how good they'll feel about a decision or an action. Moral appeals are less common in business, but are based on the notion "It's the right thing to do."

Whenever you are making a persuasive argument, you should anticipate what someone who disagrees with you might say. Think of the reasons why you might be wrong—anticipate objections. You must then refute these objections by disproving or rejecting them through clear, solid arguments. For example, "Now, you may have noticed that this product is priced 10 percent higher than the competition. But since it lasts twice as long, the monthly cost of ownership is actually less!"

If it's true that you can get across only three main points in informative speech, you should aim for no more three or four main *positive* points in a persuasive speech; then you should think of two or three likely objections and refute them. Note that you don't have a choice of objections. If you choose trivial objections while ignoring the one major drawback to your position, you won't win over the audience.

As you craft your speech, make sure that your arguments actually prove your point (and achieve a desired result). One model for persuasive reasoning is "Problem, complication . . . solution." This is rather trite—it assumes that every problem has a complication, and indeed that every complex business situation has a single, credible solution. But there's a grain of truth to the model. If you can't show that you have a solution, either you haven't correctly identified the problem, or your solution isn't viable. As you identify problems and solutions, make sure you have accurate research to make your case. For example, instead of saying "Most homes now have Internet access," be able to quote that "For middle income families, more than 65 percent of homes have Internet access and of these, more than 15 percent have broadband connections."

Sometimes you have to get people to care about something that may seem too small to worry about, or something that is a low-probability problem. Without distorting or exaggerating a problem (that is, without making up statistics), you can make your point. One technique is to *multiply*. For example, the statistic that one in five US high school graduates has problems with reading is alarming. But to state "This year, more than one million students will complete high school without the ability to read a daily newspaper" is truly compelling. A second technique is to *aggregate* (add up a number of small occurrences)—for example, "If each department can cut just one out-of-town trip, we'll be able to report our target 10 percent growth in profit." For low-probability events (for example, the chances of your house burning down are actually very small), you should go into detail of the consequences of the event, no matter how rare.

Again, your logic flow is important in persuasive reasoning. If you begin with a touching story about one small example (Ronald Reagan grew up in rural Illinois), you should move toward the underlying principle or general lesson (anyone has the potential to be president). Conversely, if you decide to begin with a broad description of the problem (secondary education in the US is ineffective), then be sure to make the general statistics compelling by including some individual examples (little Ronnie won't go to college because his high school couldn't afford new math books).

The conventional wisdom is that a persuasive speech should end with a call to action: "Vote Democrat!" or "Buy War Bonds!" However, in business, when managers are trying to influence attitudes and beliefs, the desired "end" may not be an action. In essence, you want to be able to conclude: "I'll hope you'll agree with me that. . . ." As in an informative speech, your talk should end with a recapitulation, preferably one that doesn't just recite the same words. Make use of the moment to re-emphasize the positive results of what you have to say.

6-9 Using Notes or a Script

You should be able to deliver your talk from notes, either typed on a sheet of paper in front of you or hand-written on index cards. If you are using overheads, you'll find it easier to use the transparencies as your notes, rather than juggling them and also a separate set of notes. In almost all circumstances, using a script is a very bad idea. When you write out your speech word for word, you'll use a sentence structure that is inappropriate for spoken delivery (most likely too long with too many complicated subordinate clauses). Worse, you will speak head down, without making eye contact with your audience.

Box 6-1

Speaking with a Microphone

For most business meetings with up to three dozen people in the audience, you really don't need amplification for your voice. Remember that Roman senators in the forum and medieval bishops preaching in large cathedrals managed just fine without modern electronics.

But where you are a guest or invited speaker, you may be under some pressure to use the setup that is provided by your hosts or that other speakers are using. Of course, speaking to large groups (hundreds of people) invariably involves microphones (see Figure 6-1). Here's how to use amplification well.

Figure 6-1

Speaking with a microphone can require some practice in order to be clearly heard and understood.

First, understand the type of equipment that you'll be using. The best type of microphone is a "radio mike": a small microphone that clips to your tie, jacket, shirt, or blouse and that feeds a small radio transmitter which you can clip on a belt or put in a jacket pocket. So if you anticipate this type of equipment, you'll dress accordingly—don't wear something such as a dress with no pockets. The microphone itself needs to be directly below your mouth at about the level of your breastbone. It's the responsibility of your hosts or technicians to adjust the level of amplification so your voice sounds good with that location. If it's not loud enough, ask for "the level to be raised a bit" rather than unclipping and moving the microphone. Be careful if you clip the microphone to a coat collar—it'll usually face away from your mouth and give a poor sound quality. With a radio mike, you have complete freedom of movement, and the sound quality is usually good. The only thing you have to worry about is making sure the microphone is turned off when you are not speaking—you can easily get caught making private comments if you don't realize it's on.

A hand-held microphone (the type used by sports reporters) is probably second best. Although there are some radio hand-held microphones, most will have a cord or cable, and the rules for effective use are the same for both. You need to position the mike at about chin level and about six inches in front of your face. Don't hold it closer to your mouth, or "p" sounds will sound explosive. A hand-held microphone should have an on and off switch. Before you start to speak, make sure you have a "pool" of loose cord (two or three loops) next to your feet. Then if you want to move forward for emphasis, you won't pull the equipment apart.

If the equipment is a microphone on a stand, or at a podium, take a moment when you first step up to adjust the microphone to the correct height for you (just below the level of your chin). Never duck down to get close to a mike as this destroys your professional stance. If you are especially short, arrange for a small stool (or at worst, a stack of phone books) to stand on behind a podium so you can be seen and are not disadvantaged relative to taller speakers.

In some conference settings you'll be seated at a table with a "desk microphone" on a stand in front of you. These mikes rarely work well. If there's only one mike, it gets banged around as it's passed from one speaker to another. Even if there's a microphone in front of each speaker, it is often hard to adjust the volume so that each speaker can be heard equally well. As much as you can do is to make sure the microphone is placed squarely in front of you, and again, try not to duck down to speak into it. Speak clearly and to the audience, and hope that the technicians will do a good job of adjusting the level for each mike.

Probably the worst kind of microphone is the "Lavaliere": a microphone with cable that attaches to a cord and hangs around your neck coming at mid-chest point. This old-fashioned type of equipment doesn't work very well. It doesn't pick up speech clearly but does get a lot of extraneous noise from clothing. Try to adjust the cord so the microphone is a little higher up, clear of your jacket, and then try to ignore it (don't look down at it). The same rules apply to managing the cable—try to have some slack on the floor just to your side before you start to speak so you can use some movement, and be careful to avoid getting tangled when you step back to your regular position.

Testing the microphone: Whichever type of microphone you are using, your public speaking will go much better if you have tested it before you start to speak. Don't tap the microphone with your hands (it's a sensitive device designed to pick up small vibrations of the air, and thumping it won't do any good) and don't say, "Is this thing on . . . ?" which looks tremendously unprofessional. At stage shows you've probably noticed that the set-up crew usually just counts into the microphone: "One . . . two . . . three, etc." But probably as good a line is to say, "Good morning! This is a mike check on the podium mike . . ." and so on. Try to test the mike before the meeting starts or during a break, and the start of your speech will look much more professional.

Interference: When radio mikes work, they work wonderfully well. Occasionally, they suffer from brief interference from police or taxi radios. If you have a single interruption, you can handle it with humor ("If there's anyone here from Car 96, please respond to that call"). But if it happens repeatedly during your presentation, all people will remember is the interruptions. So if you experience this problem, or bad static in the radio reception, the only way to handle it is to turn off the microphone. "Clearly, this is not working for us today" is what you'd say. Then speak a little more slowly, very distinctly, and loudly enough to fill the whole room. Again, remember that public speaking went on for centuries before the invention of electronic amplification. Your audience will be grateful.

A more common type of problem—which can affect any of the microphone types—is the howl and screech called "feedback." This occurs when the volume of the amplifier is turned up too loudly. A small sound is amplified and played by the speakers, and is then picked up by your microphone and re-amplified. A nasty screech results. If your microphone has an on/off switch, turn it off as quickly as possible to stop the howl. When you turn it back on, ask your hosts or the technicians, "Can you take the level down a bit, please? We're getting bad feedback here." If the people running the meeting can't fix the problem, once again, it's better to dispense with the amplification completely and do your speech "unplugged." A screeching microphone is so aversive to members of the audience that no one will be able to concentrate on your content.

However, in a few circumstances your talk will be written out in full ahead of time. First, if you have a legal responsibility—for example, announcing layoffs—the exact wording of what you say may have important consequences. Your speech may have been written by others and reviewed by your firm's lawyers and other outsiders, and you'll have no option but to stick to the script. Second, if you are asked to give a speech in a language in which you have some speaking abilities but not fluency, you may want to make sure that both your choice of vocabulary and your use of grammar will not cause offense to your audience. Third, you may be asked to give a reading from something that someone else has written. The way to handle this situation is to make sure that you look up and make eye contact with your audience right before you start, and from time to time during your talk (about once each paragraph).

If you practice speaking from notes, you'll soon find that natural turns of phrase occur to you better when you're on your feet delivering your talk, rather than when you're sitting at your desk typing. Unless you make formal speeches every day as a routine part of your job, you should plan to rehearse your speech. For a "mission-critical" speech (such as to an audience that'll be hard to win over, or to an unfamiliar and rather large audience), you should try to rehearse in the actual room where you'll be speaking. But don't over-rehearse your speech. If you try to memorize every line, then when there are interruptions or distractions, you may completely lose your train of thought and have difficulty in restarting.

After you've prepared your talk, you may have plenty of time before you are due to speak. Make use of the time to do some "wordsmithing." Which technical terms need to be repeated and defined? Have you used the same phrase too often, and can you add some variety? Make sure you've avoided clichés—common expressions that, while true, are trite and overused, such as "in this modern world of ours, change is always with us." Clichés rarely add anything to your talk and could mark you as an unoriginal, boring speaker. Then work on transitions: An eloquent summary of one section and an appealing "lead" into the next section will show your expertise.

6-10 Delivery

No matter how carefully you prepare your talk, it won't be effective if people can't hear you! Yes, when you are speaking in public, you must speak somewhat louder than you do in conversation. But you don't have to shout. The key is to enunciate clearly. You can do this by slowing down (that is, reducing your **rate of speech**) and by taking pauses between phrases. If you are doing this right, it will feel as if the whole world has stopped spinning on its axis. Try watching yourself on videotape: A pause that felt like infinity when you were speaking looks like a tiny moment to someone in the audience. You should heavily emphasize consonants. For example, in conversation, we often pronounce the word "technology" almost as "teh-nolgy"; but in a speech it has to come out as "teCK-no-lo-GY." In sum, although you need to be "loud enough," speaking slow and clear beats shouting.

Before you begin (ideally during your practice in the room), make sure that there are no distracting sounds that can be eliminated. For example, in many hotel function rooms there is background music (Muzak) that doesn't seem noticeable when people are gathering and talking but is completely distracting when you are giving a speech. If you are a speaker, you should make every effort to eliminate this distraction, by finding the volume control, or a hotel manager who can help you. If you are called on to speak and you notice this problem, politely ask someone to go and have it turned off. Similarly, if there's noise from an open window, you could say, "It's a little hot in here, but I wonder if we could close the windows for a few minutes; I think it'll be easier for us all to hear."

Plan to keep your talk interesting by varying the tone and pace of your voice. That is, you should not speak too rapidly, but you can say some familiar phrases or expressions quickly, while you must introduce new terms carefully and slowly. In addition to a slight increase in volume (you'll already be speaking medium-loud, so you don't have too much room to adjust your sound without shouting), you can emphasize important terms by preceding them with a slight pause. If you listen to radio commercials, you'll hear experienced announcers doing this:

> ". . . and that's just [pause, pause] 99-cents a day!"

You can practice this by saying "pause, pause" *silently* to yourself right before the words you want to emphasize.

If your talk is going to be more than five minutes long, vary the lighting as much as you can. For example, if you are the third speaker in a row, and the previous two speakers have set the lights low to show slides, take a few moments of introduction with the lights fully on to wake up your audience. If you have a long, complicated presentation (for example, financial material), break it up in the middle by blanking the projection and raising the lights while you make some narrative comments.

When you're speaking, work very hard to eliminate "**placeholders**" in conversation, such as "um, err, you know." One or two are acceptable, but if you have a severe problem with this, your audience will become irritated. One way to cure yourself of a bad "um" habit is to take a stack of quarters (or dollar bills, depending on your income level) and practice giving a talk with a friend playing the role of audience. For each time you say "um," your friend gets a quarter. You'll find that although you may still use placeholders in casual conversation or phone calls, your public speaking will be greatly improved.

If you make a mistake, correct yourself quickly and naturally as soon as you notice it. For example, "I just said *Panama* and, of course, I should've said *Patagonia*." And then move right along. Don't make your mistakes worse than they are: "Argh! I'm completely stupid! Of course it's not *Panama!*" We call this "**catastrophizing**"—treating a small slip as if it were a catastrophe. Most people don't like to listen to people who are completely stupid, so you shouldn't label yourself that way. The same advice applies if you show the wrong slide or have some other problem. The correct approach is to acknowledge an error, correct it, and continue with confidence. If you carefully watch star athletes (especially ice skaters), you'll notice that they all make small errors—the winners are the ones who can recover well.

6-11 Stance

For small audiences, you'll probably be sitting—as much as you need to worry about is making sure that the desk in front of you is uncluttered and that you are sitting upright. For medium-sized groups, you will likely be at a table. It's a good idea to stand at the beginning of your talk—this helps draw attention to you and to signal that irrelevant conversations should stop. If there is a podium at the front of the room, you can consider using it, based on your comfort level, what you've seen other speakers do, and the level of formality you wish to signal. In a large-audience setting, there'll undoubtedly be a lectern or at least a table at the front of the room. You should stand, and probably begin behind the podium. An exception would be where you wanted to signal informality. For example, suppose you have a meeting of everyone in your department, and your task is to get everyone to agree to work over a holiday weekend to meet a deadline. In that case, you would probably want to stand away from the podium to signal that you are "one" with your audience and not lecturing at them.

Practice a **stance** at the podium that is comfortable for you. For most people, that involves resting your hands on, but not gripping, the sides of the lectern. If you are in front of the podium, you may have note cards or a prop in one hand, or on a table in front of you. Some people hold their hands behind their backs (this stance can look uncomfortable and limits your ability to make gestures), and others lightly catch the thumbs of each hand on their pants pockets. However, you should resist the temptation to stuff you hands deep into your pockets—it looks too informal and can be distracting for the audience. Serious debaters keep their arms straight down, with the fingers slightly curled in (about one quarter of the way to making a fist), absolutely motionless. If you can do this without paying too much attention to yourself, the effect is dramatic when you move from this stance to making a gesture. The exact position of your hands at rest will depend on your height, your personal style, and what you like to wear. Practice and find a solution that is comfortable for you, and remember to implement it. Your goal is to look confident and unflustered. Make sure that your hands never fidget with your notes or your clothing—if you are in any doubt about this, videotape a practice speech and watch yourself.

Make an "entrance," even if you are sitting at a conference table, and merely rise to speak. Make it clear from your body language when you are taking control of the room. If you are walking up to a podium, stride purposefully and immediately take a strong, stable stance. The trick for how to do this is to stand with your feet about six inches further apart than usual (that is, a little wider than when you are standing in conversation with someone). This position will feel weird at first. But you will look rock-solid, like a lighthouse, and this will eliminate any temptation to bob and weave backward and forward. You need to make sure that you do not pace backward and forward. If you are unfamiliar with public speaking, you may find a certain amount of pacing feels natural and that it helps you keep the rhythm of your speech. However, it's extremely distracting.

Now that we have you immobile and frozen, it's time to add back some movement and gesture. If you've adopted a nice, professional stance, a small amount of movement can be a compelling addition to your public speaking. If you are calling for cooperation from the audience, you can step out from the podium and take one or two steps forward. You don't have to be very close—often a half step forward and a half step back to continue your speech can be very effective. In a long talk where you are not tied to the podium, it's a good idea to change your position as you change topics (about a page of single-spaced material). Be careful not to speak as you are walking and indicate the transition:

> "Now that we've covered the financials, [move a few paces] I'd like to turn to the long-term benefits for our division."

You can develop a small vocabulary of hand gestures: reaching out, emphasis, dismissal of a weak idea, and so on. These gestures can be accompanied by a lively expression on your face—a bit exaggerated from day-to-day, but not clownish. The gestures that work for you will be part of your personal style, and you shouldn't adopt a set formula. However, as you are developing your public speaking abilities, you'll be sensitized to gesture, and it's a good idea to watch how performers on stage use hand gestures. You don't want to look like a rock musician, but you can get some good ideas. For example, you can use a horizontal semi-circular sweeping movement of your arm to accompany, "I'd like to welcome you *all* . . ." with the gesture signaling inclusiveness. Be careful about clenched fist gestures and banging the podium—you don't want to come across as a third world dictator.

Eye contact is culturally determined, and is a sensitive issue. In American business culture, if you never look people in the eye, you'll be seen at best as someone who is lacking in confidence, at worst as someone who has something to hide. On the other hand, if your gaze fixes on one person for too long, you'll make that person uncomfortable, and he or she will feel as if you are a stalker. Because it's important to engage all of your audience, you should shift your gaze, from front to back and from right to left. The best way to study this behavior is to think of someone whom you think is a good speaker and watch specifically what she or he does. Practice this, have yourself videotaped, and ask friends for feedback.

6-12 Speaking with Visual Aids

If you have decided that some sort of visual aid is appropriate for your speech, you'll need to plan how you are going to stand with respect to your media. If your audience size is small, your medium may be a laptop with a slide show. It may work best if you sit side-by-side with your audience so you can point to details on the screen and comfortably control clicking for the next slide. If you are using projected PowerPoint® in a medium or large audience setting, your first decision will be whether to have an assistant control the appearance of the next slide, or whether you'll control the computer yourself. If you have help, printing an outline of your slides and a few moments of advanced planning will save you from endless repetitions of "Next slide, please." When you are projecting media onto a screen, you should stand as close as possible to the screen, but avoid getting light from the projector on your face.

Avoid blocking the view of the screen for any audience members, if you can. If the room is small, and some blocking is inevitable, you can handle the problem one of two ways. The first option is to stick your ground (hold one position)—people whose view is blocked figure it out and lean around you. The alternative, if you are talking for quite a while about each slide, is to make half of your comments, then move, and conclude. The one thing to avoid is interrupting yourself with questions such as "Can you see back there?" and bobbing around from side to side in a way that robs you of your professional demeanor.

If you are using visual aids, you may want to draw attention to specific parts of a graphic using a laser pointer. This technique can be very effective if you use the pointer in moderation and can avoid any fiddling with the pointer. If you are not using a pointer, you should gesture toward a point you are discussing. For example, with a Power-Point® slide projected on a large screen, as you move through bullet points, turn and extend your arm toward the point you are making. You don't need to actually reach the specific bullet with your hand (it may be several feet above and behind you in a large room). The goal is just to acknowledge your own slides. Gestures can help you achieve this objective.

6-13 Question and Answer Periods

The key to a successful "Q&A" session is to manage, or control, the situation. Your host may choose which audience member can ask each question, but you should not allow one person in the audience to dominate the discussion with several follow-up questions or by attempting to debate you. Saying "Perhaps we could take some other questions before my time is up?" while pointedly turning to face other parts of the audience is a polite way to handle this situation.

It's always good to restate a question. All members of the audience may not have been able to hear the questioner, and restating gives you a moment to collect your thoughts. You verify that you are about to address the questioner's chief concern, and you can "edit" a question to your advantage:

> "Well, I heard a number of concerns, but if I can summarize, your question is: How can we propose a major capital expenditure at a time when operating budgets are being cut?"

If a questioner points out something you haven't considered, don't try to dismiss the question as unimportant. "Thank you—that's an aspect of this proposal we didn't address today" is gracious and sufficient. If a questioner points out that there's an error in your reasoning or in your math, it may be very hard for you to think through the correct solution on your feet. Responding "You're right, those numbers don't add to 100 percent; clearly, we're going to have to check that" would be a good way to handle a potential embarrassment. If you've worked hard, you'll actually enjoy defending your ideas, but you should never appear "defensive."

6-14 Polishing Your Performance

Before you give a speech, you may be anxious that you do well, and you'll want to know what you can do to make sure that it is a success. Of course, practice is helpful. But be careful of over-practicing (it may only add to your anxieties). Instead of going over and over your speech, put some effort into some of the sub-tasks such as experimenting with a variety of gestures. It's much better to have a lot of practice in many different settings with speeches of different lengths and purposes (informative or persuasive). You can get more practice by volunteering at work to be the person in your group who'll speak on behalf of your colleagues. In addition, you can find many opportunities in social settings to give a short speech, and the nationwide association called Toastmasters exists solely to give its members regular and varied public speaking opportunities. For example, if you and your cousins are attending your grandmother's eightieth birthday, instead of joining in when someone else says, "It's time to say 'Happy birthday, Grandma!'" make it into an opportunity for a brief informative speech. Gather your facts (10 grandchildren, 4 great-grandchildren, etc.), make a few notes, step to the center of the gathering, take a break, and begin, "If I could have your attention . . . I'd like to say a few words on behalf of my sisters and brothers. . . ."

Videotaping can help you see annoying habits such as fidgeting and pacing, but could make you more nervous than you otherwise would be. So consider videotaping an actual speech when you feel you are doing pretty well at public speaking and you want to become expert.

You may be wondering when we are going to address "nerves," fear of public speaking, and stage fright. The answer is: We don't. Although you'll hear all sorts of anecdotes about how professional speech coaches encourage you to overcome nerves, the best solution is simply to concentrate on the mechanical aspects of your talk: the topic, the points you are going to make, your stance, gestures, and so on, and you'll be surprised that you'll do much better than you ever imagined.

Take notes during the next speech you hear. Is the goal of the speech merely informative, or is it aiming to be persuasive? How well has the speaker achieved the goal?

Put This Chapter into Practice

1. Try to deconstruct a speech: What were the main points? What was the supporting evidence? Did the speaker give signposts, and how were transitions handled? Was the conclusion compelling, or was it just a restatement?

Chapter 7

Rules for Group Presentations

Key Terms

| Brainstorm | Butterfly format | Drilling |

Outline

Many business presentations require group efforts

Most businesses encourage the use of teams working together on projects. There's ample evidence that teams produce a superior result, by bringing together people with different expertise.

But teamwork is difficult. In most business situations, there are two or three possible courses of action—and you could make a good case for any one. Of course, when the team members can't agree on overall strategy, the group effort is a disaster. Disaster can be avoided by making a firm commitment to avoid jumping to a conclusion. Instead, a team should gather information, **brainstorm** all possible solutions, and then carefully choose a strategic direction. Beginning to plan a presentation before there is a clear agreement is a great mistake.

A political scientist once observed that the success of democracy does not depend as much on contested elections, as it does on the losers' willingness to support the winner after a fair fight. The same should be true for a team project. Remember that most firms face a choice of credible strategies (for example, low price-high volume, *or* high-price niche market) and that success comes from the execution of the chosen strategy.

There probably hasn't been a team in history in which some members didn't feel that some other participants in the group were being "free riders": people who claim credit for working on the project but who haven't made much of a contribution. Probably the best way to deal with this variation in effort is to embrace it—enjoy it like going for a run in the rain. Understand that not everyone can care as much about every project and that variation in enthusiasm is natural. Complaining that some people aren't working hard enough is destructive. In team meetings, ask "What would you like to work on?" Get commitments to sub-projects that are readily achievable, and make sure the deadline is clear. If the freeloader tries to hide behind a vague statement such as "Well, I'll try to look at that before the next meeting," it's best to confront that response head-on: "We need this work done—can you commit to it?"

It may help to understand why some people are being unhelpful. Most likely, they have substantial competing demands on their time for projects which they consider to be more important (very few people are constitutionally lazy). When a team member is offering very little positive contribution, you'll have to decide whether the project is so important that more active members of the group will take on a bigger workload, or whether you'll settle for a less-than-complete result.

7-1 Before You Present

The basic rules for strategic analysis and planning apply to group work. And just as in the case of a written report, a team should work to an outline. However, using the word-for-word text of any speech—including a group presentation—will guarantee that your effort will fail to attract the attention of your audience. It's much better to complete a presentation knowing that you've missed a couple of small details (you can probably recover during a question and answer period in any case) than to bore your audience. You should plan to speak from notes, and in many cases, referring to the text of your own visual aids will be sufficient to prompt you.

7-2 Presenting Your Work

Most business presentations are quite short. Even a multimillion dollar, six-month consulting project will often end with a 20-minute presentation of key recommendations, and many billion-dollar acquisitions result from board discussions which have followed a presentation that was less than an hour in length.

When a team has worked together on a project, one possibility is to use one team member as a spokesperson. But this approach has liabilities. Where the team was made up of professionals from different functional groups (say, finance, marketing, and manufacturing), a presentation by one person inevitably is seen as "this is the Finance position on this proposal."

Group presentations take some effort, but involving four to six people in an actual presentation can produce a very professional and persuasive result. It takes some skill to get several speakers "on" and "off," to keep to time, and to rotate answers to questions. But the result is a powerful demonstration that the project team has thought through the issues carefully, and their proposed solution is the best.

Group work can be presented in many possible formats. Sometimes consultants issue a written report and then schedule an unstructured meeting: "We're here to answer any questions you may have." Clearly, this approach is very cold and is likely to be unpersuasive. A team can distribute handouts and then lead listeners through the material. Often this is necessary for at least part of a presentation involving complex financial statements (such as a merger proposal).

But there's no doubt that the gold standard is a PowerPoint® presentation, in which all team members take a part. When the team has four or fewer members, everyone should take a turn in presenting part of the work (for example, four people take 5 minutes each, making a 20-minute presentation). When the team is as large as six members, some teams relegate one or two members to the mechanics of running the computer and distributing handouts. This approach is probably not ideal, as it may give the unintended signal that some members weren't important in the work that was done.

7-3 Know Your Equipment

Checking out the equipment that you'll be using takes only a few moments—and this step should be completed well in advance. Nothing will destroy your professional image faster than plugging and unplugging cords into laptops and portable projectors, while an audience waits for you to get set up.

Some conference rooms have computers built into a podium. In others you may be working from a laptop, and to avoid uncertainties and the risk of incompatibility, many consulting firms plan to bring their own computer and portable projector. In most PowerPoint® presentations, the presenters use the keyboard to pull up the next slide, but some presenters prefer to use a radio mouse. This is a matter of personal preference, but you need to make sure the equipment works reliably, or stick to the keyboard.

When the group is larger than four people, some teams choose to designate one individual to manage the computer, while the others present. Typically, this approach guarantees a smooth presentation of the visual aids, at the expense of giving the appearance that at least one group member was "out of the loop." The alternative is to alternate who is in charge of the computer. Of course, this must be rehearsed ahead of time, or confusion is bound to result. So some groups arrange their speaking position so that the speaker also controls the PowerPoint® presentation. This method guarantees that the next slide appears at just the right moment, but it has the disadvantage that the speaker is tied to the podium and cannot use movement to emphasize speaking points.

When using PowerPoint®, many teams dim the room lights too low. It's important to check the room ahead of time. Adjusting window shades and reducing room lighting to about half the normal working level will usually be about right. And with rooms that are well designed, it's possible to have quite bright lights for the audience (for note-taking), while leaving the projection screen relatively dark. Presenting in the dark is a mistake: Even the most attentive audience will get sleepy, and they will miss the facial expressions and gestures of the speakers.

You should be careful and thoughtful about how the light from the projector strikes the speaker. In general, you should stay out of the way of the projected image. In some rooms it is impossible to move sufficiently far to the side. It's then better to take a position in the light and keep it. The worst is when a speaker's face is half-lit, or if the speaker bobs in and out of the image, shading his or her eyes.

7-4 Where to Stand

The team can take several possible positions, depending on the shape of the room, whether there is a table or podium for notes. In all but the smallest meetings, all team members should stand for a presentation, even when they are not presenting or controlling the visual aids.

The key success factor is the professional stance of the people who are *not* presenting. Once you've said your part of a speech, it's tempting to sigh, exchange "Glad *that's* over!" expressions with other team members, or to relax. The most effective teams don't do this. Instead, every member who is not speaking turns to the speaker and watches the presentation as if it is the most fascinating talk they've ever heard. Almost military discipline in standing still can have an impressive effect.

Figure 7-1 illustrates a typical positioning for four people when speaking from a podium. In this case, the group has chosen to have the speaker control the appearance of the next PowerPoint® slide. This arrangement needs careful rehearsal—as speaker 2 comes to the podium, he or she may collide with speaker 1. In any case, speaker 1 should join the end of the line (next to speaker 4) when his or her turn is complete.

If the speaker doesn't control the PowerPoint® presentation, a well-rehearsed presentation should not require "Next slide, please." However, if the slides are lagging, a simple request can be made to appear professional. Angry debates with teammates ("Not that one! Go back to the other slide!") seriously detract from the presentation, and the only sure preventative is plenty of practice. When the team chooses to have someone other than the speaker control the computer, it's important that other team members should *not* huddle around the keyboard.

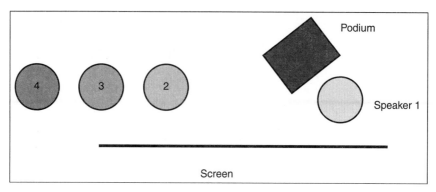

Figure 7-1   Basic position for team members during a group presentation.

For example, an improvement on the basic form is to have the waiting speakers line up at a slight angle, with an independent PowerPoint® operator, as shown in Figure 7-2.

Once again, changing from one speaker to the next without looking like slapstick comedy will take some practice, especially where the space is constrained by the seating and desks for the audience.

Where the team is large enough to have four speakers *and* a visual aid manager, and particularly where there is a stage or large space in front of the audience, the "**butterfly format**" is very effective for four speakers (see Figure 7-3).

In this format, speakers 1 and 2 take a few steps forward when it's their turn to speak, and speakers 3 and 4 step forward and to the middle (remaining out of the line of the projected image). After each speaker finishes, he or she calmly walks back to his or her original position and pays close attention to the next speaker.

7-5 The Order of Speakers

When four people give a 20-minute presentation, four 5-minute speeches are fine. But a better way is to have one person both open and close the talk. The first speaker should outline the presentation, and on the second appearance should draw a value-added conclusion, emphasizing the main points made by the middle three speakers, not merely restating them.

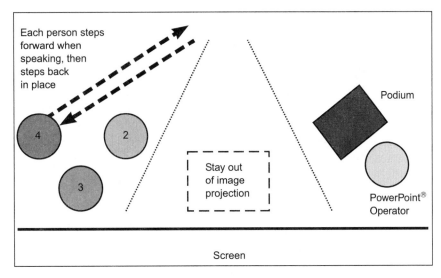

Figure 7-2 Improved position for team presentations with the speaker not controlling the computer.

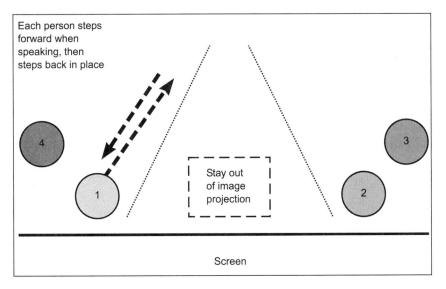

Figure 7-3 Butterfly format for team presentations—note that each team member moves forward to speak.

In every group, there'll be some variation in the talent of individual group members for public speaking. You should aim to end with your best speaker and begin with your second-best. If someone clearly has difficulties of language or articulation, that speaker should come in the middle of the group. A weak speaker should probably have a smaller percentage of the total, should practice thoroughly, and do a small part well.

As a group presentation develops, each team member will develop an expertise in an individual area, so who speaks about what will begin to become apparent. But you should work to make sure that your whole presentation appears integrated. It is invariably a mistake to assign "the financials" to one person. At the worst, three of four team members have a PowerPoint® presentation that grinds to a halt. One hapless team member is introduced to "do the numbers" in isolation, and when the audience is completely lost, the good speakers attempt to return to the main presentation.

7-6 Introductions, Integration, and "Polish"

To avoid the problem of a presentation looking "cut and paste" (described at the end of section 7-5), when a presentation is 80 percent complete, make some effort to consciously integrate the ideas. For example, if the financials are going to show that one option has a superior Rate of Return, foreshadow this point in an earlier section. If one of the possible courses of action is strategically attractive but has very high start-up costs, mention that point while reviewing the options and then go into detail when alternative "pro forma" financials are discussed.

Careful, courteous introduction of team members at the beginning of the presentation (or just after a very brief attention-getting opener) is essential. No matter how familiar you are with your teammates, the audience may not catch who's who, unless you speak slowly and their names are clearly shown on an opening slide that stays on the screen for more than a few seconds.

Spending some preparation time on the transitions between one speaker and the next can have a high payoff. A few moments of rehearsal can prevent collisions as one speaker takes over from another. Conventionally, each speaker summarizes his or her own section before leaving center stage. But a particularly effective technique that demonstrates that the team has worked together is for the *next* speaker to do the interim summary:

"Lee has just outlined three possible courses of action. Now I'm going to show you the costs associated with each of these, and then Dana will be here to explain the payoffs."

7-7 Questions and Answers

Almost all group presentations end with an opportunity for questions (often referred to as "Q&A"—the initials of "Questions and Answers"). In an ideal presentation, several questions are answered succinctly, with each of the team members taking turns with an unspoken selection of who should answer which topic. Of course, it is very hard for this shift in speakers to occur seamlessly, and only the highest functioning groups who've worked together for a long time can achieve this, and they will depend on some good luck on the order of questions.

Because most groups can't expect such good fortune, it makes sense to designate one group member to "call" who should respond. Many democratically organized groups may resist that this gives the appearance of a team captain, but the alternative is time-wasting, embarrassed silences, or two or more team members interrupting one another.

Most answers to questions are 90 percent correct. It's then very tempting for the remaining team members to jump in and add the last 10 percent. Resist this temptation. In most instances the second speaker either contradicts the first, or goes over old ground, wasting time. Most often, the hidden message is "My colleague is a fool! Here, let me save him from himself!" In short, routinely having more than one person pile on an answer usually detracts from your professional image.

When a speaker has made a clear mistake that needs correction, be brief and gracious:

"I believe Taylor just said the Fixed Costs are $400—of course, that's $400 *million*."

Try to prevent audience members from giving a speech of their own when they should be asking questions. A gentle interruption (signaled by taking two steps smartly toward the questioner) is appropriate: "So, if I can form that as a question, your concern is that. . . ." When one of the audience appears to be **drilling** only one of the team members, the team member under fire should try to gracefully introduce other team members: "I believe Leslie can give more details on that . . ." and other team members should be prepared to draw hostile fire. At the limit, where one line of questioning has gone on too long, it's best to get the discussion going again by moving on:

"Well, it's clear we have some more thinking to do on that topic . . . I wonder, does anyone else have a question we could take in the remaining time?"

High-functioning groups spend as much time planning and practicing questions as rehearsing the main part of their presentation.

Put This Chapter into Practice

1. Rehearse a group presentation twice, changing one of the parameters of group presentations: For example, try running your own slides versus using another person in charge of the computer. Or try the butterfly format versus each taking a turn at the podium.

2. Practice Q&A for a group presentation, including drilling one team member and giving a speech instead of asking a question.

Chapter 8

Business Dining

Key Terms

Brunch
Ethnic food
Regrets
RSVP

Splitting the bill
Two-martini lunch
Universal terms of reference

Outline

The correct protocol involves more than knowing which fork to use

Meals take on enormous social significance in many cultures. For example, in France, many business negotiations include a long and heavy lunch, although the protocol is that it is usually considered bad form to actually discuss business during the meal, out of respect for the chef. In China, elaborate banquets are a prerequisite to even the beginning of negotiations, and in Japan, businesspeople are likely to end a long day of work with an evening of heavy drinking in a karaoke bar.

In the US, however, there is a great deal of informality about eating. Indeed, many visitors become upset when they see how, at lunchtime, many American workers eat while walking down the street or eat at their desks while continuing to work. So it's fair to state that meals don't have as much significance in American business as in other countries. Mealtimes are simply an occasion to get food, and because Americans are universally friendly and outgoing, they often eat with co-workers, superiors, and business partners.

Americans typically eat three meals a day. Breakfast eaten at home is often very light, typically cold cereal or toast, and coffee—quite unlike the "full cooked breakfast" with bacon, eggs, and other fried food beloved by the English. However, if you are invited to a business breakfast in a restaurant or hotel, most people would expect you to order a more substantial meal.

When eating alone, most American office workers also tend to take a light lunch, often just a salad or sandwich. In many US cities, it's increasingly rare for a business lunch to feature a formal dining environment, with cloths on the tables, elaborate menus, and separate courses. There are distinct regional variations in business lunches. In New York, and Washington, DC, many formal restaurants still seem to do more business at lunch than at dinner. And in Los Angeles, the phrase "Let's do lunch!" has become a catchphrase, although the meal itself may well be quite light and eaten in a café with outside tables. In many business sub-cultures people don't like the interruption to the workday that a long business lunch implies, and they don't like the somnolence that follows a heavy meal. As Michael Douglas's character says in the movie *Wall Street:* "Lunch is for wimps!"

Because Americans tend to eat quite lightly at both breakfast and lunch, US dinners tend to be huge, with very large portions of cooked food (especially meat) as compared with both Pacific Rim and European cultures. In theory, a formal American dinner can have up to five courses: an appetizer (called *hors d'oeuvres* in French), which might be a small cooked dish or soup; then a salad; a fish course; a "main course" of meat with potatoes and vegetables; a dessert (sweet dish); and finally a "savory," such as cheese. In practice, most formal dinners are, at most, three courses, with no final course and the salad served as a side dish to the main course or in place of the appetizer. Note that in the US the salad comes before the main meal, whereas in Europe it's not unusual to have it served after the meat course.

You may be invited to any one of these meals, or alternatively it's acceptable for you to offer a mealtime as a possible meeting. For example, if a supplier is calling on your company, and you know the representative is staying at a hotel, the offer "Why don't I meet you for breakfast" is definitely within the norm of accepted behavior. Lunch is likely to be informal, and you may be invited to go along at the last minute. Similarly, if you have visitors to your firm who are spending the whole day, you may give some spontaneous consideration to lunch, but no one would expect you to make elaborate plans and reservations.

There are no special rules for what to eat or order at breakfast or lunch, except to note that you should never take alcohol at these meals, no matter what other people are doing. A generation or so ago (people who are now coming up for retirement), many businessmen (there were very few businesswomen in the 1950s and 1960s) routinely drank mixed drinks (cocktails made with spirits) at midday. This gave rise to the set phrase, the **"two-martini lunch."** Concern over drunk driving and a faster pace of business make this custom unacceptable. You might occasionally take lunch with a colleague who drinks a glass of beer or wine at lunch, but you should never join in, even if pressured to do so in a tough situation such as a job interview (see Box 8-1). Most business breakfasts and lunches are "working meetings," and although you might begin with a few pleasantries, there's no requirement to make extensive small talk or to avoid talking about business while eating.

"Brunch" is a late morning meal that, as its name implies, is a combination of both lunch and breakfast. American hotel brunches are usually lavish buffets, and stories are told of Asian visitors photographing the spread because they are unused to seeing so much food set out at once. People are more likely to go to brunch on weekend days, and often as part of a family function or celebration. But you might be asked to join such an event. Even if a superior or business associate invites you, you most likely would not be expected to discuss business at the meal; the meal is just meant as an opportunity to socialize.

Box 8-1

When You Really *Don't* Want to Drink

I n many social situations it's the cultural norm to drink alcohol, or even to drink too much alcohol. Wedding receptions are one good example. However, in business you probably don't want your business associates to see your silly side, and indeed, you may have a personal or religious reason not to drink alcohol.

You should never be embarrassed to refuse to drink alcohol or to stop drinking when you've had enough. People who are heavy drinkers may try to encourage you, and might even make fun of you. But you should be confident that they are only making themselves look bad. Your only responsibility is to be courteous in your refusal and not "preach" to those who are drinking.

Having some socially acceptable excuses may help you to avoid drinking or drinking too much. "I should stop now; I have a heavy day tomorrow" is one possibility to limit the amount you drink. Because drunk-driving laws are becoming more strictly enforced (though not nearly as strictly as in Scandinavia), one socially acceptable reason to avoid drinking at all is "Better not—I'm driving."

At the limit, if your associates are still pressuring you, all you need to say is "No, really. I choose not to drink." If you can do this with grace and a cheerful attitude, everyone will respect you.

Unless you are doing business with people outside your firm, you won't be expected to go to dinner with colleagues and associates as a matter of routine. There will be enough formal entertainment of clients and partners and enough celebrations within your firm that you will probably find little interest in additional dinner-time meetings with your workgroup. Most Americans work long hours and have long commutes. Even when someone else is paying, formal business dinners aren't valued, as they invariably steal from family or personal time. However, sometimes a formal invitation to dinner will be issued—for example, to mark the end of a successfully concluded project or deal negotiation. The meal will take place at a restaurant or the dining room of a large hotel, but it's not usual to take a private room. Such celebrations usually involve one to two dozen people. (More than that, and it's hard for the restaurant to accommodate, and people at different ends of the table won't have an opportunity to hear one another.)

8-1 Your Own Dietary Preferences

You should feel under no obligation to eat anything that by religion, habit, or personal preference you choose not to eat. When you receive an invitation, it's polite to give your hosts pre-warning of your restrictions. For example, you might say, "Yes, I'd love to come, but I should mention— I'm vegetarian." This forewarning will save your hosts from the embarrassment of taking you to their favorite steak house. But even in the worst circumstances, menus of American restaurants are quite eclectic, and you can find something acceptable to eat. For example, even a steak house will have a salad.

If you are encouraged to try something that you don't want to eat, politely declining ("Actually, I don't eat pork") won't cause offense to your hosts because American cuisine is derived from many other cultures, and upon reflection, most Americans would acknowledge that there are probably some things that they don't eat themselves. No polite host would insist that you eat something against your will.

If you are really uncomfortable with the items offered on a menu, you can probably get a good restaurant to make a substitution. For example, you could ask if grilled meat could be prepared without sauce, if you could have two (vegetarian) appetizers instead of a main course, or if rice could be served instead of potatoes. Don't be afraid to ask.

As already noted, the size of US dinners tends to be huge, not so much in the number of courses but in the sheer amount of food put on your plate. You are rarely afforded the option to serve yourself from a communal dish (as is the custom in Chinese restaurants), and your dinner plate will likely arrive at the table with more than you can be expected to eat. So, eat what you want, and don't worry about leaving some food on your plate. You should indicate that you have finished and are ready for a course to be cleared by placing your knife and fork together in either the "four o'clock" (US style) or "six o'clock" position on your plate. A good server should not have to ask, "Are you finished?" In restaurants featuring Asian cuisine, leftovers are commonly boxed up to be used at home at another meal, and in Western dining, people may ask for a "doggy bag" for left-over meat. (The dog is a fiction—diners plan to eat the meat themselves.) But carrying out leftovers would be polite only at a family outing. In most business situations you don't want to be carrying cooked food with you for the rest of the day, and hoarding a few morsels of a meal might make you look cheap. To many international visitors to the US, the amount of food carried uneaten from tables is a scandalous waste. Apparently, it's a part of the culture which signals the overall wealth of the economy.

8-2 Who Will Pay?

If a dinner marks the conclusion of a project, the team leader will make the arrangements, including getting permission to charge the firm for the meal. In general, you can charge meals to your firm only when you are entertaining a client (someone who reasonably might buy from your firm) or when you are traveling away from your home office. So managers need to seek permission to entertain only firm members. When a dinner marks the closing of a deal between two firms, the party that's making a profit (the seller or banker usually) will propose the meal and pick up the bill. In general, if some other party in business invites you to a meal, you can assume that party will pay.

However, when two colleagues go to lunch together, the expectation is that they will **split the bill,** also colloquially called the "tab." There's some protocol about this procedure. First, when the bill is presented, it's reasonable to say, "Let's split this." Because many people like to pay for meals by credit card, you may get the response, "No, let me get this one, and you can pay next time." You should graciously accept but keep track of who in your office you owe meals to, or over time you'll get a very bad reputation as a "freeloader." Be careful about splitting the bill. In general, businesspeople just divide the total (plus a tip of about 15 percent) by the number of people at the table. Haggling over who had the $7.50 sandwich or the $16.00 salad would be considered petty and poor form.

If you've invited an associate for a meal, there usually won't be too much of a fight if you offer to pay because "splitting the tab" is the cultural norm. If you find yourself the victim of someone who insists on always picking up the bill (and, for example, you don't want to appear indebted to a supplier), you can arrange to pay when you think it's your turn by slipping your credit card to the waiter before the meal or by pretending to take a bathroom break. This trick is much better than having a fight over the bill at the table which would be considered poor manners.

8-3 When You Are the Host

Even if you consider yourself to be the junior member of a team, you will soon find yourself responsible for making arrangements to host clients or visiting colleagues. Begin by being clear who should be invited. In general, spouses aren't invited to business meetings, unless the setting is a conference away from home where all participants are accompanied. Then, make a decision about the level of meal that is expected: Are you just providing nourishment while a project is in progress, or does the meal have an important symbolic function?

For most restaurants, especially for large groups of people (more than six), you'll need reservations. Calling a restaurant a week in advance is typical, but for very popular restaurants or for large groups of people, you may have to book a month or more in advance. You don't need to tip the person who makes the reservation, and the idea of tipping the *maitre d'* (host or greeter) in the hope of getting a prestigious location is amusingly antiquated. Unless you're Bill Gates, you'll be seated wherever the staff can accommodate you (see Box 8-2).

Most restaurants won't seat "incomplete parties"; that is, if you've reserved a table for six people, you won't be seated until all six people have arrived. Although you will be prompt in order to keep your reservation (many restaurants cancel a reservation after 15 minutes' delay), there may be an occasion when you and your guests are all present but the table isn't ready. Take this situation in stride—a restaurateur is at the mercy of other diners finishing their meals, especially if you have a large party requiring several tables. If you are hosting a dinner, offer to buy your guests a glass of wine while they are waiting. But you'll impress no one by insisting on your reservation or your importance.

Most invitations are issued informally, by word of mouth, phone, or by e-mail. But if the event has some specific significance, you may issue a written invitation. The form of a printed card bearing a flowery phrase such as ". . . request the honor of your presence at . . ." is only used for weddings. The wording you should use can be simple and direct:

> I'd like to invite you to attend a small dinner party in honor of Tracy Jones who'll be leaving the group at the end of the month. We're planning a dinner at Max's next Thursday, the 30th, at 6 P.M. Please let me know if you'll be able to join us."

This example uses simple wording to ask for a reply. On invitations you receive, you may see the letters "**RSVP**" (*répondez s'il vous plait*, the French for "Please reply"); it is mandatory that you let the host know whether you are coming or not. However, even when an invitation doesn't say "RSVP," whenever you receive an invitation, it's good form to reply.

If you cannot attend a function, the conventional wording is to express your "**regrets**" and perhaps mention that you have a prior commitment. You don't have to be specific as to what the commitment is. This is often abbreviated: "I'm afraid I'm going to have to send my regrets—I have a prior." Even when invitations ask for a reply, Americans are maddeningly casual about complying with this simple courtesy. So if you

Box 8-2

Becoming a "Regular Customer"

You may have noticed that some people seem to get preferential treatment at restaurants: They are seated promptly, always seem to have the best tables, and receive attentive service from the waitperson and the restaurant management. That's because they are considered "good, regular customers." Regular customers are the mainstay of a restaurant's business. They are not necessarily the people who run up the biggest bills—they are patrons who understand how the restaurant works and who are considerate of the restaurant's operational constraints. You should always aim to be considered a "good customer"—here's how:

1. Develop a "portfolio" of three or four preferred restaurants, and concentrate your repeat business on them. You could include a cheap, quick place for lunch; a more expensive place where you know you can linger; a place that accommodates large groups; and one more expensive, very good restaurant where you take your most important clients. Giving regular business to a few restaurants, rather than trying every new place that opens, will have a big payoff.
2. Always make reservations, and learn about how far in advance makes sense for each restaurant.
3. If you are going to be late, or if the number of guests changes at the last minute, be sure to call, apologize, and explain.
4. Learn the names of the owner or managers.

are organizing an affair, you should anticipate that you'll need to make follow-up phone calls to be sure who's actually attending.

8-4 At the Table

When your group is seated, the waiter will bring menus for each member of the group but probably only one wine list for the person who most looks like the host. In some sub-cultures (particularly in California and other wine-growing regions of the US), one or two people in the group may know a great deal about wine and may care a great deal what is ordered. It's not a bad idea to defer to them if they have some ideas, but you should be careful because some bottles of wine can be very expensive and may cost more than the meal itself.

5. Explain ahead of time if the meal has a special purpose, or if you need any special arrangements, such as how the meal will be paid for.

6. Get to know the size of group each restaurant can routinely accommodate and what sizes of tables they offer. If you have a very large group, you should probably rent a function room from a local hotel or arrange to have a meal catered at another venue.

7. Understand the restaurant's peak hours and try to work around them. For example, if a restaurant gets busy by 7 P.M., you can often arrange an inexpensive group meal at 5:30 that works well with plans for theatre, sports, or tours later in the evening.

8. If you have budget limitations, especially for a group meal, work cooperatively with the restaurant. The managers may well be able to suggest a special menu to suit your price point.

9. For a group dinner, decide in advance whether your firm is going to cover the costs of guests' alcoholic drinks. Make sure your guests understand if they are paying, and arrange for the restaurant to charge people separately.

10. If you know your group is going to be noisy, take a private room. If a group becomes unexpectedly boisterous, encourage them to move on from the restaurant to a bar or other social setting.

11. And, of course, tip generously. Almost all restaurants will add 15 percent service charge to the bill for a large group. It's a good idea to personally give a few dollars more in cash, especially for special accommodations or particularly good service.

Drinking wine or beer at dinnertime is certainly acceptable; you shouldn't worry too much about choosing something impressive or worry about which wine goes with what type of food. For example, although few people would choose a Zinfandel (a strong-flavored red wine) to go with poached fish, the old rule about always drinking white wine with fish and chicken has definitely been discarded. Drink what you like. You may encounter some people drinking "mixed drinks" (for example, scotch, bourbon, or gin mixed with soda) either before a meal or at the table. This is more common in the generation who started work in the 1950s, and in most business situations it's probably a good idea to avoid these "hard" drinks and stick with wine and beer.

Even if the meal is part of a celebration, you don't want to build a reputation as a heavy drinker, and if you are driving home after the meal, you need to be very cautious about how much you consume. If you are not driving, a glass of wine before the meal and one with the main course is about right, and if you're drinking beer, two medium glasses of beer is enough.

If you are a guest, you'll be asked to order first. The old-fashioned etiquette advice that you should avoid ordering particularly expensive items is probably still good advice. Because someone else is paying, appearing respectful of that person's wallet is prudent. It's typical to begin by selecting your main course and then waiting to see whether other people are having soup, salad, or another first course (often called an "appetizer"). You can always pile on at the end, "I'd like a salad too." No one would be expected to give an order for dessert at this point in the meal.

In business dining, you should avoid anything unfamiliar or exotic. When you are conducting negotiations, or when the meal is a part of a job interview, you should avoid all messy foods such as lobster (which must be cracked and eaten with the hands) or spaghetti dishes (which tend to dribble sauce over whatever you are wearing). If the food all looks strange and unusual to you, you're bound to find a "safe" choice buried somewhere in the menu. At the limit, you could choose to eat a salad.

If you are not particularly hungry, as may happen if you've traveled far and you are jet-lagged, then there's no offense caused by eating lightly. Even if your host insists that "These are the best steaks outside Kansas City!" you can reasonably say, "I'm upside down because of the time change. I think I'll have something really light." People will respect you, and doing this is much better than ordering a large dish that you don't eat.

Most restaurants make a great effort to bring out the meals of all the people at one table at the same time. But if your dish should arrive first, whether you are the guest or host, you should wait until everyone else has been served. If your guests have been served before you and there appears to be a delay in your meal, you should encourage your guests not to wait for you: "Please, go ahead and start." When the host picks up his or her utensils and begins to eat, you can also start. In family dining, and very informal social situations among friends, people may offer samples of their dishes to one another around the table. But this behavior is very informal and wouldn't be acceptable in most business situations.

Americans love the cuisine of other countries, and some **ethnic foods** come with different courses. For example, Italian meals often include an antipasto (first course), a pasta course, and then a separate meat and vegetable course, before finally reaching "dolce" (sweets or dessert). If you are unfamiliar with the fare, there's no offense in saying, "This is my first time eating (*name of the country*) food. Tell me what I should be doing here." Your host will guide you and be happy to explain the particular routine.

Figure 8-1   Typical place setting for a formal meal.

The same applies to restaurants that encourage you to use anything other than a knife and fork. For example, Afghan and some Indian food is eaten with the hand—and strictly only the *right* hand. If you aren't familiar with this custom, just ask your colleagues how to go about it.

Old-fashioned European cuisine came with multiple courses and enormous numbers of utensils: knives, forks, and spoons (see Figure 8-1). Knowing that one blunt-shaped knife was the "butter knife"—to be used only for transferring butter from a communal dish to a side plate—was one of innumerable little pieces of protocol that were used to determine who really was a "gentleman." Most Americans would agree both that this is silly and that often they are confused about which fork to use. In general, the simple rule for utensils is that where there are multiple courses, you begin with the utensils on the outside (furthest from your plate) and move in as each course goes along. But if you've made a mistake and used a utensil meant for a later course, just say to the server, "And I need another knife. . . ." For many dishes that you order, the waiter will bring additional utensils, such as a soup spoon or (sharp) steak knife.

If you usually use chopsticks at home, the protocol for a knife and fork is pretty simple. In European style, the knife is always held in the right hand, the fork in the left. Meat and vegetables are cut from time to time, and you put food in your mouth with the fork using your left hand.

A knife should never enter your mouth, and it's unacceptable to pick up a large piece of food and take bites from it (which is routine in Asian eating). In American-style Western use of cutlery, diners cut several pieces of food first (with knife in the right hand, and the left hand using the fork to position the meat or other food), place the knife down, and switch the fork to the right hand to eat. The knife and fork should be placed resting on the plate, never on the table, when not in use. You'll see U.S. businesspeople using both the American and European style of eating interchangeably.

You'll find that side plates (for bread, for example) are placed to your left, and wine and water glasses to your right, at about the one o'clock position relative to your plate. There should be a napkin at your place that you put on your lap before ordering.

In theory, strict etiquette requires that you should not talk while you are eating—although in practice, you'll see that most people do. In Asian cultures, people cover their mouths if talking or laughing at the table, but don't necessarily keep their mouths closed while actually eating. This is a big difference from Western culture, and an important one to learn. Americans may laugh or talk while eating, but otherwise, lips are firmly sealed shut while chewing. Chomping with an open mouth would be considered a distinct lack of manners.

It's considered impolite to lean on your elbows at the table, but there are no specific rules about what to do with your hands.

8-5 If Your Meal Isn't Right

If the server brings you the wrong dish, it's probably best to mention this point (the meal was meant for someone else) by asserting the positive: "Ah, mine was the grilled sea bass!" A more difficult situation comes up if your meal isn't prepared right (perhaps something is undercooked or tastes strange). In a formal business setting, you may decide to work around this situation and leave the offending item. However, if you are the guest, this causes the risk that your host may detect that you are unhappy with your food, and then the whole issue will become escalated. So it's probably better to attract the waiter's attention and quietly explain the problem and a proposed solution (either "Could you ask the cook to grill it a little longer?" or "Perhaps you could just bring me a hamburger instead?"). You should do so in a way that feigns that the problem is yours, that of course you are asking too much and you in no way want to criticize the cook or the cuisine.

If you detect a lump of gristle, or something else inedible in food that's already in your mouth, you'll have to discreetly get it out of your mouth and on to your plate, putting it to one side. You can use your fork for this, but an alternative is to bring your napkin up to your mouth, pretend to cough or clear your throat, and take the offending object away. Of course, at this point, you have a lump of something nasty in the napkin on your lap, and it's very hard to discreetly dispose of it. But many people would recommend that maneuver.

8-6 Getting the Attention of Your Server

American waiters are usually readily available throughout a meal, so you should have no difficulty in contacting them if you have any request. Indeed, most Europeans visiting the U.S. find the habit of waiters checking back and asking "And how *is* everything . . . ?" to be intrusive. But if your waiter is absent, or busy with other tables, there's always a problem of how to attract his or her attention. Perhaps your guest's meal is not cooked correctly, or you really need the bill quickly so you can settle and go on to a meeting.

Don't worry—getting a waiter's attention is something that many people find difficult. The problem is that in liberal, democratic America, any term of address that implies the "master/servant" relationship is bound to cause offense. So, although "Excuse me, waiter!" is technically correct, most people aren't comfortable using it. Almost no one addresses a waitress as "Waitress!" and "Hey, Miss" is even worse (because most women no longer use "Miss" as a title). Quite possibly, your server began the meal with an introduction: "Hi! I'm Gerry, and I'll be your server this evening." (Again, Europeans object to this behavior because they don't want to know wait staff on a first-name basis.) If you've remembered the server's name, then you can call out, "Gerry, when you have a moment. . . ." In most circumstances you won't remember the server's name. The steps then are to try first to make eye contact, then exaggerated turning in the chair to make eye contact, and if you're still being ignored, the simple phrase "Excuse me!" will usually work (see Figure 8-2). When the waiter responds to your request for attention, you can signal a great deal of "polish" by carefully choosing the words you use to refer to other people at the table (see Box 8-3).

Figure 8-2   Getting a waiter's attention is something that many people find difficult. If you've remembered the server's name, you can ask for him or her by name; otherwise, a simple "Excuse me" will usually work.
John A. Rizzo/PhotoDisc/PictureQuest

In Europe, presenting the bill before the customer is ready may indicate a discourteous haste on the part of the restaurant to get rid of the guest. In the US, it's not unusual for the server to place the bill on the table in the middle of the meal, especially at breakfast or lunch. It's just a matter of efficiency, and no one is trying to get you to rush your meal. But most people have experienced the opposite problem at one time or other. The meal is finished, and no bill has appeared. What to do? Some etiquette experts feel that pantomiming writing a bill is poor form, but it's what most people do to indicate that they need the bill.

If you are on a tight schedule, it's best to anticipate a long wait for a check at the end of a meal—and avoid it. Alert the server at the beginning of the meal: Saying "Gerry, just to let you know, we're on a 7 o'clock flight, so we need to be out of here pretty quickly" is acceptable and helpful to the server who can't guess who wants to linger at a table for a long discussion.

Box 8-3

Universal Terms of Reference

A fter you've mastered how to address your waitperson, you can demonstrate "polish" to your manners by the way you refer to other people at the table. This is a piece of courtly, perhaps rather old-fashioned protocol, but you'll observe people who have a good understanding of business protocol using this form of speech.

When you have to refer to someone else while addressing the waiter, it's considered impolite to use the personal pronouns "he," "she," and "they." So the form "She needs more coffee" is technically impolite in formal manners because you are referring to an associate as an unnamed person, "she." It's as if you don't care about her name. But the alternative—"Sheila needs more coffee"—also seems out of place because you won't want to be on first-name terms with the wait staff.

The solution is a group of polite terms which are called "**universal terms of reference.**" In this example, you would say, "And my colleague [gesture with hand] would like some more coffee." In essence, you are referring to people by their social titles: "My friend," "my mother-in-law," etc.

Although this arcane piece of etiquette probably won't mean much to your waiter, referring to a boss as your "colleague" or someone from another firm as "my colleague" is a subtle pleasantry that may be well appreciated.

Put This Chapter into Practice

1. If you are comfortable drinking alcohol with meals, try refusing a drink when you are dining with colleagues from your firm to gain skill in doing this naturally, and to learn how it feels for someone who does not drink alcohol for religious or cultural reasons.

2. Practice graciously splitting the check after a meal with a friend. Use the phrase "I'm working on splitting all checks."

Chapter

9

Social Customs

Comp day
Employee Assistance Program (EAP)
Mitbringen
Politically correct (PC)

Quid pro quo
Significant other
Tchotchke
"Thank you" notes

O u t l i n e

Understanding the complexities of interactions with business associates

Because US business operates in a friendly and informal environment, as a successful businessperson, you'll find yourself invited to many different social functions. The most common will be when you are asked to join a group of colleagues to go to dinner to celebrate some business milestone, such as the end of the fiscal quarter. Unless it's clear that a team leader is organizing this event as a symbolic reward for hard work, when a peer invites you, it's understood that each person will be paying for her or his own food and drink. There are no special protocol rules to observe, except to watch the amount of alcohol you drink, especially if you're driving. Conversely, if you know that there will be fairly heavy drinking, take care to make sure that you won't be driving home at the end of the evening.

9-1 Social Functions with Superiors

A situation that is bound to cause more anxiety is when you are invited to dinner (or a party) at your boss's house or even at the home of your boss's boss. To be comfortable, you'll want to have some idea of the level of formality of the function, which may depend on the time of day, and on its size, location, and purpose. For example, an annual holiday party in December, scheduled for eight o'clock in the evening, would usually mean that the menu would be drinks and some snack food, but probably not dinner. The cultural norm would be that you would be dressed in your very best clothes—quite a bit more smart than you would usually wear to the office. Many women at such an event would be wearing very glamorous outfits, only appropriate for evening wear.

On the other hand, if you were invited to your boss's weekend home at 3 P.M. on a weekend day, you would be way out of place if you turned up in a suit and tie (or a dress and high-heeled shoes). You might find that everyone else was in beach attire, playing at the side of the pool. So it's entirely reasonable to do a little bit of checking around to see what's expected. Some of your colleagues may have been to similar events before and will be happy to give you some guidance on what to wear and what to expect. If they can't help you, you would probably feel embarrassed asking a senior manager, "What should I wear on Saturday?" but you could certainly ask the manager's assistant: "I'm not really sure about this event on Saturday . . . could you give me some hints? How formal is it, and do you know roughly how many people are invited?"

For most large functions, it's expected that you'll bring your spouse or "**significant other.**" The invitation should be explicit about this point, and for daytime summer functions, whether children are invited too. Again, if the invitation doesn't make this point clear, you should check and make sure—most usually with the personal assistant of the manager whose name is nominally on the invitation.

Some social functions organized by senior members of a firm are quite large and are a routine part of the firm's annual calendar. For example, in many law firms, all interns may be invited to a barbecue at the end of the summer, held at one of the senior partner's homes. Such a function is likely to be catered (that is, a professional firm will do the cooking and will provide waiters), and it will be common knowledge that this lavish event is actually paid for by the firm. For that reason, social custom does not require that you bring a gift for your host. However, a "thank you" note (see section 9-6) would be a good idea.

No matter how routine and no matter how large such an event may be, you should work hard to make use of the "office politics" elements of the event. Don't slip in late and leave quietly so that no one knows you are there. Seek out and greet your immediate supervisor first, and ask if you can be introduced to senior managers. If the event is large, your host may not know your name or your position in the firm, so you should try to be introduced. But if no one is around to do that, don't hesitate to introduce yourself and describe your position and, in a general way, the work you've been doing for the firm. However, you should avoid detailed discussion of business issues at such a social gathering. Spouses and other people who don't work at the firm will be bored by endless discussion of work projects, and there's a danger that you'll violate the firm's confidentiality.

What are acceptable topics of conversation, then? The old rule that you should not talk about sex, politics, or religion in polite society doesn't hold true at all. Indeed, you may think that Americans talk of nothing else! (In practice much social talk is also about sports.) Of course, we cherish freedom of speech, so you can express any opinion you want about any political person, issue, or position. Common sense will dictate that you should be polite about colleagues and customers, even if their behavior is sometimes frustrating. It's perfectly acceptable to make comments about the differences between US customs and other cultures, as long as you are "politically correct" (see Box 9-2 on page 146).

9-2 Dining at Home with Your Co-Workers

If you get along well with your co-workers, the time will come when you are invited for a meal at a colleague's home. Just as in social functions with your superiors, you'll be most comfortable if you have a reasonable idea of how big the function is going to be, whether it is for some specific purpose (for example, a birthday party or to celebrate a promotion), and what the level of formality is. This will give you some idea of what to wear, whether to bring a gift, what food will be served, and how long you'll stay. You would be expected to bring a spouse or significant other—a boyfriend or girlfriend or someone you live with—although you might want to check that if the invitation doesn't make this point clear.

There is a wide range of possibilities on whether you should bring some food, something to drink, or a gift. The expectation will depend on both the broad culture context of your firm (for example, whether the firm is located in Manhattan or in Silicon Valley) and the specific company culture. This is one area of etiquette where you may worry that you are always about to do the wrong thing.

At one end of the scale, for example, a spontaneous party suggested by one of the junior—and hence lowest-paid—members of your workgroup, you may be expected to contribute substantially to the food at the event. This is explicitly so if the event is designated as a "potluck." For many parties among peers, it's expected that you bring some alcohol to contribute—either wine, beer, or a bottle of liquor, roughly equivalent to the amount you and your guest will drink during the event. The way to handle this uncertainty is to ask the host directly when you accept the invitation, "And may I bring something?" You should take the answer "No, just bring yourself" at its face value. There are few things more embarrassing than turning up at a party with a casserole dish in hand, only to find that the event is being professionally catered.

9-3 Giving Gifts

If you are not bringing food or drink to contribute to the occasion, the cultural expectation may well be that you bring a gift. In German, a small gift that you bring with you is literally called a **mitbringen** (brought with). In Asian cultures, there would be an intolerable imbalance created to accept a meal without having offered a small gift in return. Often the gift itself is of little value, and is merely a token. However, in Anglo culture, there is a risk on the other end of the scale: Insisting on presenting a gift the moment you arrive may seem as if you are trying to "pay" your host for the meal. Although people often bring small gifts, it's by no means mandatory because there is an unspoken cultural expectation that you will at some point in the future repay your hosts with a return invitation. Traditional mitbringens are cut flowers or a bottle of wine. But they are by no means riskless choices. If your hostess is welcoming quite a large group of guests, or if the setting is a formal dinner party, thrusting a bunch of flowers into her hands on the doorstep requires her to stop preparations and go to find a vase. Moreover, in sub-cultures where a well-trained host-ess would be expected to have already thought about appropriate flower arrangements (Chicago and Manhattan would be examples), arriving with flowers in hand subtly implies that you expect your hosts will be deficient in this area. The same can be true for arriving with food; although in Asian American circles, arriving with an elaborate dessert in hand would be customary politeness, in many other US homes, it would be taken as an implication that the hosts couldn't be expected to plan a complete meal, and hence it is an unintended insult to their menu-planning abilities.

One way around this situation is to bring a small gourmet item of food that demonstrably is not meant to be part of the actual meal. In John Guare's play and movie *Six Degrees of Separation,* Will Smith's character says that "Rich people like jam," and he ingratiates himself with his hosts by bringing chichi jars of compote. For as much as it is a joke, bringing something edible but not immediately perishable probably gets mitbringen right. Unlike bringing a permanent object (like a vase) where you have to guess at your hosts decorating preferences, this type of gift is something that doesn't require much knowledge of your hosts' tastes. A small, interesting edible item can be set aside and doesn't require special handing.

If you are confident of your wines, or if you recently took a trip to a wine-growing region, a bottle of wine is an acceptable mitbringen in most cases. Don't be surprised if your wine is not served at the meal—your hosts may already have selected something else. If you have any reason to suspect that your hosts are expert *oenophiles* (wine lovers) and you know very little about wine, don't embarrass yourself by picking up a bottle of non-vintage wine at the supermarket.

Unlike in Asian cultures, where the wrapping is sometimes more important than the gift itself, in America, most people don't pay too much attention to wrapping. You may well see people hand over a bottle of wine unwrapped or in a brown paper bag. However, some small effort in wrapping your mitbringen would always be appreciated. The one "killer" is to make sure that you have removed the price tag from whatever you bring, and this is probably true in all cultures in the world. You don't want to seem either bragging or "cheap."

One reasonable alternative to arriving with a gift in hand is to send a gift afterward. For example, if you were on a business trip, and to your surprise a business dinner turned out to be an invitation to an associate's house, you might have little chance to repay the hospitality. So a particularly gracious gesture would be to send a small souvenir from your home office, or perhaps an arrangement of flowers to your hosts a week or so after you return. This is also a good way to demonstrate your thanks when you've been a houseguest (stayed overnight at someone else's house).

In general only close personal friends exchange birthday gifts beyond childhood years. However, it may be the custom in your office for everyone to get together to buy a single gift to acknowledge the birthday of a team member. This piece of sub-culture often begins when several managers depend on the work of one support person who should be recognized—there's no better time than a birthday to say "thank you" for months of loyal service. But you may come across a situation that has escalated to the point where there is a group gift for every birthday, engagement, promotion, retirement, anniversary, and so on. Before long, it seems that every other day there is a solicitation for someone or other. The burden falls unequally on lower-paid staff: Because everyone on the team chips in $5 to $10, this is "pocket change" for executives but a significant amount of money for hourly paid support staff. You may end up giving money toward a gift for people you don't know very well or don't particularly like. So if you are a manager or have an opportunity to influence the culture, try to minimize gift giving and limit celebration of personal events to a card and some modest token of appreciation such as a cake for the whole workgroup. If you become responsible for buying a gift on behalf of a group, try to avoid "gag" gifts and anything that is overly personal (such as presenting lingerie).

Figure 9-1 In US companies, gifts are often limited to small items, especially those that are printed with your firm's name and logo.

In US companies, there is no need to arrange for elaborate gifts for business associates from other firms. Indeed, presenting a purchasing officer with any gift of value, such as an expensive bottle of Scotch, might be seen as an attempt at a bribe. With the possible exception of the Hollywood movie industry, firms do not go to elaborate efforts to send gifts to individuals. Usually, gifts are limited to little **tchotchkes,**[1] especially items that are printed with your firm's name and logo. Note that it's illegal to give anything of significant value (even tickets to sporting or cultural events) to a procurement officer of the military or government, so if your firm is selling to institutional buyers, make sure you are trained carefully on the rules.

9-3a Gifts of Money

In most Asian cultures gifts of money are common. However, you should be careful with simple cash gifts in most US business settings. They can look like a bribe. In almost all cases in which you are expected to give a gift to a colleague, a cash gift would look out of place and might cause embarrassment. Within families, people may give cash gifts to close younger relatives such as nephews or nieces, often with a specific designated purpose.

---

1. *Literally* "trinkets," that is, things of little real value.

When a group of employees is giving a gift (such as at a senior col-league's retirement), and they really don't know what the recipient would like, then a gift certificate issued by a retail store is reasonable. An exception to the "no cash gifts" rule would be when you are giving a gift to an employee such as a janitor or gardener. In the case of a very low-paid worker, cash might be welcome—but for a worker paid on salary, such as your secretary or assistant, a cash gift would at best seem thoughtless. When you decide that a cash gift is best, choose a round number such as $50 or $100, go to the bank and get a nice, crisp new bill, and enclose it in a card with a note acknowledging something personal about the work that the employee has done.

9-3b Holiday and Year-End Gifts

You will encounter a great deal of variation in the practice of gift giving at the holiday season at the end of the year. In general, no gifts are distrib-uted at Thanksgiving, although mining, manufacturing, and retail firms often used to supply their workers with free turkeys. The practice is fad-ing away as workers are better paid, they may be dining with family, might prefer the cash, and so on. Being invited to attend Thanksgiving dinner with a colleague would be a special honor because this meal is tradition-ally a gathering for extended family only. You probably would want to acknowledge this kindness with a small gift, as described in section 9-3.

Your firm or your supervisor may give you a small gift at Christmas time although it likely won't specifically mention Christmas as many employees may celebrate other religious or cultural holidays. The gift will likely be small and impersonal—for example, chocolates, something else to eat, or a desk calendar. You should not respond with a similar gift to your boss. You are not expected to, and in any case, your firm probably paid for the gifts. Within the work environment, most companies dis-courage people from exchanging gifts among peers. The reasons are that someone invariably gets left out, and inevitably there are disparities in the values of the gifts.

There are two exceptions to this rule. Among lower-level, hourly paid workers, you may see a gift exchange organized as part of a holiday party. Often this is done by a system called "Secret Santa" in which co-workers draw names for other people in their workgroup so that each person receives one gift without knowing whom it was from. You will be given some guidance on the price range and should stay within that range. You can choose something thoughtfully to match the co-worker's interests and hobbies (such as a book), but you should try to stay away from overly personal items such as lingerie or joke gifts.

The second exception concerns when a support person does work for a whole group and receives little recognition for an extraordinary effort. For example, a mailperson or custodian may deserve a reward at the holidays. If this seems like a good idea, try to make the gift from the work-group so that you don't look like you are trying to show off or to gain special favors.

In apartment communities, you may find an extensive, well-organized system of gift giving for the staff, or you equally well might find that none are expected. You should make discreet inquiries from friendly neighbors well before the end of the year. Find out whether most people give the doorman and mailman a holiday gift, whether you are expected to join in the expense of a community gift, or if none is expected. If you employ a housecleaner, you should plan to give a holiday gift. Most workers appreciate cash, and a gift up to one week's wages is appropriate for someone who has worked all year for you.

9-4 Receiving Gifts

If a visitor to your firm brings a gift that is outside the norm in your line of business, you are faced with a difficult situation. Unless you're working on a government contract, you can reasonably accept the gift as long as it is of moderate value, whether or not your firm has something of equivalent value to offer in return. If the donor is from another country, you can both accept *and* simultaneously indicate that a gift really isn't necessary. In some cultures, it is considered unseemly haste to unwrap a gift at once—but Americans always unwrap a gift as soon as it is presented. If an international visitor hands you a beautifully wrapped gift, the polite response would be to comment on the wrapping and ask, "May I open it now?"

If the gift is too generous, or too personal, you'll have to decline with great tact. For example, instead of a plain vase, you are presented with a complete set of crystal. Or your visitor makes a big joke of the pornographic nature of a little statue that's been presented to you. You'll have to be both gracious and clear in your refusal: "Oh, it's lovely, but I'm afraid I simply can't accept!" You can explain your firm's strict rules or, at the limit, state the truth: "It's a cultural difference . . . we usually don't give and receive such generous gifts at work. But I do appreciate the thought." Beware that in some cultures, every gift that is accepted is preceded by at least three ritual refusals and re-offering of the gift. So anticipate that your gracious refusal will have to be firm and persistent.

Receiving an overly extravagant gift by mail might really embarrass you. Returning and rejecting the gift could lead to the greatest offense. But the gift will indeed have to be returned. For instance, say you are the lead negotiator for a joint venture between your company and another firm, and a beautiful gold necklace arrives at your hotel suite. This gift is doubly unacceptable because it's both too valuable and too personal. You will have to use your highest diplomatic skills—perhaps with both a gentle phone call so the return of the gift won't be a surprise, and also a pleasant, but businesslike note. Sticking to the line "No, I can't! It *really* is too much" is the best approach. Then you'll have to restart the business relationship as cordial but "strictly business" and demonstrate that your rejection wasn't angry and your feelings are not hurt.

If you receive a gift for a social occasion (for example, your birthday) and it's accompanied by a card, the polite protocol is to carefully open and read the card first (etiquette teaches that the kind thoughts expressed are more valuable than the gift). In US culture it's expected that you'll open a gift immediately after it's presented. In some Asian cultures this is considered greedy and grabbing; however, you can handle this by saying, "May I go ahead and open this now?" You will always be encouraged to do so.

9-5 "Thank You" Notes

Is it almost impossible to write too many **"thank you" notes?** Well, at the limit, a beautiful card with the following message clearly diminishes the value of all the other "thank you" notes that you write:

> Dear Michelle, I want to thank you for loaning me your stapler this morning when I couldn't find mine. Sincerely, Tom

But a card left on a colleague's desk with the following message might have a big impact:

> Tom, Just a note to thank you for the extra effort on the presentation materials for this weekend's sales force team meeting. You caught that we had omitted page 13, and stayed late on Friday to reprint the packets. Thank you for your dedication to the team and for helping make the meeting a success. Michelle

You should send a "thank you" note for any gift you've received, and for any event that had a specific invitation, unless you are really sure that it was a big corporate event paid for by your firm (and even then, a brief note to someone who made the arrangements isn't a bad idea). It's a good idea to keep some small greeting cards in your desk with generic scenes (for example, landscapes) that you can use for such notes, although a handwritten note on plain paper is fine (see Box 9-1). (In strict etiquette,

Box 9-1

Should All Notes Be Handwritten?

Yes, all notes should be handwritten. Well, that's the simple answer, but like any rule, there are exceptions. If your handwriting is simply unreadable, you can write a note on your computer, as long as it is very carefully formatted. (And you should probably think seriously about improving your handwriting in the meantime!)

In a few circumstances e-mail thanks would be acceptable: If your workgroup routinely uses e-mail, and if a colleague has provided you with information or assistance, a short "e-thanks" would be appropriate. If you are interviewing and the firm has been communicating with you through e-mail, then e-mail thanks may be necessary if the recruiters have indicated that a decision will be made in the next couple of days.

For everything else, a handwritten note is best.

---

the formal style is to use a "correspondence card"—a nice piece of stationery with your own name printed in calligraphy or a stylish script.) You don't need to buy cards that specifically say "Thank you" on the front.

The form of a "thank you" note is as follows:

- Express your thanks for the event.
- Say what you particularly liked.
- Close with something personal.

For example, the following would be appropriate for dinner at someone else's home:

> Dear Raji and Amalia, Thank you for the wonderful dinner at your house last week. I really liked meeting so many members of the firm who I just knew by name. The Indian food was great, and I enjoyed trying so many new dishes. With best wishes, Sujin

9-6 Attending Business Conferences, Trade Shows, and Conventions

The number of business conferences you will have to attend will depend on the exact job you hold and the line of business your firm is in. Some people in sales may attend as many as ten out-of-town conferences a year, whereas other executives may rarely attend even one trade show or convention a year. A good approach to attending a conference is to ask, "What is the result the firm wants to achieve?" Although the firm may just want to reward you for six months of hard work by giving you a few days of recreation in Las Vegas, it's more likely that the firm has a specific agenda, possibly some of the following items:

- Attract new customers
- Show off new technology
- Maintain contacts with existing customers
- Understand industry trends
- Assess the capabilities and strategies of key competitors

Many firms don't do enough pre-planning to think through their objectives, or attending an annual trade show may have just become a routine. You'll position yourself well in the firm if you begin a discussion on the outcomes you want to achieve.

You need to be aware of a couple of potential pitfalls at conventions and trade shows. First, you should be very clear what new products and technologies you can talk about and at what level. For example, your firm might have a specific plan to scare off a potential competitor from entering a line of business in which your firm is successful, and you might have a strategy of announcing publicly, "We've found a new way to make a product that is twice as fast, at half the cost." On the other hand, your cost structure might be considered to be "top secret." Make sure you understand before you go.

Second, any discussion of pricing with competitors leads your firm open to a charge of anti-trust violation. You should check on your firm's rules. Some firms have adopted a rule that there are to be no meetings (either open in hotel bars or private in your hotel suite) with competitors' staff. Even innocently remarking in casual conversation "Well, we're certainly hoping to keep our prices high for quite a bit longer" could be construed as attempting to set up an implicit agreement in a competitive industry that everyone will "stay high" and not compete on price. A firm can avoid the accusation of collusion by making a public (press conference-style) announcement: "We plan to defend pricing, by adding features and avoiding discounting." But it's a dangerous area, and you should make sure you are well briefed before you go.

9-7 True Love at the Hyatt

Conferences are held at hotels, and everyone has, yes, a bedroom just upstairs. You are away from familiar constraints (such as having to explain to your roommates or family members why you didn't come home last night). The atmosphere is convivial, and alcohol may be freely flowing. In short, romance is in the air. No one can dictate affairs of the heart, and no doubt many happily married spouses have met one another at trade shows and conventions. But some common sense and restraint are good ideas. You should anticipate that a few people specifically go to conferences looking for short-term liaisons. You don't want to come home heart-broken, with your colleagues snickering about your adventures. You don't want to become the subject of office gossip.

9-8 Dating and Business

In Victorian society, many spouses met one another through family connections or through church or temple. But the truth of the matter is that in the last half of the twentieth century, most husbands and wives met each other either at college or through work. Dating between people in the same firm runs up against a desire by many large companies to limit workplace romances. The reason for this is a great fear that the firm will become the target of a complaint alleging sexual harassment.

Dating someone from work is not illegal. What is illegal is either offering "*quid pro quo*" ("Come out with me on Friday, and I'll put in a good word about your promotion") or creating a "hostile work environment." A hostile environment is one where unwanted sexual comments or materials (for example, "girly" calendars) are routinely displayed, or one where an employee is subject to repeated sexualized comments. Merely saying "You look nice today, Carol" probably won't get you into trouble, but "Ow! I just go *crazy* when you wear that red dress!" almost certainly will. For that reason, many US managers avoid any comment—complimentary or not—on other people's appearance (see Box 9-2).

Inviting a co-worker on a date definitely does not constitute sexual harassment, and you should be relieved to know that many romances are formed in large American companies. However, repeatedly asking out someone who keeps telling you "No" could be considered badgering and unwelcome attention. However, because the conventional form for a "polite refusal" is to claim to have a competing engagement, it's hard to know if you are being turned down, or if there is a genuine conflict. "Oh, I'd love to, but my Spanish class meets on Thursdays" isn't a clear "No." So it's probably reasonable to ask someone out two or three times for different sorts of activities, and if you are still getting "regrets," you should hear the message that your attentions are not welcome.

Box 9-2

Better Watch Out—Being "Politically Correct"

M any international visitors are anxious about doing business in the United States because they are afraid of running across some unwritten rule of "political correctness." On the other side, US managers who are hosting colleagues from other countries may cringe when a visitor starts a joke that makes fun of people of one ethnic group or gender.

However, a newcomer to the US shouldn't be anxious. Being "**politically correct**" doesn't mean anything more than using common sense and good manners. Here's where the "PC" movement came from. Social interaction in the workplace often involves the expression of personal opinion and sharing jokes (Americans tell a lot of jokes). During the Civil Rights movement of the 1960s, liberal Americans (of all ethnicities) realized that jokes that demeaned all members of a race as being slow or stupid were really just a covert way to express deeply held hostile feelings. The excuse "Aw, c'mon! It was just a joke!" didn't take away the real damage that these jokes caused, and indicated that the joke-teller may have held serious underlying prejudices.

This period was followed by the women's movement of the 1970s, when educated women began to point out to their male university contemporaries that jokes that portrayed all women in a certain way (for example, as poor drivers or mechanically inept) were neither factually accurate nor very funny. Later social movements drew attention to similar prejudicial attitudes toward issues of sexual orientation and disability.

Jokes about the imagined characteristics of an entire group of people present a "hostile environment" for work or study for members of that group. Under various federal laws, workers can sue for discrimination if they can point to attempts to restrict

---

If a colleague appears to be pursuing you romantically, but you are not interested, you should work to make sure that your polite refusal is quite clear. In the previous example, your being "busy on Thursday" implies that other days might be possible. So you should practice an unambiguous turndown:

> "Oh, that's kind of you to ask. But I'm really so busy with my work and responsibilities, I just don't have time to take on anything new."

If you become seriously romantically involved with someone at work, your firm may have strict policies about "office romances." You can't even think about dating when there is a direct supervisory relationship. You can't ask your boss out, and you should never ask a subordinate to see you after work in any setting that could remotely constitute a "date" (that is, when the two of you are socializing without other people present).

their admission to, or advancement in, certain types of jobs or education. Evidence of a "hostile work environment" would support a claim, and the financial damages assessed against large companies can be huge.

If you are working for a large US corporation, you'll undoubtedly be offered "Diversity Training" (which will explain "political correctness") as part of your orientation. But if you are working for a smaller company, or are just visiting a US firm, the rules for "politically correct" speech can be summarized as follows.

Remember that politically correct speech is no more than common courtesy and good taste. You should never make a comment or joke that implies that everyone knows that all people of a certain group behave in a certain way, suffer from the same character defect or limitation, and so on. For example, you'll be in trouble for the sentence "Well, he probably does that because he's . . ." that ends in any of the following identifications:

Race, ethnicity, or national origin
Gender or sexual orientation
Religion
Disability

If you realize that you've made a mistake and have offended a business associate, you should apologize quickly and completely, and perhaps explain that you are working to adapt to the US culture. Then move on with the business at hand. You won't help the situation by allowing it to grow out of proportion, so make sure that your behavior toward other people shows that you are not prejudiced and that the verbal slip was an isolated incident.

Fortunately, the US is not a totalitarian state, and your firm cannot control whom you fall in love with. However, the firm may have a rule that the two of you may not be on the same work team. If romance blooms, see your supervisor together and ask for a reassignment, according to the firm's policy. Both of you will probably appreciate being able to focus on work while at the office. A very sensitive issue occurs when there is a supervisory relationship between two people who are romantically involved. If the junior is promoted, the other members of the workgroup suspect favoritism; if the junior is held back, the firm can be accused of discrimination, with the allegation that romantic disappointments spilled over into the workplace. So if you find yourself attracted to someone you supervise, you should seek advice quickly so that one or the other of you can be transferred. Of course, this is not as easy as it sounds, as both of you may have a strong commitment to your current projects.

Whenever you take a new job, if you are single and looking for a life partner, it makes sense to learn the rules carefully during your orientation. Smaller firms tend not to have official policies on dating at the office, but there will likely be some unwritten rules or strong opinions that you can uncover by some discreet questioning.

9-9 Ceremonies

Although the boundary between business and personal life often seems permeable in American business, the boundary between what is considered "business" and what belongs to "family" is much more clear. So, unless you have developed a personal friendship with a co-worker, there is little requirement that you should attend or even acknowledge many of the ceremonies that mark the major life events for a co-worker. Weddings, engagements, births, baptisms, first communions, graduations, and funerals of family members may go completely unremarked by co-workers. This is in contrast with the culture in Japan, where the presence of company officials at a worker's funeral is considered essential, and Latin America, where co-workers might be invited (and expected to attend) important family celebrations.

Now, keeping in mind that your presence isn't going to be *required* at any of these rites of passage, you may well encounter an invitation to one of these events. Let's begin by looking at the happy events. When a co-worker becomes pregnant, people in the same workgroup will get together and hold a small party, called a "shower" (for showering the recipient with gifts), and each guest may be expected to bring some modest baby-related gift (for example, an item of clothing), or the whole group might join together to get a more substantial item (such as a car seat or stroller). If you can, it'll be less work for you if you can join in the "from all of us" gift.

A shower might also be held for a colleague who is getting married, although by custom, usually only for the bride. The gifts would traditionally be items for the home, but because many couples now live together before marriage, or may be merging two existing households, there is less need for basic household items such as pots and pans. If you are invited to a wedding, you will be sending a personal gift, so you can opt out of any group gift at the office. The couple who are about to get married will likely let you know where they are "registered"—they'll give guests the name of one or two stores where their "wish list" for gifts is set up. You go to the store and choose something in the price range of what you are prepared to pay. How large a gift you should send is a complex function of your wealth and how well you know one or both of the bridal party. It's not wrong to bring a gift with you to a wedding, but because you'll have to balance it on your knees during the ceremony, and the bride and groom will be busy welcoming guests at the reception, it's preferable to send the gift ahead of time. By tradition, gifts were always sent to the bride, but if you know only the groom, sending the gift to the groom, with both names on the accompanying card, would be fine.

It's most unlikely that you would be invited to a baptism or first communion—the separation of "church and state" is reflected in keeping most religious belief separate from the workplace. However, if you decide that the personal relationship is strong enough that you want to attend, you may be at a loss to know what is expected of you. Because the US is a pluralistic society, no one will expect you to be familiar with the protocol details of all faiths. You'll need to know what clothing is appropriate and what you'll be expected to do and not do. Don't be afraid to ask before the event, and then carefully follow the behavior of other people.

You might receive a "graduation announcement" when a co-worker's child finishes high school or college. It's a protocol error to send out such announcements to people at work, and unless you personally know the student through friendship outside the workplace, you can safely ignore these announcements. Don't allow yourself to feel "put on the spot," as if you are obligated to send a gift.

If a co-worker suffers the death of an immediate family member, you probably would neither be expected to turn up at the funeral nor to send flowers. However, most people would express their concern with a personal or group card. More importantly, the workgroup would make a tangible expression of concern and support by temporarily taking on the colleague's duties. When the co-worker returns to work, the cultural norm would be to make the briefest mention of the bereavement, something like, "I'm sure this has been a tough time for you," and then not go much further into personal details.

Similarly, if a co-worker has a parent, spouse, or child who is seriously ill, you can express your concern and think about practical help that you can offer in the workplace to support your colleague.

A different situation exists when a colleague dies. If a co-worker is in an accident, either while traveling or at the workplace, the entire workgroup may close the office and attend the funeral, while also contributing flowers. If a colleague dies of natural causes (say a heart attack), the work group would probably send a fairly extravagant floral display to the funeral ("from all of us at XYZ Corp."), but whether to attend a funeral is not as clear. The funeral may be held according to a religious rite with which you are unfamiliar or may be considered a "strictly family" affair.

So your presence, no matter how well-intentioned, might be perceived as an intrusion onto a period of private grief. On the other hand, having no representatives from the workgroup might be considered disrespectful ("They worked him into the ground, and this is all the thanks we get!"). It may take some very tactful negotiation with the survivors, ideally with the member of the workgroup who knows the family members best. Be guided by their wishes.

In general, senior managers don't make an appearance at the funerals of people who didn't work directly for them. However, an exception to this is when there is an on-the-job accident resulting in death, when the highest company official (such as the CEO) would be required to attend the funeral. In such circumstances, a token appearance at the religious service is sufficient, and the official might leave before any graveside services or other function where only the family would be expected to be present.

9-10 Other People's Business

In the workplace you are bound to become aware of your co-workers' personal problems (see Box 9-3 for a discussion of related issues). Although you may want to appear concerned or even sympathetic, you don't want to cross the line between business and family life and to become over-involved in someone else's problems. So in general, if you feel you're being drawn into the role of confidant in some hopeless domestic drama, it's best to be busy and to try to deflect all issues to a group response. For example, instead of being a reliable "shoulder to cry on" for a colleague who is going through a divorce, you could acknowledge the topic when your co-worker brings it up but refuse to get over-involved: "This must be a difficult time for you. If you need a few days off to move into your new place, I'd be happy to speak to the boss for you."

If a colleague appears to have a problem that is affecting his or her ability to function at work, your first inclination may be to ignore the situation and hope that it gets better. But if marital discord, spousal abuse, alcohol or drug dependence are involved, the situation is very unlikely to resolve itself. No matter how tempting it is to offer your advice, you should not become over-involved with someone else's difficulties. Most firms have an "**Employee Assistance Program**" or "EAP" (you can find out about it from the Human Resources department) that has trained professionals who can direct your colleague to appropriate resources. If you allow someone to share too much information about personal prob-

Box 9-3

When It's Always Your Turn to Stay Late

American business is demanding, and many people work long hours. Only a handful of executives head for the door at 5:00 p.m. This causes special problems for managers with young children. Although they can make childcare arrangements, very few people have a "nanny" taking care of their children at home. More likely, their children are in a commercial childcare arrangement with the children from many other families. In that situation, there'll be a strict time limit when the center closes and when parents must pick up their children. Six o'clock is typical. Working parents learn to drop everything at work to make the deadline, or they'll face stiff "fines" from the caregiver.

In some firms, childless workers have found that they take on a disproportionate share of the after-work projects. When something just has to be done, the manager pleads, "Harry has to leave and get his kids . . . Can you stay and do this?" If you find yourself in this situation, you are in a difficult position. If you complain about the extra workload, it looks as if you are complaining that "Harry" is a slacker. However, if you say nothing, you may end up working more for the same salary. Keep a note of these extra impositions. If they happen once in a while, hope that the workload will eventually even out. But if they are a substantial, continuing burden, you'll have to speak privately to your boss. With your notes as evidence, make an "appeal to equity." You can't change Harry's childcare situation or the need to take care of urgent projects, but with documented overtime, you can reasonably ask for a "**comp day**" (a day off in "compensation" for extra hours worked) from time to time. If you schedule your requests for comp time in a way that respects the workflow of your team, your request is likely to be granted. At the limit, if you feel you are endlessly abused and your boss doesn't see your side of the problem, you'll have to look for a different job.

lems, returning the relationship to a well-functioning business rapport later may become very difficult for you.

If a colleague has a serious illness, most workgroups will reassign duties and will "cover" for the absent team member. How long the team continues to cover the workload will depend on how long the absence is expected to continue, the nature of the work, and the company culture. You may be provided with quite a bit of information about the ailing colleague's health status, hospitalizations, recovery, and so on. However, you shouldn't be too intrusive when questioning if information isn't offered to you. For example, if you are told that a colleague has been "hospitalized," it may be considered impolite to ask, "Oh, what for?" Leave it up to the person involved to decide how much information to share.

If you have been ill yourself, details of your illness, discomfort, surgeries, relapses, and so on are likely to be more information than people at work want to know. You should use some discretion and generalities in describing your illness. For example, you could say that you have a "nasty infection" that requires you to stay home and be on antibiotics, rather than describing where and in what circumstances you caught the disease. If you need to be absent from work for more than a few days, you'll need to give your boss some reasonable information about the severity of your illness and your expected return to work.

Put This Chapter into Practice

1. Stock your desk with some blank cards to use for "thank you" notes.

2. Ask a friend to role-play and practice politely turning down a gift that is too generous and that might make it look as if you were accepting a bribe.

Chapter

Chapter 10

Bodily Fluids and Functions

Key Terms

Calling in	Euphemism	Sick leave

Outline

You should never have an embarrassing moment

Rules for dining behavior are fairly easy to discuss. But other bodily functions are private, sensitive, and potentially embarrassing. All humans have certain physiological needs, and they include the need to excrete and get rid of the body's waste products. However, in a civilized society, we go to no end of trouble to deny the existence of these physiological functions, perhaps because they remind us of our fundamental animal nature. Although most of us have to work in some kind of group setting, there are some bodily functions which are still quite private.

10-1 "I need to take a break . . ."

Let's approach this topic by addressing a simple physiological need: thirst. Most American offices are air-conditioned, so the air may be quite dry. There are water fountains close to most offices, and many firms offer bottled water from coolers. However, you may not necessarily be offered water when you most need it, and you will present yourself as polished and professional if you know how to ask for a moment of refreshment at appropriate times.

At the other end of your body, nothing can be more embarrassing than attempting to sit through a day-long meeting or a series of back-to-back interviews with the discomfort of a full bladder and an urgent need to use a toilet. If you try to soldier on without taking a break, you'll end up squirming and looking inattentive. So the first thing to practice is being able to make polite interruptions. Choose a tactful moment in the schedule between specific interviews and say with confidence, "I need to take a break here." Don't worry, interviewers and bosses have bladders too, and in contemporary American business (where strict hierarchy does not bind relationships), there's little problem in taking control and interrupt-

Box 10-1

The "Etiquette Bell" Saves Face

 recent innovation in Japan and Korea allows women to mask the noises of bodily functions in the rest room. Pressing the button on the "Etiquette Bell" gives a 20-second burst of recorded sound, much like the sound of running water. Public bathrooms in the new Inchon airport feature this device in the women's bathrooms—but not the men's.

ing. In social settings, although everyone knows where you're going and what you're about to do, it's ungracious to announce the specifics of your intentions. The phrase "I need to excuse myself for a moment . . ." is a sufficient courtesy.

In many countries in the world, toilets are referred to by **euphemisms** (a "beautiful sounding" word for something less-than-beautiful). Every culture has its own "polite" term, and it may be obscure. For example, consider the differences between US and British English. US speakers of English never refer directly to a "toilet" and would be modestly embarrassed if you used the word. Instead the preferred terms are "rest room" or "men's (women's) room." A common euphemism in UK English is "Would you like to use the facilities?"

In US business, if the purpose of your request to take break is not obvious, and your host does not offer directions—"The rest room is down the hall . . ."—you'll need to ask. You can do so without embarrassment as long as you use the correct euphemism. You can ask for the location of the nearest "men's (or women's) room" without further explanation. The room may be referred to as the "bathroom" or "rest room," although there is no bath in there, and the function of the room is certainly not to "rest"!

In general, men do not accompany one another to the rest room, and you may cause offense if you volunteer: "I'll come with you!" Women don't seem to follow this rule (perhaps because their toilets come with separate stalls), and indeed, in social settings, women may excuse themselves en masse to go to the rest room (see Box 10-1). However, even for two women, in business settings, offering to accompany your boss or an interviewer to the rest room might be uncomfortable.

To avoid the social embarrassment of being in the rest room with a superior, most men plan their breaks when they can see that their boss is clearly occupied. In interview situations, a good trick is to take advantage of the rest room facilities on the floor below your scheduled interview, so there's little chance of running into the person who ends up being your interviewer. If you do run into someone in the bathroom, you are faced with the unpleasant choice of either ignoring him or her, or making small talk—either way, it's unlikely to put you at ease. If you enter a bathroom and find yourself "caught" because a superior is using a urinal, a nice pleasantry is to pretend that you just have something to wash off your hands so that you are at the sink and not side by side in uncomfortable closeness with your boss.

The same kinds of euphemisms work if you are invited to a private home, and you may encounter the additional phrase "powder room." Again, saying "May I use the toilet?" would cause either laughter or offense. Although parts of public spaces in America are notoriously dirty with street litter, private bathroom facilities are scrupulously clean. So if you experience any spill or accident while using the toilet, you should take some folded toilet paper and clean up carefully after yourself, and then wash your hands. You could be deeply embarrassed if someone else uses the rest room immediately after you if you left it in a mess.

10-2 Other Bodily Fluids

If you need to blow your nose, doing so in public is within acceptable behavior, although most people would turn aside and mutter "Excuse me" to do so. However, picking your nose when anyone else is present is considered highly offensive. If you feel a sneeze coming on, you'll need to turn your head aside and excuse yourself. If, like many people, you don't carry a handkerchief, you may have to use your hand under your nose and immediately excuse yourself to a bathroom to clean up.

In many cultures in the world, coughing up phlegm and spitting it out are considered reasonable behaviors, especially on public streets. But spitting anything in America in any setting is considered highly offensive. What, then, do Americans do with phlegm that accumulates in the back of the nose or throat? The answer is that in most cases they quietly swallow it. If that seems unacceptable to you, the alternative is to turn your head and quietly cough up the nuisance into a folded handkerchief.

It's very bad form to cough without covering your mouth, ideally with a handkerchief, or at least with a cupped hand. In most professions, people keep working and do not take **sick leave** if they have a simple cold, but everyone is aware of the likelihood of sharing germs with co-workers.

Using a surgical face mask, as is common in Japan and other parts of Asia, would seem very weird in America, no matter what the potential benefit.

10-3 Belching, Burping, and Breaking Wind

In many parts of the world, a hearty belch during a meal is considered a great compliment to the host—but not in the Anglo-Saxon countries. Of course, US and English diners do get gas trapped in their stomachs just the same, so this leaves you with some potential embarrassment if you feel a big belch coming on. Most polite diners would handle this situation by bringing their napkin to their lips and covering their mouths. A mumbled "Excuse me" after the fact requires no response from other people at the table. Many people will try to cover a small burp by bringing one hand to cover the mouth and making a small cough.

At the other end of the intestines, gases want to escape too. But breaking wind" in public (the colloquial term is "farting," but it's definitely slang) is considered the worst bad manners. What to do? Most businesspeople would tell you that they have had times when they've had to work hard to physically suppress passing gas. If you are caught with this problem, after eating spicy food perhaps, the socially appropriate solution is to make an excuse to leave the room and to seek out the nearest rest room, or even walk outside. If you very commonly have this problem, you may have to consult your physician and may need to limit your diet to avoid certain foods.

If the worst happens, and you surprise yourself by emitting a loud and vulgar noise, the best advice on how to handle this comes from Judith Martin ("Miss Manners"). In this case, instead of begging pardon from those around, Miss Martin's rule is that "Some things are just so awful that they are unspeakable—and so, we simply just don't speak of them." The best thing to do may just be to carry on as if nothing has happened, and hope that everyone else will ignore the matter too. If they are true professionals, they'll act as if nothing has happened.

10-4 Illness

Most Americans are surprisingly healthy, and although US companies have generous policies for "sick leave," most executives rarely stay home from work with illness. We treat common colds either as if they are not infectious (they are, of course) or as if their germs are so endemic (you probably caught the cold from someone else at work) that they are just a

Box 10-2

"I'm feeling a little queasy..."

I n January 1992, President George Bush (Senior) was facing a serious re-election challenge, and to show that his administration was getting tough over the issue of a mounting trade deficit between Japan and the US, he arranged a state visit to Japan. Unfortunately, during a formal dinner he apparently suffered food poisoning (although his press office later referred to it as "stomach flu"), and he collapsed at the table and threw up.

Worse, as he sank into the arms of his host, Japanese Prime Minister Kiichi Miyazawa, according to some press reports, Bush threw up onto his host's lap. Although Bush gamely went on TV the next day and asked, "Which of us hasn't had an upset stomach from time to time?" the incident hardly helped US-Japan relations and undoubtedly weakened Bush's presidential image at home. He lost re-election.

The moral of this story is, no matter how important a business function is that you feel you must attend, if you are feeling ill, better to make polite excuses and stay home. And if you feel unwell at a function, get yourself to a bathroom as quickly as possible.

If you're feeling ill, it's better not to attend a business function.

---

hazard of daily life, to be ignored. Minor sports injuries requiring a sling or a cast are considered to be a badge of courage, and no one would expect you to stay home to recuperate.

It's appropriate to stay away from work if you have a fever or if you are actively vomiting (see Box 10-2). But in that case, you would certainly want to let your supervisor and your co-workers know as quickly as possible. Even when someone has been advised by his or her physician to rest at home, that person is likely to at least stay in touch by e-mail and may indeed "work from home" for a few days.

In the case of serious illness requiring hospitalization, although such matters are theoretically private matters outside the workplace domain, it would be very strange for an American employee not to fully explain the circumstances of an illness, the severity, and likely prognosis. For interview situations, there may indeed be rare times when you are just too ill to make an appointment. And you wouldn't want to lose the chance of a good job by interviewing when you are not at your best. But beware of using illness as an excuse for anything else, such as mistaking directions or having another interview offered at the same time. In general, Americans show little sympathy for someone who begs off because of a cold (over-the-counter remedies can mitigate the worst symptoms, no matter how bad you feel), and if you lie about illness, the potential for being found out is enormous. For example, in a culture where both spouses often are professionals in the same industry, you may not know who is married to whom at rival firms, and if you falsely claim to be ill to balance a tight interview schedule, you may well be found out. In the workplace, "**calling in**" (that is, phoning to say that you are sick and must stay home) when you are not sick could lead to instant dismissal if you are seen attending a sports match on sick time.

10-5 Chewing Gum Is a Particularly American Habit

More than 50 percent of Americans chew gum at some time or other; indeed, many other cultures consider gum chewing to be a cultural hallmark indicating that another person *is* American. Despite the large proportion of adults who chew gum, it is in essence a private activity. You should never chew gum when talking with someone else and never use or offer gum to other people in a formal business setting such as a planned meeting or conference.

The chief problem with chewing gum is what to do with the gum after you've finished with it. Used gum is unsightly and very hard to remove from furniture, floors, or sidewalks. So many US private schools restrict gum chewing; and in the Republic of Singapore, the government has banned its sale. In business settings, because it's impolite to talk with gum in your mouth, you'll need to plan for some way to spit it out. It would be a big mistake to throw out gum unwrapped, covered in saliva. Even if the people you are speaking with chew gum themselves, they would consider this behavior unmannered. So it's best to keep the wrapper the gum was sold in, spit it out discreetly into the paper, wrap it up, and dispose of it in a trashcan.

10-6 Smoking Is Generally Discouraged

Only about 25 percent of Americans now smoke cigarettes, and because smoking is more popular among people who have non-office jobs and among people who grew up when smoking was more popular (say, people over 60), you are likely to find that fewer than 10 percent of your co-workers smoke. Smoking is universally prohibited in airplanes, almost all offices, and restaurants in most states. Smoking is not permitted in

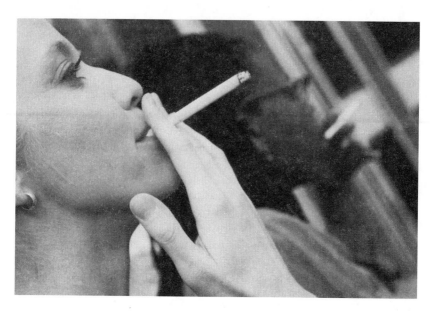

Figure 10-1 Smoking is prohibited in most office buildings in the US, and employees who smoke must do so outdoors.

©Andrew McCaul & Sarma Ozols/Brand X Pictures/PictureQuest

cinemas, theaters, and hotel lobbies. Indeed, German visitors have joked that "California is a 'no smoking' state." Smoking is prohibited in many hotel rooms and rental cars. You will probably find that your firm bans smoking not only in meetings, rest rooms, lunchrooms, and cafeterias, but also in your private office, due to the risks attributed to "second-hand smoke" (smoke exhaled by others).

Although airports have designated "Smoking Lounges" and some states permit smoking in bars, if you are a smoker, you will experience considerable problems in the office environment in the United States. Because your company will not allow you to smoke in your own office, you will be required to take "smoking breaks" outside the building (see Figure 10-1). In large cities, even in winter, you will see clusters of workers gathered outside the entrance to office buildings, having a smoke. But even this activity is becoming regulated as many non-smokers don't want to walk through a gauntlet of smokers on their way into the building, and people complain if smoke drifts in through windows or ventilation. In California, regulations recently adopted have banned smoking within 15 feet of a doorway to a building, so the cluster of smokers outside office buildings have become even more remote and forlorn.

So if you are a smoker, in theory, you manage your habit by planning to take regular "smoking breaks." In practice, in most businesses, taking these breaks becomes quite difficult. You have to interrupt the flow of meetings, and because most of your colleagues won't be taking these breaks, it is true that they'll resent you constantly leaving the work setting. You can see that there is tremendous pressure on executives to quit smoking, and this is one of your options. Alternatively, you'll most likely have to cut back your frequency of smoking and work hard to try to take advantage of natural breaks between meetings to grab a few moments to smoke outside. Many young office workers have resorted to nicotine gum or nicotine patches to handle their craving between smoking breaks. Becoming a non-smoker would probably be better.

Unless you have seen someone else smoking, you should never offer him or her a cigarette—to do so wouldn't cause great offense but would be considered strange. And you should never ask "Do you mind if I smoke?" since you would be expected to know that there are strict rules against smoking in most places. Although colleagues might give you permission, they might feel "put on the spot" (asked to say "yes" to something they didn't like).

Put This Chapter into Practice

1. If you are bashful about attending to your own needs, give yourself some easy practice by excusing yourself from social gatherings. If your circle of friends usually handles bodily functions by trading slang and making jokes, work hard to practice common, professional ways of speech.

2. Lead a discussion with your friends on "most embarrassing moments" in the workplace. Sharing information should help the group understand that many people have had similar experiences. Keep the tone of the discussion professional and lead the group to problem-solving: Apply this chapter to come up with courteous solutions to difficult situations.

11

Looking the Part: What to Wear

Broadcloth
Business attire
Business casual

Costume jewelry
Oxford cloth
Twin set

Outline

Balance your personal style with local norms

There's been a huge movement toward casual dress in the workplace. Even at the most conservative New York banks, you are quite likely to encounter businesspeople who no longer wear dark-colored formal suits. However, it's hard to know whether this is a non-stop trend to informality or whether it's a temporary situation that will be followed by a return to more conservative **business attire.**

If you came to the US from another country for the first time, you would probably observe that most Americans dress quite casually—even sloppily. As you went from one region to another, after a while you would see that there are substantial variations in dress from one city to the next, and indeed, between different industries in the same town. For example, in Denver, Colorado, and Houston, Texas, bankers and lawyers may well wear cowboy boots with business suits (and the boots are likely to be very fancy and highly decorated). It's a cultural norm. In the South (Atlanta, Georgia, for example) button-down collars on shirts are common, even in the most formal business settings, whereas on the West Coast, such a shirt would be seen as somewhat less than fully formal, more of a "weekend" look.

Compared to most places in the world—even wealthy countries in Europe and Asia—Americans have enormous numbers of clothes. They change costume frequently and have their clothes laundered often. For example, no US businessman would wear a dress shirt for more than one day, and it would not be exceptional for someone on an out-of-town business trip to change shirts between daytime and evening activities. Americans are influenced by fashion over long time periods—if you look at business magazines from 10 or 20 years ago, you can see substantial changes in skirt lengths, hair styles, the width of lapels, and so on. But compared to Europe (especially Italy and France) businesspeople in the US aren't really fashion-conscious. The good news about this is that a suit or dress that you buy for this year can probably be worn next year, and it'll still look smart.

To be successful in contemporary American business, you should be aware of the possible options for what to wear and then make some effort to diagnose the preferred style in the firm where you'll be working. Your firm may permit (or encourage) **business casual** on some days or in certain circumstances (for example, if you have a day when you are not expected to meet with clients). However, the term "business casual" can mean anything from neatly pressed pants and a plain dress shirt without necktie in a firm of East Coast lawyers, to shorts and T-shirts with cartoon characters in a California software company.

In theory, no US employer could force an employee to dress in any particular style, but in practice every firm has a dress code. In a large company the expectations will be written down (quite often in terms of what is *not* acceptable), but in a smaller company the code may be unwritten, but nonetheless be taken seriously. If you don't understand the code, you may look as if you don't fit in, and that may limit your effectiveness in projects where you need to engage the cooperation of your peers. You may be overlooked when it comes to prestigious assignments that involve presentations to clients or to senior management.

You may be wondering, is it possible to be overdressed? The answer is clearly "yes." If you are invited to a weekend function at your boss's house and you are the only one wearing a suit, while other people are dressed in jeans and sweaters, you'll feel tremendously out of place, and your hosts may feel ill at ease for not having communicated better with you.

11-1 Dressing for Interviews

The old standard was that you should wear "business attire" for job interviews: a dark suit, white shirt, with a "conservative" tie (that is, one without a distinctive color or pattern), brightly polished shoes, and a matching belt. But if you are interviewing with a technology company in Silicon Valley where everyone is wearing shorts and T-shirts, it's hard to imagine you would be comfortable in this formal costume. The trick is to wear one level *above* what you would actually wear on the job. In the case of the technology company, you might wear very smart jeans and a plain T-shirt to an interview. If you were recruiting with a bank where a strict interpretation of "business casual" is the norm (Dockers-style pants—everyday pants in khaki, gray, or blue that are not jeans—and dress shirts without tie), you might dress "one up" by choosing a sports coat, plain colored shirt, and a fairly bright necktie. For women, the "one level up" also applies: If people at the firm wear jeans, then to interview, you wear tailored slacks and a smart blouse.

Because the interpretation of "business casual" can vary, and the term "business attire" is subject to subtle variations, you can understand why some job candidates make a "scouting trip" to the company and hang around in the lobby of the firm's headquarters building to get a feel for the dress code.

In an interview situation, you need to pay attention to the details: Your shirt should be professionally laundered, starched, and ironed, and your shoes should be properly polished. Pay attention to the discussion of perfume and cologne in section 11-4—in general, you should carefully avoid any strong scent. Many people wear sunglasses, especially to drive, and on the street they look "cool" (fashionable). But they prevent eye contact, so you should always remove sunglasses when greeting someone. The cultural associations with sunglasses are to dictators of third-world countries and "bad cops" (corrupt police officers), so you should remove them when you're interviewing with people. Indeed, many people feel that the same rule applies to "photochromic" lenses on eyeglasses. (These lenses automatically darken in sunlight.) Because they darken moderately under the fluorescent lights used in most offices, you should avoid them if at all possible.

If you have several rounds of interviews on different days with the same firm, it's a good idea to keep track of what you wore on each day so that you can rotate your choice of shirt and tie (or blouse and jewelry). You want to give the impression that you know how to dress professionally, not that you have one nice outfit.

11-2 Types of Clothing You May Encounter

Figure 11-1 summarizes the possibilities for what to wear, organized from most formal to informal in terms that might be used on an invitation, for example, "Please come and meet the new Treasurer. Attire: Bus. Casual."

11-3 Developing a Personal Style

When you are working in business, you are not in the military, and you don't have to wear a uniform. Indeed, as soon as you are comfortable that you know the norms in your city, firm, and workgroup, you can choose something that is your personal trademark. For example, you might be the only person in your group who wears suspenders rather than a belt. When everyone else is wearing golf shirts, you might be the only one who regularly wears Hawaiian "Aloha" shirts. You might be the only woman in your group who wears heels with jeans. If it's your personal style, you look good, and you are comfortable, go for it! If you do this right, you'll signal,

F I G U R E **11-1**   Types of Attire for Business Situations

How it might be referred to	What it consists of	Who might wear this
"Tails" or "White Tie"	Black tailed coat, black pants, waistcoat, black polished shoes (or "patent leather," which is shiny); stiff white shirt, white bow tie. *Ladies* would wear ball gowns (ankle length) and heavy jewelry.	Almost exclusively for symphony orchestras and soloists in classical music concerts. No businessperson would wear this.
Morning Dress	Dark or gray jacket usually with long tails; striped gray pants; waistcoat, stiff shirt, bow tie in any color, *or* "four in hand" tie (looks like a folded silk scarf). For weddings these costumes are invariably rented—no one owns this or regularly wears it. *Ladies* wear a day dress or very smart suit; probably not pants. Modest jewelry.	Exclusively for member of a wedding party (e.g., a best man or usher). Invited guests who are not part of the official party might wear tuxedos or business suits.
Tuxedo, or "Black Tie." [Called "Dinner Jackets" in British English]. Also called "Formal" when it's an invitation to an evening event.	Black or off-white suit-coat length jacket, black pants with a silk strip on the side; stiff white shirt and cummer-bund or waistcoat. Tie of any color (even if it says "black tie") often in a fancy pattern matching the cummerbund. Often rented but some peo-ple whose business requires them to attend many formal functions might own this. *Ladies* wear "cocktail dresses"—probably knee length, and very smart; often plain fabric but possibly with embroidery or beaded deco-ration. Jewelry can be flashy.	Standard for formal evening events such as charity balls, galas, and banquets. Rarely used for just going out to dinner. Still expected in some cities for opera or "serious theatre" hence "Dress Circle."

continues

F I G U R E **11-1**   *(continued)*

How it might be referred to	What it consists of	Who might wear this
Business Suit, Business Attire, or Business Formal. ["Lounge Suits" in British English] 	Business suit, most often dark gray or navy blue, possibly with a faint stripe. Plain shirt, probably white or pale blue. Smart necktie. Dark socks— even in summer. Shoes and belt match, often black but dark brown is acceptable (although a little less formal). *Ladies* wear women's business suits (pants suits are acceptable) or skirt and jacket with a formal blouse or **twin set** of a matching cardigan sweater and fine knit short-sleeved shirt (popular where outside temperatures are hot, but buildings are air-conditioned, such as in Hong Kong or Miami). Modest jewelry.	The "default" for US business. That is, if you are not sure what dress code is expected, choose this.
Blazers 	Navy blue blazer (brass buttons are considered flashy— most people avoid them) and gray pants (most of the year). Off-white, or plaid pants are acceptable in summer. Shirt can be any color, patterned or plaid. Necktie optional. Shoes are usually slip-ons ("loafers") or "deck shoes" (leather shoes in a moccasin style with leather laces and flat soles); socks should be dark except in summer. *Ladies* wear smart tailored pants or "designer" jeans and short-sleeve or sleeveless tops (but not "spaghetti straps") and have a cardigan sweater often draped on the shoulders (sleeves not used). **Costume jewelry**—that not made of precious metals or stones—is acceptable.	Very popular in Europe for everything from the opera to casual poolside barbecues. Slightly casual for "serious" US business (for example when first meeting a client, or when negotiating a contract.)

continues

How it might be referred to	What it consists of	Who might wear this
Sports jacket	Actually, not much to do with sports. A jacket that looks like the jacket of a business suit, but in a different fabric and pattern to the pants. Shirt can be colored or patterned; necktie usually optional, but may be required in some restaurants and clubs. Golf shirt (without tie) also usually acceptable. Leather shoes usually brown and any color of socks except white are acceptable. *Ladies* smart tailored pants with blouse or finely knit sweater, or, day dress. Costume jewelry.	Not frequently designated in the US, although this level of dress is typical of older Americans dining or attending routine religious services on the weekends. Most US firms use business suits or business casual, day-to-day, depending on whether there will be client contact.
Business Casual (*see text for more discussion*); might be called "dress down" 	*In general*, khaki pants or "Dockers" (pressed cotton pants of any color); shirt with collar in any plain color. No necktie. Leather shoes which match belt. White or light-colored socks possible. Usually jeans and T-shirts are not acceptable. Sweaters are acceptable if they don't have lettering or logos. *For ladies*: Slacks with blouse or simple top with at least short sleeves. Cardigan sweater OK. Any leather shoes. Very little jewelry.	Becoming the routine for West Coast and East Coast businesses, but still used only occasionally in the Midwest and South. In some firms, permissible only on certain days ("Casual Fridays") or during the summer. Even firms that embrace business casual often revert to suits for important meetings with bankers and clients.
Athletic Attire (might vary for specific sports such as tennis or swimming)	Typically, sweat suit or jogging suit over T-shirt and shorts. White socks and sneakers ("trainers" in British English). "Logo" sweatshirts from college or favorite teams are acceptable.	Might be mentioned for some active social event. You might also see "outdoor gear" for something that involves camping or hiking.
"Come as you are" or "Dress: casual" The phrase "cas-nice" (pronounced "cazsh" as in "casual") is one up from this, close to blazer or sports jacket.	For both genders, a range, from business casual down to T-shirt and jeans. Clothes should be clean and carefully chosen, for example, avoid T-shirt slogans that might offend.	Frequently used for invitations to neighborhood functions (e.g., "potluck" suppers). It doesn't really mean, "to come over as you are," if you were just cleaning out the garage or gardening.

say, 90 percent conformance to group norms, plus a little piece of your outfit that expresses your individuality. The advantage of having a consistent but personal "look" is that it becomes easy for people in your firm who interact with you intermittently to recognize you.

11-4 Grooming

No matter how casual the workplace, you should always be impeccably groomed. For example, you can have your hair long or short (or even choose to shave your skull—it's fashionable in some circles), but your hair should always be neatly trimmed and not unkempt. The same applies to shaving: In almost all industries it's permissible to wear a beard or mustache, but if you choose to do so, keep it neatly trimmed.

All US office workers take at least one shower a day, and many bathe more often. For example, someone who goes jogging at lunchtime or someone who goes to the gym at the end of the workday will often take two or more showers a day. Americans are highly sensitive to body odors and are likely to be offended by smells that would be considered natural in other parts of the world. So you should always use a deodorant after showering.

On the other hand, avoid strong-smelling perfume or cologne (aftershave). Although it's true that many people enjoy and admire a subtle fragrance, unfortunately not everyone has the same taste, and your co-workers may find your favorite to be overwhelming and annoying. Most businesspeople don't wear a fragrance at work; if you really want to do this, you had better plan on checking with a trusted colleague to see if your choice is acceptable and not too strong. Because some people have allergies to certain scents, some firms have resorted to banning the use of any fragrances.

For women, whether to wear makeup at all (hospital nurses often wear none, for example) and how much to wear (some department store sales clerks are heavily made up) will depend on your firm and the culture within your industry, together with your personal preference. If, for example, you are working in an accounting firm where everyone seems to "put on a face" every morning, but your hobby is hiking and you hate makeup, you should probably steel yourself to at least using lipstick at work. On the other hand, if you enjoy makeup, but it seems against the norm, try to come up with a simplified "look" using only light makeup for the workplace, and save your most glamorous efforts for evenings and weekends.

Figure 11-2 Body piercing is a form of self-expression that may make some colleagues uncomfortable. Consider temporarily removing piercing rings in the workplace.

11-5 Jewelry, Piercings, and Tattoos

In Table 11-1, there are notations on how much jewelry is acceptable. For ladies, this is definitely an area for personal style, and you may wear a little more or less than your co-workers. However, don't try to show off wealth with excessive amounts of gold jewelry, and don't wear pieces that would be distracting in the workplace. Very often, women wear what is called "**costume jewelry**," that is, jewelry that looks as if it's made out of precious metals and stones but is actually made of plastic and cheap metal. For men, in very conservative firms *any* jewelry beyond a nice watch would be considered strange, but in some industries (such as the West Coast entertainment industry) men routinely have not only gold necklaces, but often metal bracelets too.

Pierced earlobes for earrings are now more common than not for women in the workplace, and many men have one or both ears pierced too. However, men don't wear earrings in the most conservative settings. Although there are differences by region and generation in the acceptance of piercings (such as eyebrow rings), most middle-aged people are not accustomed to seeing—and are not comfortable looking at—lip, nose, or tongue piercings (see Figure 11-2). Be warned that if this type of self-expression is important to you, it may limit your choice of employment.

Although some piercings are permanent, many can be temporarily removed and replaced with "keepers," which make the piercing unnoticeable during work hours.

In conservative businesses, piercings other than women's ears may not be accepted.

11-6 Building a Wardrobe

When you first start into the workforce, you may be overwhelmed at the thought of all the clothes that you have to buy. Don't despair—you don't have to buy them all at once, and you should be able to buy most of them on sale. Let's begin by considering the circumstances in which you need "business attire"—for example, if you were beginning work as an accounting auditor where it is expected that most of your time will be spent in clients' offices. Whether man or woman, if you are required to wear a suit, the minimum number you'll need is two. Conventionally, one of them should be dark, charcoal gray, and the other navy blue. To add some variety to your wardrobe, choose one of them to be completely plain and the other with a subtle stripe (pin stripe). Stay away from broad stripes (chalk stripes) that look like clothes from a 1930s gangster movie. They are a fashion statement that can look dated very quickly.

If you have just a couple of suits, try to avoid plain black, with the possible exception that you live in New York, where black, black, black, black seems to have dominated business attire for the last 10 years. Although black is fashionable in some circles, it doesn't suit everyone's coloring (complexion) and is a look that goes better for "clubbing" (that is, after-hours entertainment). Men can choose a single-breasted or double-breasted style (one side of the jacket overlaps the other). A double-breasted coat looks good when you are standing up (so it makes a good first impression), but it should be unbuttoned when you're sitting. This makes for some awkward "stage business" (unbuttoning and rebuttoning) if you have multiple seated meetings, so it's not best for interviewing. A double-breasted suit looks good on people who are large (it can break up the bulk of a large torso), and the formal padded shoulders can help to bulk up someone who's very slender. But it's hard to tailor one well for someone with a very athletic shape (broad shoulders and narrow waist). At present, almost no one wears a vest—"waistcoat" in British English—(so-called three-piece suit) even in winter, although this is subject to fashion, and three-piece suits might return.

Most of the time that you are required to wear a suit, you'll soon remove the jacket. Make sure you put it on a hanger to keep its shape. One trick is to buy two pairs of pants with one jacket. Although you shouldn't dry clean a suit too often, you'll be able to send one pair of pants out to be cleaned while using the second pair.

Women must make a big decision about skirt length. Whether fashions are short ("micro-mini skirts") or long ("peasant length" to the ankle), it's best to be conservative and choose a length close to the knee. A skirt that's too short will require very careful sitting and movement if you are not to embarrass yourself, and one that is too long will be an inconvenience when you're commuting to work.

Don't be afraid to buy good-quality brand-name clothes on sale or from discount stores. Department store sales of business suits are frequent (at least twice a year), and many designers have stores in outlet malls, where you can pick up a bargain. Don't hesitate to get something that doesn't fit right. For a little money, you can have a tailor make alterations so that the suit fits you perfectly. Careful alteration is probably more important than the price you pay in achieving a strong professional image. A skilled tailor can accommodate any body type and make your clothes enhance your appearance.

When you have your two basic suits, you can begin to branch out. A suit with a faint check about two inches square ("window-pane check") might be next, followed by a more casual type of suit with a subtle plaid (usually called "Prince of Wales check" if black on gray, or a "Glen Plaid" if brown). Be careful that these suits can be used only on semi-formal occasions, but they can be a nice change from the gray/blue routine. Most suits will be suitable for "three seasons" (fall, winter, and spring), and you might then move on to some lightweight suits for summer, depending on the climate where you live. Women might expand their wardrobes with a beige or olive-green suit, depending on color preference. When you've built up a collection of five to seven suits, that's enough for even the most formal work environment. You can wear your suits in rotation and buy two or three new suits each year, while retiring some that you've owned longest. That way, you can keep a substantial business wardrobe without bankrupting yourself.

After establishing the basic "formal" business wardrobe, men should add a blazer and a sport coat to their wardrobe. These items of apparel are useful for a "not-quite-formal look" (see Table 11-1.) Women should shop for nice **twin sets** to pair with skirts for the same "semi-formal" look. A twin set is a smart, tailored sweater or T-shirt with a matching cardigan.

If your firm embraces "business casual" dress at least part of the time, you'll need an inventory of pants and shirts (or skirts and blouses). In some climates you'll also add a sports jacket or plain sweaters, depending on the norm you observe in your firm. In business, most people have their shirts or blouses professionally laundered. This gives a very crisp appearance because the laundry uses starch (stiffening), high temperatures, and special ironing machines. Of course, this pounding is stressful for shirts, and they tend to shrink substantially over the first two or three launderings. To counteract this problem, buy shirts that are one full size larger than you would buy to run through your home washing machine. Dress shirts for business can probably withstand only about 15 to 20 launderings and still look smart. This suggests that you should aim to quickly have at least a dozen shirts in your wardrobe. Half will be at the laundry at any one time. With this rotation, you need 12 to 14 new shirts at least each year.

Most shirts and blouses are made of cotton "**broadcloth**," but some people prefer a fabric in which the strands of thread are doubled in the weaving, called "**Oxford cloth**." Oxford cloth shirts usually have button-down collars, a slightly less-than-formal look. Most broadcloth shirts for business wear have plastic collar stays to keep the points smart and uncurled (you remove these stays before sending shirts to the laundry and put them in again before wearing). Cuffs can be "barrel cuffs" (what you would expect on a collared shirt for leisure wear) or "French cuffs," that is, with an extra length of material that is folded back and secured with cuff links. This particular style is highly favored in some firms (such as in certain investment banks) but might be considered old-fashioned in many industries and cities.

You can build up a collection of nice shoes, again, often shopping on sale. A glance at your colleagues will give you an idea of what middle-of-the-road styles are acceptable, and your own common sense will tell you which fashion-forward styles should be reserved for after-work entertainment. You can choose black or dark brown (which may be called "Chestnut" or "Cordovan" if it has a deep red tone) for most business purposes, although black is always more formal. Light brown or tan shoes go only with casual attire. For men, shoes and belt should match in color, and for women, shoes and purse should match. Women may have more color options than men, if the leather goods are chosen as part of an ensemble.

The conventions for socks are that the socks should match (or at least not detract from) the pants. So navy-colored socks with navy pants and dark gray socks with a gray suit would be typical. However, in all but the most formal or fashion-conscious industries, you can simplify this convention by choosing one color and always wearing black or very dark navy socks. Light-colored socks (for example, beige) may be acceptable with casual dress, as can be some subtle patterns. However, no matter how hot and humid the weather, in the US, businesspeople never wear white socks with pants or suits. The only exception would be when boat shoes or sneakers are worn with jeans, and even then, many people might still wear dark socks. Ladies are expected to wear pantyhose in almost all circumstances with business attire, even when it's hot. Because hose snag and run, it's prudent to keep a spare set in your desk drawer or purse. Unless you're aiming for a particular fashion statement (for example, black hose with a black suit), you should choose one flattering color that matches your skin tone (it may be called something like "nude" or "tan").

If you commute by car, you won't need much in the way of outer garments such as overcoats, scarves, and hats. However, if you commute by public transportation, your purchases should include one very good-quality heavy overcoat in black, dark gray, or navy, and one nice raincoat that can be in almost any color. If you live in a very cold city such as Minneapolis or Chicago, you'll need a hat too, although in practice, when the weather is really cold, even professional people resort to ski clothing such as anoraks with attached hoods. If you're wearing a hat, remember that men are expected to remove their hats at once upon entering a building, whereas ladies can keep their hats on. There's no justification for this behavior; it's just an etiquette rule, for which the only exception is religious dictates, such as the choice to wear a turban.

11-7 Caring for Your Business Clothes

As you begin to build your business wardrobe, invest in some systems to keep your clothes properly. Leather shoes will last much longer if you put in "shoe trees" (shoe keepers that return shoes to their natural shape) when you're not wearing them. Good-quality wooden hangers will keep suits in the proper shape, and hanging pants upside down with the correct hangers allows them to naturally shed wrinkles.

Business clothes are expensive, and maintaining a professional wardrobe can be a big hit to your budget. However, the good news is that most people dry clean their clothes way too often. Yes, if you have a spill or have sweat profusely into a jacket, you'll have to send your clothes to the cleaners. But if you have arranged a wardrobe with a selection of suits, you just need to carefully rotate your suits and shoes so that you are not wearing them day-to-day. Hang them carefully in your closet and allow them to "rest." If you decide that cleaning is necessary, perhaps only the pants of a suit need to be cleaned (see the two-pairs-of-pants tip in section 11-6). If you send your suits to the dry cleaners too often, the fabric will become shiny as the outer fibers get lost and only strong thin fibers are left.

Sending your suits to the cleaners no more than four times a year should be enough if you are careful with sweat and spills, and you could achieve just twice a year if you have a large collection of suits. If you can minimize the number of trips to the cleaners, your suits should last for more than two years, and of course, this fits with trying to build up a good-sized wardrobe with lots of different choices.

Put This Chapter into Practice

1. Make an inventory of your current business clothes, and develop a long-range plan. Comparing the two lists, develop a list of fundamental business wardrobe items that you'll look out for at the next department store sale.

2. Interview friends about their understanding of the term "business casual," and see whether you can develop a consensus for your community.

Chapter

12

Recruiting

Outline

No matter how much you love your current job, you should always be looking for your next one

American business runs in cycles of boom and bust. In one year everyone is getting multiple job offers and switching companies after just a few months in a position, and the next year, no firms are hiring. So even if you've just landed the job of your dreams, you have to be aware of the process for recruiting and constantly be prepared to begin your search for your next position.

It's helpful to think about the process of getting a job from the perspective of three different situations. First, there's **"on-campus recruiting."** Whether you are completing a bachelor's degree or graduate training, the firms that want to hire will come to you. This is an enviable position to be in, and will be the easiest recruiting experience of your life. You should be sure to take advantage of scheduled on-campus recruiting. Make sure you understand the rules for your university's career center, which may require you to sign up, or to "bid" preference points for certain employers. It's likely that you'll be required to submit a resume in a particular format that is common to all students. Many firms use a process called "resume drop": You indicate your interest in a firm by submitting a copy of your resume only (without **cover letter**), and the firms then decide which candidates are to be invited for interviews. Many—but not all—schools permit recent graduates (or any graduate from their school) to participate in on-campus recruiting, sometimes for an additional fee.

The second situation is when you are "between jobs" (a euphemism for "unemployed"). Many specialized books on job hunting are available, so this brief summary should not be considered a substitute in this situation. The main features of this type of job search are that you should actively seek out job leads from as many sources as possible. Experts say that, after the first post-college job, most people find their jobs through personal contacts, not through applying to jobs that are announced in newspaper advertisements or on the web. If your period of unemployment from your main profession is likely to last for more than a few weeks, it's a good idea to take on temporary or contract work so that you have some income while you're looking. (You can omit such work from your resume, and if you are asked at an interview, you should answer honestly but label the work as unimportant in the whole context of your career.) You should make sure that your resume is available on-line at the major job-search web sites and on any site that is specific to your skills.

In some industries, professional recruiters (so-called "**headhunters**") can be helpful intermediaries. They may know of positions that are vacant but not publicly announced. Sadly, headhunters invariably try to switch people who are employed from one firm to another (they use internal contacts and phone around), and they often shun people who are currently out of work. However, if you get the name of a headhunter, submitting a resume and attempting to set up a meeting can be worthwhile.

You are much more likely, then, to hear from a headhunter in the third situation, when you are employed. You may be happy with your job and not actively looking. Although headhunters quite often call people at work, it's not a good idea to discuss new jobs from your current office. Headhunters know this and can arrange to talk to you outside business hours. If your search for a new job gets serious, and you need time to go for interviews, you'll have to plan how to take the time off. You can take vacation days, and you don't need to be specific about why you are taking the time off. But you shouldn't "call in sick" when, in fact, you are not. To your surprise, you may find yourself interviewing with someone who knows your current boss. When a rival company from your industry is recruiting you, the new firm will understand your situation and will respect your wanting to keep the overtures confidential. So it's not unusual to have preliminary meetings outside work hours—over breakfast, for example. You'll have to be discreet about recruiting. If your current manager learns that you are "looking around," you'll be unlikely to get good projects assigned to you, you won't get promoted, and yours may be the first name that comes to mind if there are layoffs.

Even when you're satisfied with your current position, and your promotion prospects look good, keeping your eyes open for new opportunities makes sense. American business is simply not structured for lifetime career opportunities. (If you want to get a picture of this situation, look up which firms were at the top of the Fortune 500 list 10 years ago.) So you should be looking to develop your own career, independent of the success of an individual firm. Make sure you keep your resume up to date. At the very least, review it twice a year (say at the beginning of the year and at the Fourth of July). Does it reflect all your skills and interests? Does it include your most recent accomplishments? Does it include details that are now irrelevant? Even when you're not looking, there's no harm in having your up-to-date resume posted on-line; this way, you have a version ready if you are asked to apply for a position.

12-1 Networking

In the 1980s the term "**networking**" gained popularity—indeed it became almost a fad. Young executives would dash around ever-larger "networking events" handing out their business cards to anyone within reach. Then when they needed some advantage in business, they would call someone whose card *they had* been given and feign friendship. Of course, such superficial contacts don't really give you much advantage in business. However, you should learn what could be called "smart networking."

If you would like your career to move in a particular direction (for example, away from mere technical work, into general management), you should actively seek out people who can give you advice, both within your firm and in the industry in general. If you want to switch firms, think about who you know who might know someone at the firms where you would like to work. You're unlikely to be introduced at once to just the right person, but you can ask, "Who *should* I be talking to?" Most people like talking about themselves and their firms, so most will welcome an opportunity to talk with you. One key is to end every such discussion with "Whom else should I be talking to?" If you are actively looking for a new position, people who don't have an opening themselves may think of other managers who might be able to hire you.

Jobs come and go. You should always be recruiting.

12-2 Resume Basics

Each industry has some cultural norms about the format and content of a resume. You should ask for copies of resumes that recruiters liked and didn't like, and be prepared to ask specific questions, such as "What do you think about the bulleted format?"

First, you should know that your resume may be referred to as a "Vita" (especially in British English), which means "Life," or as "Curriculum

Vitae"—in essence, "the story of my life." And you may see the French form, résumé, which could be loosely translated as "A summary." In any case, the convention in the US is *not* to use any of these words at the top of the page—just begin with your name.

In many parts of US business, you will be expected to submit a one-page resume. Prepare a longer document only if you are sure that it's acceptable in your field. In Europe and other parts of the world, it is customary to include some pieces of information that should not appear with a resume submitted in the US. Do not include a photo or mention marital status, children, or your citizenship. Federal law requires that you have the right to work in the US (in general, a US passport, appropriate visa, or permanent resident status ["Green Card"]). But employers cannot discriminate against you on the grounds of national origin, so most people leave off such information on their resumes.

You will encounter two main types of resumes: a **chronological resume,** in which information is presented in the order "most recent first" within specific sections, and a so-called **functional resume,** which lists abilities (in any order that seems to make logical sense) and then provides details. There's an overwhelming preference for the chronological resume, and some firms may require you to re-write a functional resume in the other style. People who have had unpaid work experience and those who have been out of the workforce for a long period of time favor the functional resume.

Many firms receive more than 2,000 resumes for each position that they are trying to fill, and large companies receive several thousand resumes each week. So you should not be surprised to learn that most large firms scan resumes they receive and convert them to electronic files. Even when resumes aren't scanned, they are likely to be photocopied, faxed, sent as e-mail attachments, and so on. This means that formatting and your choice of font are important. Although you want your resume to stand out, above all you want to achieve clarity.

When resumes have been scanned and sorted, a firm's Human Resources department frequently presents managers with from 60 to 200 resumes. Suppose that a manager has to sort through a stack of resumes from her briefcase during a three-hour plane flight. Deducting time for boarding and landing, some time for a meal, and so on, you can estimate that the stack must be processed in no more than two hours. You can calculate that your resume will get *at most* a couple of minutes of attention. So you want to aim for a good, quick summary, rather than overwhelming detail.

Many firms now ask for resumes to be submitted electronically. Although the Adobe .pdf (portable document format) has some advantages, there's a small chance that your recipient may not be able to read that file type, so you should submit your resume (and cover letter) as an MS WORD .doc file, unless the firm specifically requests that you submit material as text in the body of an e-mail. This last option presents quite a challenge: All formatting is lost, and your resume will no longer have the attractive layout that you worked so hard to achieve. However, firms that ask for e-mail text submission of your resume probably aren't going to "read" it in the conventional way: They'll likely use a sophisticated computer program to search for certain combinations of skills. If you believe that this is the likely fate of your resume, it will change the words that you use. For example, instead of saying that you are "expert in many operating environments," you would say, specifically, "Experienced with Novell, Unix, and Windows-NT systems." Because the process of scanning a paper resume is to generate a computer file version of a paper resume, this suggests that the use of specific technical terms for skills and experience may lead to your resume being pre-selected for review by a recruiter.

When you know that the fate of most resumes is to be scanned by machine, you can readily answer many common questions about resumes:

Should I use a special paper?   The scanning machine won't care that you spent a fortune on special linen paper. It just cares that the ink is black and sharp and the paper is white. Using decorative paper may cause problems with readability. An exception to the "plain white paper" rule concerns resumes that you physically hand to recruiters at interviews or career fairs. You can certainly use a heavier "weight" of paper (that is, thicker) to make a good, professional impression. Keep copies of your resume in a portfolio, nice and flat, rather than folded in your pocket.

Can I submit multiple copies of my resume?   Absolutely! There are some chance elements to the submission process. For example, if you hand a resume to a recruiter at a career fair, your resume might be mislaid. You should definitely submit a clean copy to the recruiter's office and also to the firm's Human Resources department. The "worst that can happen" here is that someone checks and sees that the resume has already been entered into the system. If you think you are under consideration at a firm, and it's been a long while since you've had contact with the company, it's legitimate to use some minor improvement in your resume (such as being elected to a leadership position in a club) as an excuse to re-submit your resume.

Can I have different versions of my resume? Yes, in fact, most professionals probably have more than one version. For example, someone trained as an engineer probably has one resume that emphasizes technical skills and another that highlights managerial experience. As long as the two versions are not contradictory, there is no problem here. If you get to interview and are asked about having two versions, you can state the truth: "I have a lot of experience as an engineer, and I've been working for some time in management—the two versions emphasize the two different skill sets."

How do I apply on-line? Many firms now ask candidates to submit digital versions of their resumes. Unless you are given other instructions, such as "include your resume in the body of your e-mail," you should submit your resume as an MS WORD .doc attachment to a simple e-mail note that clearly indicates the position you're applying for. The company may well be using a computer program to sort through applications and choose a subset of resumes. So you want to make sure that you have all possible words that an employer may be searching for and the names of specific computer programs or machines that you know how to work. Including all this information may make a version of your resume that is longer than the usual one page, especially if you clip the text and include it in an e-mail. If you're sending your resume as unformatted text in an e-mail, you'll have to use line spacing between headings (such as EXPERIENCE) and detail. You won't be able to lay out material in columns. Although the Adobe Acrobat .pdf file format preserves your layout, it may be incompatible with the systems that a firm is using to receive and sort resumes, so don't try sending in this format unless you've checked with the firm.

12-3 Resume Conventions

Resumes are written in a peculiar shorthand style of sentence fragments that are linked together ("concatenated") in groups of logically related parts. For example:

> GREAT CORP. *IT Manager* Expedited customer service requests, developed three new applications, eliminating more than two dozen legacy programs. Maintained 99 percent uptime under strict budget, implemented new off-site backup. Supervised staff of 9 graduate engineers, voted manager of the year award.

This form avoids wasting space by endlessly repeating the word "I." In general, resumes leave out the subject of the sentence ("I" is implicit because it's your resume) and often avoid conjunctions such as "and."

The standard for what to include in your resume is this: With the exception of the section labeled "Interests," what is on your resume should be the result of an examination—or could be. In the case of your employment, it can be verified. So you can say "Expert knowledge of C++" whether or not you've actually taken a course in this programming language, and you can say "Native-level fluency in Spanish" (even if you weren't born in Spain, as long as your Spanish is "as good as" someone who was born there.) But you can't say "Reliable, hard worker." Although this statement may be true, it's not subject to examination, so it belongs in your cover letter, not in your resume.

If you were called to be a witness in a court of law, you would raise your right hand and swear to tell "the truth, the whole truth, and nothing but the truth." On a resume, you are expected to tell "the truth and nothing but the truth," but you don't have to tell the whole truth. For example, if one of the main ways you spend your time outside work is in the deeply religious pursuit of spirituality, you might choose not to mention that. Similarly, if you worked as one of Santa's elves at a department store to earn extra money while you were in college, you might choose to omit that job. Selecting what part of "truth" to present is a major part of preparing different specifically targeted versions of your resume. When you have to fill out a firm's own application form, you have to be more complete; this issue is discussed in Chapter 13.

Experts on resume writing encourage you to use strong, active verbs, and the description of positions that you held should always lead toward a *result*. For example,

> *Sales Manager*   Responsible for Twin-Cities territory for a leading
> industrial products manufacturer.

doesn't convey as much information as

> *Sales Manager*   Directly supervised four salespeople with $3 million
> combined sales; increased active accounts by 20 percent to more than
> 200 in 18 months.

Lastly, in chronological resumes, the order of information is backward from the way you would tell a story. It's called "reverse chronological order," and within each section your most recent accomplishments (education or position) come first and then so on back through time.

12-4 Sections of a Chronological Resume

You may well encounter some variations in the order of sections in resumes that are common in your industry. Your industry may use some unique sections (for example, actors might have sections for Films, TV, Plays, and Commercial Work). However, the following is a general guide of the sections that are routinely encountered, especially for young college students being hired into their first positions in US business.

Identification Objective Education Experience [Additional Experience] Activities Awards and Honors Skills Interests

Note that the words "Education" and "Experience" do not take an "s" to make a plural form in this case. Although you may have had many different experiences, the abstract noun "experience" is often treated as a plural (like one sheep, several sheep.)

12-5 Identification

Although we talk about the "Identification" section of your resume, unlike the other sections, we don't use the word "Identification" to label this part.

At the head of the resume, you place your name and contact information. Most people put their full legal name, such as "Charles Edward Windsor," but you can use a shorter form if you prefer. If you usually use a nickname, you might choose to put it in quotation marks:

Edward "Tug" Maddingly

Under your name put one e-mail address that you check regularly. Try to prevent your word-processing program from adding an unnecessary underline that may make the e-mail address hard to read or scan.

You should have at least one good mailing address, although these days it's rare for a recruiter to contact you by mail. Students often have two addresses, with one labeled "College" and the other "Home" or "Permanent." You can use the cover letter to indicate when you'll be where. Place phone numbers under the appropriate address and be sure not to use too small a font for them (10-point minimum, 12-point is better) as most recruiters who want to set up an interview will phone.

You can include a personal web page URL if your site is thoroughly professional (no "funny" pictures of friends), but you should never send a cover letter or e-mail and tell the recruiter "You can download my resume from. . . ." Asking the recruiter to download your resume makes the recruiter do extra work, and if he or she is reading your application while traveling, then your application may be passed over.

12-6 Objective

There are two schools of thought on whether you should use an objective on your resume: You'll hear some people say that a resume without an objective is unlikely to succeed. On the other hand, many people believe that an objective is likely to limit your opportunities. For example, you have good spreadsheet and analytic skills and you announce your objective as "Financial Analyst." Then your resume is passed over for an analyst job in the marketing group of a major retailer that you would have really enjoyed.

An additional reservation about the "Objective" section is that it takes up a lot of space on the page that could be used for giving more information about yourself. You can make the case that the same information could be conveyed in a cover letter. However, thinking about an objective could be helpful if you are writing two versions of your resume—say, one technical and one managerial. You could begin drafts of the two versions by including an "Objective" section such as "Objective: Line management position with P&L responsibility," and then write your resume, selecting facts which match that. Then, repeat the same process for the technical resume. At the end, you could delete both "Objective" sections. They've served to guide your writing and are no longer needed.

A clearly stated objective is useful when you would accept only a certain type of job. For example, if you were trained in several different computer operating systems but, for career development reasons, want to work in only one environment, then using an objective such as "Database systems developer for Windows-NT" makes sense. This is particularly true in computer programming, where resumes are often circulated by e-mail without cover letters.

12-7 Education

The "Education" section begins with your most recent degree, and if you are currently enrolled, you include the degree that you hope to obtain. You can use the phrase "candidate for BA in History, May 2003" or simply append a date that's in the future: "BA History, May 2003." For a US resume, you don't need to spell out the specific years that you attended college—except if you have completed your studies in an exceptionally short time, such as just three years for a US bachelor's degree.

If you have a double-major, or an **academic major** (specialty) or **minor** (sub-specialty), you would mention that fact here, along with any honors you achieved at graduation, such as *cum laude* (with honors). However, be careful about any spurious honors[1] that mean more in college than in the real world (for example, most good students are on the "Dean's List"—it doesn't mean very much to employers).

You'll find cultural norms with respect to reporting your GPA (Grade Point Average) and your SAT (Scholastic Aptitude Test) scores. Some industries (such as financial services) expect to see both, but in other industries reporting your GPA on your resume is seen as tasteless bragging. Ask among friends and colleagues, and particularly try to look at copies of resumes for people who've been successfully hired in the industry that you want to join. If reporting a GPA is typical, you can include two or more GPAs, such as your GPA in your major or your GPA in science classes. Put the best one to the right, especially if you're trying to "bury" a less-impressive overall GPA (sometimes called "cumulative GPA") in the middle of a line.

In the "Education" section, you can give details of coursework that you've taken (often with the sub-heading "Relevant Coursework"). This information is useful if your degree is in one subject, but you've actually taken a lot of relevant coursework in another field. If you've studied abroad as part of your education, you would place this information immediately after the institution that will grant your degree (even if the study abroad is "most recent"). Be sure to say what courses you took and imply the benefit of this experience.

In the "Education" section, some people note that they've won scholarships (although these details may be in a separate "Awards and Honors" section). People who have worked hard at odd jobs to support themselves through school will sometimes make a notation in this section to that effect, such as

50 percent self-supported through on-campus employment.

Most US resumes do not mention high school or earlier education. If you have special distinctions, such as being a national champion athlete in your pre-college years, you may consider including that information further down the resume. The reasons for ignoring high school are that there's a presumption that anyone at a competitive university graduated from high school, so mentioning this fact doesn't add much value.

---

1. In recent years, more than 90 percent of Harvard bachelors' degree candidates have graduated "with honors," so the distinction has lost its meaning.

12-8 Experience

The key to the "Experience" section is remembering the rule "not necessarily the whole truth." Both in your selection of jobs and in the description of jobs held, you will be making strategic omissions. For example, many summer jobs include chores such as photocopying and getting supplies. These tasks aren't really relevant to career positions.

For jobs that you've held, begin with the most recent and work backward. You will show the dates of each employment using the form "1999–present" or "1999–continues" for a job that you still hold. If you've held more than one position at the same firm, try to group the positions under a single statement of the firm's name and location. You can use a similar form for positions that you held concurrently:

> INVESTMENT FIRM, INC. Tiburon, CA   *Retail broker* (1995–continues) and *chairman of the investment committee* (1996–1998).

Firms will be concerned about any gaps in your employment. You shouldn't lie (starting and ending dates can easily be confirmed by talking with your old employers), but you should attempt to have a good "cover story" for interviews, even if you were unemployed and looking for work. For example, "Well, I'd planned to go back to graduate school, but then I heard about my next job, so I decided to begin work there."

Because the title "Experience" doesn't specifically say "employment," some people include volunteer experience and unpaid internships in this section. The word "intern" is routinely inflated, so you can apply it to almost any short period of employment, even if your job title was technically something else. Indicating which experiences were unpaid and which were paid is not essential, but you should know that many people do put the word "unpaid" immediately after job titles to be sure that they are not accused of misstatement on their resumes. If you have a mixture of paid and unpaid experience, you may choose to add the next section, "Additional Experience."

12-9 Additional Experience

You may have heard this old joke: "You need to have experience to get a job. If you want to get experience, get a job." It's circular. Many young people find themselves crafting a resume in the face of very limited work experience. Using a section titled "Additional Experience" can allow you to describe work-related activities and demonstrate what you've learned:

St. Joseph's Hospital, *Volunteer* In more than 240 hours of community service, assisted ward clerk and triage nurse in an urban Emergency Room with more than 1,200 nightly visits. Responsible for checking insurance eligibility and explaining covered benefits to family members.

Some elected college positions, such as Student Body President, amount to a full-time job, so you could make entries in this section to describe them.

12-10 Activities

In the "Activities" section you describe clubs and associations to which you belong, and your role in them. Recruiters don't expect everyone to be the president of every club he or she belongs to—but they do hope to see some significant contribution. Many college students are daunted by the task of resume writing because they can't truthfully say much more than "active member" in describing their roles. Recruiters want to see accomplishment and progression. They are more impressed by results in one or two groups, than in membership in dozens of different organizations. So the moral is that when you work hard for a club, take responsibility for a specific function with your resume in mind.

Young Business Club Active member responsible for managing parking for annual career fair with more than 200 professionals attending.

12-11 Awards and Honors

No section means more to resume writers and less to recruiters than "Awards and Honors." If you are a good student at a competitive university, it goes without saying that you won the prize for best reader in your kindergarten class. Honors that merely "pile on" (you have a good GPA, so you are on the Dean's List) don't convey information to employers. Almost all applicants can point to local high school prizes which they won—such a listing doesn't set any of them apart, and a long listing merely looks self-congratulatory. Many scholarships are awarded without much personal effort as a routine part of financial aid. So the standard for inclusion is this: How comfortable would you be discussing this information at an interview? If the best that you can say about the HJM Alumnus Scholarship is that it's a part of your financial aid package this year, and you don't know who HJM was—leave it out.

On the other hand, if you've been selected for a highly competitive scholarship or have won a regional or national championship, then that information belongs here:

> *Morehead Scholar* One of 12 scholars selected from 2,000 applicants for a full tuition scholarship in a statewide competition.

> *National Collegiate Debate Champion, 2002* Won individual forensics title in field of 200 contestants from all 50 states.

12-12 Skills

In the "Skills" section, you will list specific lab, computer, and foreign language skills that you possess. Remember, the standard is "examined, or could have been." So, for example, if you know how to operate an electron microscope, although there probably isn't a corresponding course with a final exam, there *could* be an exam for this skill. It's a skill that few people have and is worth mentioning. There's an old line from newspaper advertising copywriting: "The more you tell, the more you sell." So list all skills that you think might possibly be of use in the workplace. However, for professional positions (managerial work) most people don't list skills such as typing and "current driver's license," which are presumed for all Americans. (Listing these basic skills detracts from other, more special skills you have.)

You should list as many computer programs that you know as will fit, and you can consider adding qualifiers such as "basic," "intermediate," "proficient," or "expert." The same applies to foreign language skills—try to accurately describe your level of proficiency. There are many levels from "basic" through "reading knowledge" or "traveling knowledge" of a language through "fluent" to "native speaker." Try to elaborate on languages that are useful to an employer, such as "fluent written and spoken Spanish." Unless you know that an employer has a particular need for your skills in a dialect that isn't used much in business, you should be thoughtful about how much you emphasize this point. Suppose you grew up in Wales in the United Kingdom and you were fluent in written but not spoken Welsh (a type of Celtic language). Unless you are applying to be the rare books librarian in a university language department, this is an interesting personal characteristic that doesn't mean a great deal to a potential employer.

In this section, and in the next, the order of your ideas is not "reverse chronological," so you don't have to put your most recent skill first.

Instead, you should think about the most important ideas and have them come at the beginning and then the second most important at the end. "Bury" incidental, or less important, information in the middle.

12-13 Interests

The "Interests" section is the great exception to the rule of "examined, or could have been." So why does it appear on a resume? The purpose of the "Interests" section is to convey something about your personality. For example, listing intra-mural indoor soccer and basketball as your activities signals that you are a team player. If you list mountain climbing, an employer can see that you are not afraid of hardships and efforts that require great endurance.

There's a small chance that an interviewer will be interested in the same activities as you, and that's always a good starting point for a congenial interview. But even when there is no good match, an interviewer can often refer to interests as a way to get you talking about yourself: "So, tell me about your figure skating hobby. . . ."

It follows that you should not list anything that wouldn't be a good lead-in to a pleasant discussion at an interview. You can be selective about the interests that you list and avoid any that you feel might side-track an interview. Be thoughtful about activities and interests with a strong political or religious element. In general, it's best to say "Active in volunteer work with church group" rather than "Elected twice as lay member of Lutheran Social Services" unless you accept that some interviewers might not relate to this particular denomination. Worse, over-emphasizing a group identity could imply that you are seeking preferential treatment as a member of that group.

12-14 References

In the conventional modern form of a US business resume, there is no standard ending phrase. Because it's assumed that a resume will be one page, there's no need to indicate that you are at the end, and this is the purpose that the phrase "References available on request" possibly served. This phrase is invariably omitted now because it's assumed that any credible candidate will have some references.

You should arrange to have three or four people who will give you a reference, if asked. Technically, the person who gives the reference is a "referee," a written letter about you is a "reference," and you are "referand"—although in practice, people refer to the person who will say good things about you as the "reference." In practice, few firms ask for references (see Chapter 13), and they are mainly used in academic circles, such as for applicants to graduate school. But you should be prepared just in case.

Try to choose a group of people who know you from different backgrounds. There will likely be some overlap. For example, two or three people could describe you as hard working and conscientious. However, you should suggest to each referee the area that you would like him or her to be responsible for covering. Make sure to talk with the referee in person if possible, or at least by phone, and if it's been a long time since you worked together, remind her or him of the key facts of your association. Never ask referees to comment on something they don't know from their own experience. For example, don't ask a college professor to comment on your community service work, unless you worked together in the same association or club.

You can use a well-prepared reference list as a way to move the hiring process along. If you've been talking back and forth with a company, and you are not getting to the point of an offer, you can ask, "Would you like me to provide you with references?" Presenting a neatly formatted list, as shown in Appendix 3, can signal your seriousness about a position.

In the US, no one uses the "To whom it may concern" general letter of reference that is common in other parts of the world most often for domestic servants. Most employers would consider a letter that is carried by the job applicant and not personally addressed worthless. Moreover, presenting such a letter in an interview would seem strange to most Americans who are not familiar with this form.

For an example of a chronological resume, see Figure 12-1 on pages 194–195.

12-15 Format for a Functional Resume

Career coaches recommend functional resumes for people who have been out of the workforce for a long time, or for people who have had many different jobs and it's hard to see a coherent pattern. A functional resume begins with the same "Identification" section, and most experts who prefer this form encourage the use of an "Objective" section.

Then the sections that follow can be anything you choose, and are based on groups of skills such as "Office Procedures," "Team Management," or "Supervision and Training." You could even imagine a section such as "Cooking for large groups" for someone who had raised a family and done a lot of volunteer work. Of course, the sub-headings should relate to the specific skills you imagine are needed in a particular job.

Some functional resumes have jobs grouped under each category or separate sections for employment and education, although these usually come toward the end of the resume.

It's worth saying that many employers don't like this format, and will demand that an applicant re-submit a chronological resume or fill out a chronological employment application. However, the functional resume might be a "foot in the door"—it may create an invitation to interview.

12-16 Cover Letters

Professional recruiters will tell you many things about cover letters. Some recruiters believe they are more revealing than the resumes themselves, some feel they are useful "at the margin—to choose between two similar candidates," and others still rate them as irrelevant. If you can, try to find out from a firm's presentations and background information how much weight the firm gives to a cover letter. But given the number of applications that firms process, if a resume receives only a minute or two of consideration, you should know that most cover letters are looked at for less than a minute in many instances.

Very occasionally, a job announcement will ask for specific material to be included in a cover letter, such as detailing why you want to work for the firm, or whether you would be prepared to relocate. In the absence of specific instructions, keep your cover letter short, and organize it in these three sections. (Each section should be about a paragraph long, but in some circumstances, such as when you want to explain a unique experience, you might use two paragraphs in a section.)

First, you identify who you are, your place in the universe, and the exact job that you are applying for, such as "Summer Intern in Corporate Finance in the Houston Office." This information should help your resume to be sorted into the correct pile. If you have some geographic preferences but also some flexibility, you could elaborate that here. If there is a specific reason why you want to move to one city, it's appropriate to mention that point here: "My fiancée has been accepted at Albert Einstein University for medical school, so I am enthusiastic about moving to New York."

The middle section is the most important part of a cover letter. You should use it to get across the *personal characteristics* that can't be included on a resume. You use the facts of your resume and tie them into what you believe to be the demands of the job:

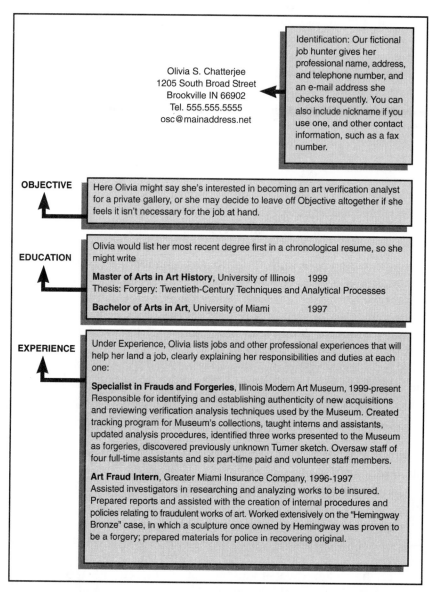

Olivia S. Chatterjee
1205 South Broad Street
Brookville IN 66902
Tel. 555.555.5555
osc@mainaddress.net

Identification: Our fictional job hunter gives her professional name, address, and telephone number, and an e-mail address she checks frequently. You can also include nickname if you use one, and other contact information, such as a fax number.

OBJECTIVE

Here Olivia might say she's interested in becoming an art verification analyst for a private gallery, or she may decide to leave off Objective altogether if she feels it isn't necessary for the job at hand.

EDUCATION

Olivia would list her most recent degree first in a chronological resume, so she might write

Master of Arts in Art History, University of Illinois   1999
Thesis: Forgery: Twentieth-Century Techniques and Analytical Processes

Bachelor of Arts in Art, University of Miami   1997

EXPERIENCE

Under Experience, Olivia lists jobs and other professional experiences that will help her land a job, clearly explaining her responsibilities and duties at each one:

Specialist in Frauds and Forgeries, Illinois Modern Art Museum, 1999-present
Responsible for identifying and establishing authenticity of new acquisitions and reviewing verification analysis techniques used by the Museum. Created tracking program for Museum's collections, taught interns and assistants, updated analysis procedures, identified three works presented to the Museum as forgeries, discovered previously unknown Turner sketch. Oversaw staff of four full-time assistants and six part-time paid and volunteer staff members.

Art Fraud Intern, Greater Miami Insurance Company, 1996-1997
Assisted investigators in researching and analyzing works to be insured. Prepared reports and assisted with the creation of internal procedures and policies relating to fraudulent works of art. Worked extensively on the "Hemingway Bronze" case, in which a sculpture once owned by Hemingway was proven to be a forgery; prepared materials for police in recovering original.

Figure 12-1   Sections of a chronological resume.

In my work on the US Census, I had responsibility for checking numeric data and submitting material according to strict deadlines. I demonstrated that I'm able to work hard with great accuracy under pressure.

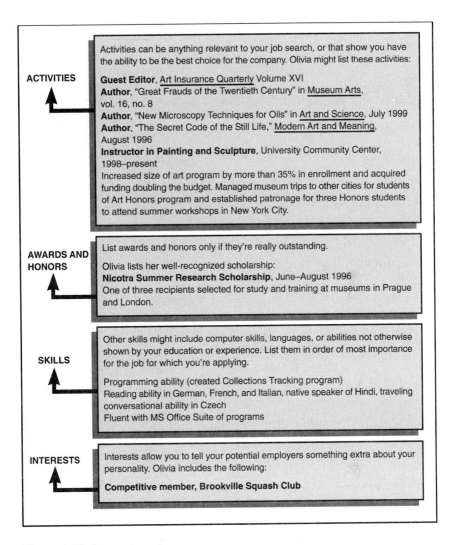

ACTIVITIES

Activities can be anything relevant to your job search, or that show you have the ability to be the best choice for the company. Olivia might list these activities:

Guest Editor, <u>Art Insurance Quarterly</u> Volume XVI
Author, "Great Frauds of the Twentieth Century" in <u>Museum Arts</u>, vol. 16, no. 8
Author, "New Microscopy Techniques for Oils" in <u>Art and Science</u>, July 1999
Author, "The Secret Code of the Still Life," <u>Modern Art and Meaning</u>, August 1996
Instructor in Painting and Sculpture, University Community Center, 1998–present
Increased size of art program by more than 35% in enrollment and acquired funding doubling the budget. Managed museum trips to other cities for students of Art Honors program and established patronage for three Honors students to attend summer workshops in New York City.

AWARDS AND HONORS

List awards and honors only if they're really outstanding.

Olivia lists her well-recognized scholarship:
Nicotra Summer Research Scholarship, June–August 1996
One of three recipients selected for study and training at museums in Prague and London.

SKILLS

Other skills might include computer skills, languages, or abilities not otherwise shown by your education or experience. List them in order of most importance for the job for which you're applying.

Programming ability (created Collections Tracking program)
Reading ability in German, French, and Italian, native speaker of Hindi, traveling conversational ability in Czech
Fluent with MS Office Suite of programs

INTERESTS

Interests allow you to tell your potential employers something extra about your personality. Olivia includes the following:

Competitive member, Brookville Squash Club

Figure 12-1 *continued*

In the third section, you should ask for the interview. You don't need to thank people for their consideration—they're being paid to read your resume, and your application should be welcome. Try not to be vague. "Feel free to contact me for additional information" is very weak. At the least, end with "I look forward to an opportunity to meet with members of the firm to discuss this position." At best, you should announce your intention to phone and ask for an interview. Many job applicants feel this approach is too pushy, but most firms would take it as a declaration of serious interest.

In the final section, include information about how you can be reached, especially if your resume has two addresses: "I will be traveling in Europe until the end of May, but after June 1, I will be at the Atlanta address."

Put This Chapter into Practice

1. Collect three or more resumes from successful professionals in the industry you want to enter. Analyze them and try to generate rules for the cultural norms for resumes in that industry.

2. Critically edit a friend's resume to conform to the general rules set forth in this chapter.

Chapter 13

Interviewing and the Hiring Process

Key Terms

401(k) plan
Airport Test
Employment application
Fired, "let go"
Group interview
Job description
Offer letter

Outplacement
Portfolio
Reduction in force, "riffed"
Shadow an employee
Taking up references
Vesting

O u t l i n e

Many interviewers are as nervous as their candidates—help them do their job well

Most research on interviewing seems to show that it's not a very good personnel selection technique—everyone is on his or her best behavior during an interview, and even the worst candidate can sound motivated and charming for half an hour. However, almost all companies still put a great deal of emphasis on interviewing as part of the recruiting process.

Sadly, many interviewers are poorly prepared. They've had no formal training in interviewing and make up some type of approach based on all interviews that they've experienced themselves, from a social chat to a "Stress Interview." They haven't thought through the purpose of the interview and its place in a series of interviews. You can address these problems by preparing well and by having an action plan yourself. To prepare, at the minimum you need to research the firm and the specific unit that is hiring. An Internet search can yield a lot of factual information, and discussions with industry insiders at other firms can tell you about the target firm's corporate culture and perhaps some details about the decision-makers. Make sure you've clearly understood the **job description** and be prepared for questions about areas where you don't quite meet the company's needs. Remember that a job description is an "ideal" but that all firms have to operate in the real world. So if the firm ideally wants someone with five years of experience, and you've had only three but with increasing responsibility, approach this issue with confidence in the interview.

Although you may see an interview as a passive process, or at least one over which you have no control, you should begin by planning what points you want to get across. Write down three points you want people to be sure to know about you—for example, that your enthusiasm and willingness to learn make up for modest experience, that you have fluency in three languages relevant to the firm's business, and that you are willing to relocate. There's a good probability that these issues will come up naturally in the conversation, but if not, you should work them in, especially if the interviewer appears unprepared and is just asking "generic" questions. If the interview doesn't cover some of the points you think are important, the firm may have a strategy in which someone else will be asking you about that issue (for example, whether you are willing to work in certain geographic locations). However, there's no harm in slipping in these points at the end of an interview, during your closing:

> "Well, thank you for meeting with me. I just wanted to mention— one area we didn't cover—I know that most of your operations are in Hawaii, and I wanted to be clear that I'm prepared to move if that's where the job is."

The most important point to understand about interviewing is that there are many different formats for interviewing, and many different types of interviews within each format.

13-1 General Interview Rules

Whatever the setup a company has chosen for your interview, you'll want to be well-dressed and neatly groomed, as described in Chapter 11. You should aim to arrive about 5 to 10 minutes before the time of your appointment (see Figure 13-1). However, you should always allow for delays in travel, so in practice you may arrive much earlier than that (for example, if you've set out one hour early to allow for a canceled train or bus). If you know that a firm is interviewing several candidates, you should check in with the receptionist and, because you're early, volunteer to go and get coffee and return, or some such pleasantry. If another candidate is running late, you'll be asked to start early; you'll be a hero, and you'll have an advantage over the competition.

If the interview is in an unfamiliar location, many people check out the route and destination the day before. There's nothing worse than arriving with 10 minutes to spare before an interview and finding that the building you always thought was MegaPlaza is in fact MondoPlaza and you are in the wrong place. A scouting trip like this is also a good opportunity to learn about the firm's dress code.

Figure 13-1   When you're interviewing, dress appropriately, arrive
early, and be sure to have extra copies of your resume
in a professional-looking portfolio.
©Stockbyte/PictureQuest

Try to travel light. You don't want to arrive with a suitcase, briefcase, computer case, and overcoat over your arm, looking like a traveling merchant on the way to a bazaar. If you are interviewing out of town, and you must bring your belongings with you from a hotel, ask for help from the receptionist:

> "I wonder, is there somewhere I could store this? I don't want to be carrying these bags around all day."

The same applies to overcoats—you want to look like you belong at the firm, and not look like a visitor. The most you should carry with you is a "**portfolio**" (a leather or imitation-leather folder) in which you have copies of your resume. You should always arrive with as many copies as people you think you are going to meet, plus one extra for yourself (you can easily forget details of how you worded things and be caught off guard by questions). Quite frequently, interviewers will have seen your resume but may be unable to lay hands on it at once. You'll help your interview go much better if you are prepared and can hand over a copy.

Whether you have one interview or several during a day, never fail to introduce yourself firmly and fully and to shake hands with each new person that you meet, as described in Chapter 1. If you are going to have a full day of interviewing, make sure to take care of physiological needs such as stopping for a drink of water or taking a bathroom break (see Chapter 10).

You should try to learn as much as possible about the format for the interview and the type of interview before you start. If there is a whole day of interviewing, the firm will have a typed schedule—ask for a copy if it's not offered to you, and ask polite questions about who the various people on the list are. The people in the firm will know who is the vice president and who is the junior assistant, but you may not have a clue. The approach you take to each interview and the questions you will ask will depend on whom you are talking with.

13-2 Format for Interviews

Most companies' recruiting process involves several "rounds." Many people are invited in for a "first round" interview, and then selected candidates are advanced to a "second round." There can be many subsequent rounds, and for interviewing that begins on college campuses, there is invariably at least a final round at the firm's offices. There are very few industries in which formal, written tests are part of the assessment, although these tests are common for certain types of civil service jobs.

The first interview may be a short one-to-one meeting in an on-campus interview suite or at a hotel. It's increasingly likely that a first interview will be by phone. It's important to treat a phone interview the same as a real interview. First, understand if the phone call is a brief scheduling call ("Can you come in next Tuesday at 10 o'clock?") or if the call is itself an interview. If it's not a convenient time, or if you feel unprepared, make a polite excuse ("I'm afraid I was just on my way out . . .") and ask to reschedule. Of course, if an interviewer says that rescheduling is difficult, you must go ahead with the interview. Make sure you are in a quiet place (turn off the TV or music). Get yourself properly seated with a copy of your resume in front of you. Imagine that you and the interviewer are face to face. Sit up straight and respond formally. Because you are likely to be in your own home when the recruiter calls, there's a great temptation to lapse into informal chatting instead of properly presenting yourself.

Some in-person interviews may have two or more people firing questions at you. This type of interview can have several purposes: It may be an expedient so that two people hear what you have to say at the same time; one interviewer may just be acting as an observer; or there could be a conscious effort for the two interviewers to take different roles ("good cop/bad cop"). While you should try to diagnose the format as quickly as possible so that you can respond appropriately, the main action step in this situation is to include all of the interviewers in your eye contact and gestures, even if only one is asking the questions.

Most candidates find a "**group interview**" to be anxiety-provoking. A firm may want to see how candidates act in group situations or may simply be trying to save time in the early rounds of a selection process. The format is for several candidates to be invited at the same time, to interact with one or more people from the firm. There may be some problem-solving exercise for the group to work on together. This is a difficult situation—there is pressure on all candidates to speak up, and many quiet, thoughtful candidates have been passed over in favor of less intelligent "hotheads" in this situation. Worse, there are no group processes or cultural norms from which to work, so the interactions are likely to be stilted and unnatural. At best, this type of situation is a measure of how you do under pressure with strangers. As much as you can do is to anticipate the situation and act calmly and pleasantly, perhaps by reminding yourself that this is just a preliminary round and you'll be able to demonstrate your personal qualities better in a later round of interviews.

13-3 Interview Styles

When junior members of a firm are assigned to conduct interviews, they may have no thought about what type of interview they are planning to conduct. The result is likely to be that the interview dissolves into a pleasant chat—as you might say, a "non-interview." If the firm is strategic, and plans better, the interview could be one of the following specific types:

- Fact Check
- Getting to Know You
- Technical Skills
- Behavioral
- Stress

Many telephone and first-round interviews just serve the purpose of checking the facts of your resume and cover letter. For example, a resume may state "Junior standing" (that is, the third year of a US university), but a student may have been on campus for only two years, having arrived with additional credits ("Advanced Placement units") from high school. The firm wants to be sure when the student is planning to graduate. In the Fact Check Interview, the recruiter may press for more details about gaps in your resume. For example, if you had summer jobs two years in a row, and nothing was shown in the third year, you could expect to be asked about how you spent the time. You should have a good answer prepared: "I wanted to graduate early—so I enrolled in summer school."

If you have special circumstances, such as a period of incarceration, or have been dismissed from a job where you know you won't get a good reference, you should carefully plan your strategy. The rule "not necessarily the whole truth" should still guide you—you don't need to tell people more than they need to know. But you definitely cannot lie in an interview. Suppose, for example, you have had several different jobs and have moved from one state to another to avoid a former spouse who was being abusive to you. This is a key point in your life but yet not a level of information that an interviewer needs to know. You should anticipate the interviewer's unspoken concerns (in this example, that you won't last long on the job) and attempt to reassure him or her: "I had some family problems, but thankfully they are behind me now. I've bought a new home here, and this is where I plan to stay."

In the Getting to Know You type of interview, the interviewer wants to get a sense of your personality, beliefs, and attitudes and will be trying to assess whether you fit with the firm's culture. This style of interview is sometimes conducted early in the interview process, in which case it may be colloquially referred to as "the smell test" (an unflattering reference to an imagined simple check that you don't smell too bad to work with). The questions are likely to be easy, and it is your style of responding, rather than anything specific, that the interviewer is looking for. So you should plan to relax and be yourself. You can anticipate that later rounds will give you a more strenuous interview. If you have already been through several rounds of interviews, late in the process you may be introduced to senior management (your future boss's boss) for a brief interview. Again, this is likely to be pleasant and low key and is just to get the manager's final approval of you as a candidate. Another late-in-the-process version of this style of interview is called the "**Airport Test,**" and it goes this way. After deciding that you are technically qualified for a position, the members of a workgroup have to decide this: If they were stuck in an airport with you for three hours due to a flight delay, could they stand your company? It is quite likely that you have to meet all members of the team during this process. If you determine this is what is going on (or if a friendly insider tells you, "It's just the Airport Test"), you should be relaxed and friendly, open, cheerful but not too pushy or "bubbly." Because every interviewee tends to be on his or her best behavior during a formal interview, some firms take input from front desk staff about a candidate's general behavior. One firm deliberately makes candidates wait and assigns a junior staff member to be a "greeter" who talks casually about the firm. Be warned: Although these conversations may seem incidental and unstructured, the firm may be using them as a formal part of the assessment process.

Surprisingly few interviews focus on Technical Skills. Recruiters may decide that they know enough from your previous work history or schooling and can assume that you can do the work. However, when the interview is designed to test your knowledge and problem-solving abilities, you'll likely be given some advanced warning. Financial services firms assess mathematical abilities with mental arithmetic puzzlers, and strategy firms ask candidates to "solve" a business problem. In both cases, it's your line of reasoning rather than the correct answer that the recruiter is most interested in. So make sure you talk through your thinking and don't sit in silence for several minutes before blurting out the answer. Most firms have given up using the element of surprise as a diagnostic tool—it only demonstrates that even the best candidates can be unnerved if treated badly enough. So you should pay attention to information that the firm gives in presentations, brochures, or web sites so that you can practice and prepare for the interview.

Behavioral Interviewing is very popular. It consists of a series of general business situations; each question begins with "Tell me about a time when. . . ." For example, "Tell me about a time when you made a mistake at work." The appropriate structure for your response is to begin by briefly outlining the situation:

> "Well, on my first warehouse job, I was responsible for making sure that the forklift trucks were plugged in so that they could recharge over night."

Then comes the problem:

> "One day, I got home and realized that I'd forgotten to do this."

Next comes the action you took:

> "So I called the night security guard and asked him to do it for me."

(At this point, you've demonstrated your responsibility and a little bit of creative problem solving.) Finally, you should end with "What I learned from this. . . ." In this example:

"So I decided each day I'd leave my car keys in my locker and that was my little reminder—I couldn't start my car to go home until I'd taken care of the forklifts."

You should collect a list of potential Behavioral Interview questions by talking with friends and business associates, but here are some examples. Tell me about a time when

- You had a disagreement with someone at work.
- You were working as a member of a team and other people weren't pulling their weight.
- You had conflicting deadlines.
- You had to deal with an irate customer.
- You discovered an error in a colleague's work.

In a Behavioral Interview, expect some follow-up questions, such as "How did other people react?" or "Have you encountered a similar problem?"

Few firms routinely subject candidates to a Stress Interview—one in which there are endless challenges and arguments to see whether you get nervous under pressure and whether you can still think clearly. However, you are quite likely to experience a challenge to your thinking if an interview is well-planned. If you make a logic error, it will be brought to your attention. Are you defensive? Do you continue to stick to your position, even when it has been shown you're wrong? Do you break down? If you don't make any errors, you'll find yourself challenged on an assertion of fact ("Well, German cars are expensive." "Really? What about Volkswagens?") or opinion ("Nixon was a great president." "Really? Most people don't think so."). In general, you have to defend your thinking without being defensive. If this is difficult for you, try to get a lot of practice with friends and colleagues before you start interviewing. Remember, it's not about winning a point in argument—this game is about winning a job.

13-4 Have a Flexible Narrative Style

Nothing is worse than having to listen to someone go on and on at length in excruciating detail about a story that could be simply summarized. In an interview, you should plan to have three versions of a story. First, the *standard version* is the three- to five-minute story that will be used in most circumstances. Second, you may have to make a condensed version, especially if the story covers a matter of fact that you want to make sure doesn't take up all of the interview time. This is similar to a business term when long documents are referred to "by *title only*" rather than read completely. For example, "Well, I missed a year of school. There was an accident and I was hospitalized—but I'm fine now, thank you." You may also have to summarize stories if the interview schedule is delayed and you have less time with a key decision-maker than was originally planned. Finally, you should prepare an *extended version* of stories to fill time if, for example, you and your host arrive for lunch and other people will be joining you but they are much delayed. You don't want to be sitting in stony silence.

The conventional wisdom that you should avoid religion and politics holds true for interviews. No matter how funny the latest joke you've heard, you should probably avoid that too. Although you don't want to be bland, you don't want to cause offense with people whom you don't know well.

13-5 Generic Interview Questions

You may encounter some standard questions that, even though they are expected, are nonetheless stressful for most people. The first of these is "Tell me about yourself." You should approach this question in much the same way as your cover letter: First, provide a brief summary of where you are in life ("just graduated," "learned a lot on my first job") and what you're looking for ("I'm planning to move from technical sales into district sales management"). Then permit yourself some non-boasting recitation of your accomplishments, and end with the reason you are approaching this particular firm or particular position.

Nearly as bad is the question "What's your biggest weakness?" You may find yourself tempted to wallow in self-deprecation: "I'm never as good a friend as I plan to be." But you should try to avoid the urge to be self-revealing—an interview is not a group therapy session, and no one wants to hire a loser. Also, resist the urge to be facetious: "My biggest weakness? Donuts!" And don't be self-serving: "Sometimes I just care too much! Every Saturday last month, I came into the office to check the invoices. I should really just let it go sometimes!" The conventional wisdom is that you should acknowledge some small imperfection and note what you are doing to overcome it. For example, "I'm getting better at public speaking, but I realize that it needs work—I'm still a bit nervous. I'm always looking for ways to practice."

Many interviewers end with "So, do you have any questions?" This question is difficult for many candidates—they may have researched the firm well and have no questions except for "Will I get the job?" In general, recruiters don't like it when a candidate has no questions. You should make sure to have a few that show your enthusiasm for the position: "I was interested in your expansion into Eastern Europe. Which countries do you think you'll be going into next?" Avoid intrusive questions such as "How much bonus did you make last year?" and generic weak questions such as "So, what's a typical day like?" (You should know the responses already from your research.)

If you really can't think of any questions to ask, say that all of your questions have been answered and reflect on some detail: "I was really interested to hear about your new product line." Unless you know what the next stage of the recruiting process is going to be, you should end every interview with an enthusiastic inquiry: "What's the next step?"

13-6 Taking Up References

Many large US companies will give out very little information about previous employees. America is a litigious country, and firms have been sued for what they've said and not said. Some large corporations instruct their executives not to write letters of recommendation, and the company will only confirm dates of employment and whether an ex-employee is "eligible for re-hire" (if the person is *not eligible,* that implies that he or she was terminated for some misdeed). As a result, many employers no longer ask for references, and of those that do, fewer than 1 in 10 firms actually goes through the process of "**taking up references**" with the names they've been given.

Just to be on the safe side, have a reference list ready, as described in Chapter 12. Be sure to contact "referees" (the people who'll be speaking for you) to alert them to the possibility of a call so that they are not surprised.

13-7 Interview Follow-up

Even when an interviewer has told you, "We'll be in touch next week," more often than not, as a candidate, you don't hear in the time span the firm has described. Many candidates assume they've been passed over, or that the offer has gone to another candidate and the firm is just waiting to have a signed contract before dismissing all other candidates. Although this may be true, it's not always the case. Indeed, when a company's management staff have agreed to hire someone, the individuals often go back to their primary duties and assume that someone else is working on the offer. At other times, there may be debate about which candidate is the top choice. Of course, you don't want to be a pest, phoning repeatedly, and pushing people for a decision. But you may well improve your chances by following up politely. Identify one person as the decision-maker (manager) or your contact person (someone in Human Resources), and when the deadline for calling you has been reached, give a very little slack out of politeness (one or two days at most) and phone. If your contact person tells you there still hasn't been a decision, be sure to ask when you should call back and check again. Some gentle persistence may work in your favor.

If you get bad news—that the firm has chosen another candidate—try to position yourself as the person the firm would call if there is a new, similar opening, or if its first choice backs out. "Oh, that's too bad! I really enjoyed meeting members of the team. Well, let me just say, I'm still interested in working for Bigco—do call me if anything else comes up." Many successful executives have earned their first "lucky break" by responding well to a rejection.

13-8 The Job Offer

Congratulations! You are the top candidate and a firm wants to hire you. You are likely to get an informal notification first—either a phone call or an e-mail message. Surprisingly, you should be cool at this point. Although you're excited, many candidates have regretted making an oral commitment to a job, when a better offer was on its way. The phone notification isn't really an offer. The offer can only be made in writing. So the correct response is to thank the person who's contacting you and say, "I look forward to receiving the offer."

The **offer letter** is formal and contractual. It will specify the job title, work location, and salary, and is likely to refer to company documents for benefits, vacation, and so on. Most often, there will be two copies of the letter, and you'll be asked to sign and return one as your indication of acceptance. Be careful—this letter amounts to a legal contract, so do not sign if your mind is not made up. Most offers will have an expiration date: If you do not sign and return by a specific date, the firm will conclude that you have rejected the offer. (For this reason, you should either hand-deliver an acceptance or send it by overnight delivery.) An offer with a due date is called an "exploding offer" in colloquial speech.

Before you sign the letter, you should be sure that you understand all of the terms of your offer and get them in writing. For example, if you are joining a small firm, and during the interview the manager said, "Oh, everyone takes about four weeks of vacation," you should politely ask for that point to be put in writing, even if it means sending you a second, revised offer letter.

13-9 Negotiating the Offer

You may just receive a letter that announces the terms of your offer in a one-sided manner without any negotiation, or you may have been talking with a firm's representatives for weeks about the details of an offer. No matter, just because an offer is written, it doesn't mean that you can't negotiate terms. Most recruits concentrate on salary alone—there isn't anyone who has ever been hired who doesn't think that he or she is worth at least 20 percent more! However, it's shortsighted to focus only on a single number, especially when you're comparing offers from two or more firms. Table 13-1 outlines some of the parameters of employment that differ from firm to firm. Understanding the details may be important in evaluating one offer or comparing offers from different firms.

In a large corporation, you may feel that many of the benefits, such as health insurance, and whether the firm offers a supplemental pension plan called a **401(k) plan,** are fixed, and not subject to negotiation. This is true. But other terms of your employment can often be discussed. For example, a firm may have a general rule that employees don't become eligible for participation in a pension plan during the first year of employment. But many senior managers negotiate that they will change firms only if they are offered immediate "**vesting**" (enrollment in the plan) or even credit for several years of contributions to the plan on their first day of employment. There's nothing worse than starting work and finding that everyone else in your training class received a signing bonus except you—just because you didn't ask about it.

13-10 Formal Hiring Procedures

At some point in the recruiting process (either at the beginning or, in some firms, right before you are to be given an offer of employment), a large firm is likely to ask you to complete an **employment application** on a form that the company has designed. In that case, if the instructions state "List all employment. . . ." you should carefully fill out every detail. If you are asked later "Why doesn't Santa's Workshop appear on your resume?" you would give an answer such as "I didn't feel it had much relevance for my work as an audit accountant." Firms that have fiduciary

T A B L E **13-1** **Points to Consider when Negotiating a Job Offer**

Negotiating Point	Details
Salary	Everyone wants more. Be prepared to provide evidence (from surveys, your previous employment, or other offers) if you think the offer is out of line.
Bonus, Signing	Many firms offer recent college graduates a small signing bonus to pay for relocation, new work clothes, find out what's typical in your industry and geographic area.
Bonus, Annual	Discuss whether a bonus is based on the firm's performance, the work of your.group, or your own efforts. In some industries where bonuses are common, If you are leaving mid-year, (and giving up rights to a bonus) you can negotiate a "guaranteed" similar sum from your new employer.
Moving allowance	For senior executives, this can include the actual expenses of moving, plus hotels and airfare to search for housing, and some of the expenses of buying a new home. For recent college graduates, a firm may offer a lump sum that you can spend on moving or anything else you choose.
Start date	You may be able to negotiate a delayed starting date that allows you to take an extended vacation before you begin your new job. Take an extended vacation.
Vacation	A firm is likely to have rigid policies for which holidays are observed and for how many days a year of paid vacation you are awarded; however, you might be able to get an agreement to take additional times as "leave without pay." Understand whether vacation you don't use in one year can be carried over to the next ("accrued") or whether you can be paid cash for days you don't use.

responsibility (that is, they look after valuables such as cash or stock) for their customers may fire you at once if they later discover that you've omitted something from their employment application. If there is something embarrassing or awkward (such as a long period of unemployment or dismissal from a previous job), fill out the form and ask to dis-

Negotiating Point	Details
Insurances	Almost all firms should offer health insurance, and there is usually at least one option that costs nothing to the employee. Additionally, your firm may offer life insurance and disability insurance, and these may be free or require that you pay at least part of the premium.
Pensions	Because US employees often switch firms, many companies are moving away from the type of pension awarded as a monthly payment after years of service. The firm will have a rule on when you are considered "vested": That is, after a certain number of years of service, you will be able to receive benefits from the plan, even if you leave the company. A "401(k) Plan" is an arrangement where employees contribute part of their paychecks tax-free for retirement benefits. The firm may match your contribution (put in an equal amount) or not.
Education	In some industries, part of the hiring process is for firms to agree to reimburse new employees for costs associated with getting a graduate degree. Some firms will pay for any course taken during employment others only for courses approved by the company.
Commuting expenses	The firm may provide parking, or this could be a substantial daily expense. The offer may include reduced-cost or free mass-transit tickets.
Clubs	Your offer may include a free, or reduced-cost membership to an athletic or dining club.
Entertaining and travel	If the job is likely to involve client entertainment, many people get the level agreed in advance. For example, in some companies, employees are expected to always fly on the cheapest ticket, but other companies will pay for business class travel.

cuss it with the person who's hiring you before you hand it in. "I wanted to tell you personally about something you are going to read on page 3 . . ." would be a good way to introduce the topic. As long as the bad news is not a felony conviction, or being fired for something related to the new job, most people will be forgiving. But be warned! Just as many criminals are eventually convicted on perjury, rather than on the underlying crime, a firm can use any false statement on an application to fire you at once.

At the time of the offer, the firm may ask you to undergo a physical (medical) exam and will quite likely conduct a drug test on urine samples. If you use recreational drugs that are illegal in the US, the firm has a right not to hire you. Other than that, under most circumstances, a firm cannot refuse to hire you if you have a medical condition such as high blood pressure that is not directly related to the performance of your duties. So you should look on the physical as a way to get a free check-up.

It's quite likely that a large firm—or a firm working with sensitive data—will ask to conduct additional "background checks." The firm can ask your permission to check with local police to see if you have any warrants out for your arrest. If you have a problem, such as a family situation in which the police have been called, or multiple traffic arrests, you'll have to get advice from an attorney on how to handle this situation. You may be instructed to say nothing and let the firm find out whatever it can (which may not be much), or you may be advised to tell your side of the story in person first. Many firms ask to perform a credit check. Although your company will not be providing you with loans (in fact, you'll be providing *them* with credit by waiting until the end of the month for your paycheck!), your credit records have a lot of information about where you've lived and how you run your affairs. A company could make a reasonable case that someone who's head over heels in debt might be more of a risk to sell industrial secrets and so on. In most jurisdictions, this type of background checking is legal. Your only choice is to refuse to undergo the check and give up the job offer.

If you have a disability that is covered under the Americans with Disabilities Act (ADA), the law requires that firms make a reasonable effort to accommodate your desire to work. So, if you could do a job, but you need a special type of computer keyboard, the firm is required to find out what you need and to spend the money to provide you with the equipment. Of course, the standard of "reasonable" is open to interpretation. Almost all large US firms have done a good job of complying with the Act. It is permissible for a firm to ask "Would you need any special accommodations to do this job?" but it's not permissible for a firm to choose one candidate over another, based on the ease of providing accommodations. So most firms won't ask this question until later in the hiring process, after the offer has been made. If you feel the ADA applies to you, you should seek some counseling as to how to work with your firm to get the equipment you need and any appropriate modifications to your work schedule or duties.

13-11 Handling Multiple Offers

With good luck, there will be a few times in your life when you have job offers from more than one firm. Many people try to solve this "problem" by a simple calculation of which firm is offering the highest starting salary. Of course, you should take many other factors into account, such as future prospects for promotion, the type of work, how convenient the firm's location is, and so on.

When you're experiencing difficulty choosing between two offers, you can talk with friends and business associates to get their opinions on the two firms' reputations and outlook. But at the end of the day, the decision will be yours. You should seriously consider which group of colleagues you will find most congenial for long days and demanding projects. A good way to evaluate your choice is to ask for one more visit to the firm you think you will prefer (or even two or more firms if you really are having difficulty deciding). Ask to "**shadow an employee**" in the group where you'll be working. (Shadowing means just following someone around— like his or her shadow—while that person goes about his or her routines.) A whole day would be nice, but at least visit from mid-morning to mid-afternoon, and go to lunch with your future colleagues. Ask yourself, "Is this the group I'd like to be part of?" Listen carefully for how group members talk about one another and their work. Ask them over lunch, "So what's a really bad day like around here?" If they say, "Well, at the end of the quarter, we never get out until 10 P.M. putting the numbers together, but we usually celebrate the next week by going skiing," you know you're in a good place. However, if there's a problem in the workgroup, such as a boss who's a "screamer," this is where the truth will come out.

You should not turn down one good offer until you are sure of the other. A job offer should be made in writing. So if you get a phone call, you should say, "I look forward to receiving your offer." After you've signed and returned the offer, you can let other firms know that you will be working elsewhere. Many people get anxious about this part of the process, but they shouldn't. As one recruiter said, "I'm a recruiter—I've been turned down before. It's part of my job." So begin by understanding that an offer is only an offer, and as such, it can be rejected without offense. You should contact the person you've been negotiating with (recruiter or manager) by the same medium that he or she has been using to reach you—most likely by phone. Most people feel that it isn't appropriate to leave a voice mail for such information. When you reach the recruiter, choose your words carefully. You don't need to give a reason for turning down the offer or to say explicitly what you are doing instead. If the recruiter asks, you can briefly summarize your decision and reasoning if you choose.

When you turn down an offer, your word choice is important. Bear in mind that there might be a time when you want to talk with this firm again—perhaps the firm's prospects improve, or perhaps your first-choice job doesn't turn out to be as good as you've hoped. If you have exaggerated a reason, it may cut you off from future consideration by that firm. Suppose, for example, you say to a recruiter, "I just decided to stay here in St. Louis. I really don't want to move to New York." Although this statement may be true, you won't look credible if you reapply to the New York firm in the future—the recruiter will decide not to waste time with you. If the job offer that you accept is for substantially more money, and you feel the offer you are turning down was underestimating your worth (or the market rate for such jobs), you can politely communicate this information.

The process of re-igniting interest in your candidacy with a firm you previously turned down isn't completely unheard of. If you ended the process on good terms and handled your rejection of the firm with courtesy, you can certainly see whether positions are still open. In this circumstance, there's nothing that can beat a little honesty: "As you know, I had accepted Bigco, but they just announced they're filing for bankruptcy," or "I really did have a plan to move west, but my wife has just been promoted, so we're staying here." If a firm liked you well enough to have made you a job offer in the past, most will have some interest in your re-approach.

Even when a job offer is made in writing, you don't have to decline it in writing. It's certainly good etiquette to make contact with the firm so that it knows that the offer wasn't misplaced, but you don't have to send a formal letter rejecting the offer—non-acceptance by a cut-off date has the same legal effect.

You may find yourself in the awkward situation of having a definite written offer from your second-choice firm, while you've interviewed and not yet heard back from your first-choice firm. In this circumstance, you can phone your first-choice company and state the facts: "I need to let you know that I have an offer from Second-Choice-Co on my desk, but I really enjoyed my interviews with your firm. I'm up against a deadline—when will you be able to make a decision?" Once again, recruiters encounter this situation frequently (they understand that top candidates will get multiple offers), so you shouldn't feel embarrassed about this call.

A more difficult situation exists when you have one offer but haven't yet begun the interview process with a firm that you think might be more to your liking. You can certainly call your preferred firm, explain your situation, and try to advance the interview schedule. You may be able to get the first firm to extend its deadline—but that's unlikely. At the limit, if the interviews can't be moved up, and the offering firm won't give you more time to decide, you may have the tough choice: You'll either have to turn down a certain offer and hope for a better one, or you'll have to go with a firm that wasn't your top choice. This is a difficult personal decision and one for which there is no trick or easy solution. You'll have to talk with friends and family and then make a choice.

13-12 Reneging

In the recruiting business, there's no uglier word than "reneging." This is the situation in which a candidate has accepted an offer in writing but then decides not to start the job. In theory, the company could sue the reneging candidate for monetary damages. After the candidate accepted, the firm dismissed other applicants and would then face the expenses of re-starting the search. Although few legal actions are taken in practice, the damage to your reputation could potentially be extreme if you renege. The recruiter from the spurned firm could phone the firm you've accepted and say, "I just want you to know what's going on here. . . ." If you don't lose the second job on the spot, you'll begin with a reputation for being untrustworthy.

The only possible reason to renege is when you have extraordinary changes in family circumstance ("My mother is terminally ill . . . I've decided I can't move now, I'm afraid") or when your plans to enter the workforce have changed. So, if you receive a graduate fellowship that you haven't expected, and you've decided to go to school, you could withdraw from a previously accepted offer (under the doctrine of "employment at will," which is discussed in Chapter 14). You should definitely make a phone call as soon as you know, and you should speak directly to the person with whom you've been negotiating. You will explain the circumstances and your decision as clearly as possible. Because this is not good news for the company and will cause extra work for the recruiter, you should anticipate that this phone call will not be pleasant. Because you have accepted an offer in writing and it is contractual, you must now withdraw your acceptance in writing (in addition to the phone call).

13-13 Handling No Offers

If you have been actively recruiting, and you've received lots of interviews and callbacks but no offers, after a while, you'll need to diagnose the reason for this situation. Are you really overqualified for the positions you're seeking? Do you lack a critical skill or certification? Are you holding out for too much money? As you've been interviewing, when you've received notification that you've not been advanced to the next round or have not been selected for an offer, it is very professional if you can ask, "Is there anything I can learn from this? Do you have any feedback for me?" Many recruiters will recede behind a wall of platitudes ("It was a tough decision—everyone liked you—there were so many good candidates. . ."), but once in a while you'll find someone who can give you good advice. For example, "Well, we thought you were qualified, but a couple of people said you came off as just too desperate for a job," or "You knew the answers to the questions, but some of the interviewers commented that you didn't really show much enthusiasm for our firm."

If you are finding it hard to get feedback, try to take a "practice interview" with someone in the same industry—an alumnus from your university who's not currently hiring, or a friend of a family member whom you've not met before. Many people will be willing to do this and to give you some pointers for improvement. If you are recruiting through an on-campus career center, there should be a routine for practice interviews, and the university staff may collect and summarize feedback from several recruiters. If you lack certain technical skills or knowledge, you know what you have to do to become a more attractive candidate. If you have the right qualifications but are interviewing badly, you'll need some good coaching.

There can be few life circumstances that are more depressing than looking for work and not finding it. The platitude "Everyone eventually finds a job somewhere" is probably of little comfort to you, but it's true. If your industry is in a slow-down, either it will pick up or you'll realize that your skills can be applied in a different field. The most important thing is to keep a cheerful mood—if you become dispirited, it will be impossible for you to interview well. You should think about the activities and friends that keep you energized and avoid those that depress you. If you have been laid off during a recession or industry slow-down, you'll have to make a decision of what to do until the market comes back. Some people make use of the opportunity to take additional schooling, and others travel. If you are facing a long period of unemployment, you should consider getting a simple job (such as working for a temporary agency, in a retail store or warehouse) to make money for basic living expenses while you're searching.

13-14 Termination—Being "Unhired"

There may come a time when you decide no longer to work for the same firm; Chapter 14 discusses the process for making a graceful exit. But you may face a circumstance in which your firm has decided that your services aren't needed anymore, and you will be **fired.** In many countries, the only reason someone would be fired is that he or she has done something terribly wrong. In America, that's not true. Firms make some estimate of their future workload, and add and subtract people very quickly.

The colloquial term for being fired is to be "**let go.**" (It's a silly term that implies that employees are constantly straining to be released from their work.) If you encounter this situation, you should have heard that the company is "downsizing," that your department or project is being eliminated, or at least that the industry is undergoing a slow-down. You should have begun the process of discreetly looking around for opportunities with other firms. When the end comes, it will be ugly and ungracious. You may look up from your desk to see a Human Resources person, or your boss, probably accompanied by a security guard. You may be asked to gather your personal belongings and leave at once. This process is very hard on people who are terminated and unnerving indeed for those who are left behind—they wonder "Who's next?" US companies do this very sudden firing to protect computer systems and proprietary knowledge. You'll be asked to surrender your corporate ID badge and may be searched to make sure you are not taking anything with you that belongs to the firm. The process is alarming, upsetting, and humiliating. The best you can do is to keep your dignity.

An alternative form is that all employees in a group or division are brought into an "all hands meeting." At this point, most people have an idea that bad news is about to hit. After a general announcement of the situation, employees are taken in small groups to be told whether they are retained or will be dismissed.

When a firm fires employees in a "**reduction in force**" (hence the phrase, "I've been **riffed**"), they will usually be asked to sign one or more documents in return for some severance pay. There is little requirement in law to provide much, if any, severance pay under most circumstances. About as much as you can hope for is payment for time worked, payment for vacation days owed, and as little as two weeks additional. Firms will offer something, in order to encourage employees to leave quickly and quietly. You should be careful about what you are asked to sign. The form might be a simple receipt for money paid to you, or it might contain "non-compete" clauses, saying that you won't go to work for a competitor. Because working for a competitor is precisely what you have in mind, signing such a document may not be in your best interests. You should take the document and ask that you have time to read it and perhaps consult with a lawyer. Arrange for a time when you can trade the signed document for your severance check.

You may be offered the opportunity to sign a letter of resignation. The advantage for the firm is that you then pretty much give up your right to sue for wrongful termination. If you don't sign, you'll be fired. In many countries, and perhaps in the US in an earlier age, being fired was considered a terrible thing. But so many people (you could almost say "most people") have been riffed at one time or another that there's no great stigma. You might consider signing a resignation letter in return for getting something you want, such as continuation of health care benefits for a few months. Many firms arrange for a type of counseling called **"outplacement."** This service is run by a specialized employment counseling firm to help you identify your transferable skills, to decide whether you need additional training, and to make a realistic appraisal of the type of job you can find next. You should definitely take advantage of this counseling if it is offered to you, and if it's not, try to negotiate that the firm will pay for outplacement.

Firms have a great deal of latitude in whom they hire and fire. You may be the most recent hire or the most long-standing employee; you may be the person with the best performance reviews. You have grounds for suing your now ex-employer only if there was discrimination in age (firing only older workers), gender, or race. You'll need to hire a lawyer, and any settlement will likely be many years away. So as a practical matter, although you may hope to recover from a firm for wrongful dismissal in the future, you'll need to get on with your life in the short term.

Put This Chapter into Practice

1. Subject a willing friend to a practice Stress Interview in which you play the role of the aggressive interviewer; learn how easy it is to challenge everything someone says.

2. Make a list of up-to-date Behavioral Interview questions by talking to people who have recently been through the interview process.

3. Practice telling the same story in three versions: standard (about 3 to 5 minutes), extended (20 minutes), and "by title" (summary and conclusion only).

Chapter
14

On the Job

Outline

Putting Business Protocol into practice every day

Congratulations! You got the job! Now comes the moment of your first day at a new firm. You may feel as if you don't have much control over your schedule and activities, but here's an outline of what you can expect and what you should do.

First impressions are important, so when you begin a new position, make every effort to introduce yourself as discussed in Chapter 1. Make sure that people have a context to get to know you, such as "I'm the new accountant in plant operations." Make an attempt to learn the names of the people you are working with and ask early for a written directory for the firm or at least for your workgroup.

As soon as you can—often during the interview process—try to understand who works for whom and how relationships are structured. If you are an engineer, for example, do you report to the Chief Engineer at the firm's headquarters, or is your ultimate "boss" the plant manager where you are located? If the relationship is not clear, you can ask politely, "So at the end of the day, is my ultimate supervisor Mrs. Plant Manager or Vice-President Engineer?" Then, within your workgroup, try to understand the working routines. For example, do all of your peers (people at the same level and job title as you) give work to a team assistant to perform, or is the boss the only person who can assign tasks to the assistant? Again, if the routines are confusing, you can reasonably ask.

Because most US businesses give an aura of informality, you may feel that the relationships within your group are as unstructured as a primary school pick-up game of soccer. If everyone jokes around and calls the boss by his nickname, "Buddy," it may be hard to discern power relationships. However, there are always subtle cues. In meetings, note who sits where and who is expected to sit at the head of a table. Observe whether meetings start the moment one person walks in or whether everyone politely delays until one person arrives. During discussion, pay attention to who can interrupt whom.

Next, try to get a sense for relationships between groups. Your co-workers may tell you explicitly: "Accounting always gets things mixed up," or Remember, people in Accounting control your life—and they can be very helpful." Again, if the information isn't given to you explicitly, try to learn whose advice is welcome and whose comments are ignored. Who seems to get the attention of people in your group? You'll learn where to make alliances within the firm and where you may have to brace for conflict, or at least a cool reception.

14-1 Defining Your Duties and Routines

During your first few days at a new firm, try to clearly define the duties of your position. What are you expected to do, and what must you not do? You may be given a formal **job description,** but it will likely be phrased in very broad language, such as "Prepares budgets at the direction of senior staff," and it may not give you the details. In this example, you might wonder whether you should show your work to one or more people for their review before you release it to another department in the firm or if you are to rely on your own judgment.

During your first few days and weeks on the job, you'll be given a lot of credit if you ask well-thought-out questions: "I wanted to check with you … in general, is this the sort of document you'd like to review before I send it out?" By asking specific questions, you'll convey an appropriate image—after all, no one expects you to know everything about a firm at once. On the other hand, you'll want to avoid acting "dazed and confused." So avoid making statements such as "I really don't know what I'm doing yet!" (Even if it's how you feel!)

You will learn what incidental activities you are supposed to do yourself and which tasks to assign to support personnel. For example, in Hong Kong, getting a cup of coffee for yourself may be a huge violation of protocol: Because the firm employs a "tea lady," serving yourself implies that the tea lady doesn't know how to do her job. In contrast, in the US, sitting at your desk and asking (however politely) your assistant to bring you coffee may be considered uppity and haughty behavior. You can develop information about the nuances of office routines by making casual inquiries at the right time. For example, if you are asking someone to show you how to use the fax machine, you can say, "Is this something I should be doing myself, or is it better to give it to one of the secretaries?"

14-2 The Workday

Workdays are long in the US. It's a paradox of the great wealth of the country that instead of taking increasing leisure time (as is common in Germany), Americans seem to work harder and harder the higher they move up the corporate ladder.

Most firms will expect you to be at your desk by 8 A.M. although you may find 9 A.M. is the norm in a city where everyone commutes by mass transit, such as New York. If you are in an environment where other people are working shifts (such as a hospital or factory), the implicit start time for managers may be 7 A.M. (because shifts are often 7 A.M. to 3 P.M., 3 P.M. to 11 P.M., and then 11 P.M. to 7 A.M. if there's an overnight shift).

As a new employee, you'll certainly want to be one of the first people into the office. You'll have to make a difficult decision as to whether to be at your desk before your boss arrives. In most instances, the junior staff members are expected to arrive ahead of the supervisor, who may come in quite late after meetings with colleagues or associates outside the firm. Indeed, in financial services, it's considered essential that juniors be at their desks early. For example, on the West Coast (three hours' time difference from the East Coast) because the New York exchanges open at 9:30 A.M. EST, most people are in the office working way before 6:30 A.M. PST. On the other hand, in some businesses the boss likes to be in first, to assign work to people as they come in. If you tried to beat your boss into the office, you might violate an unspoken rule and upset her or his work routine. You can diagnose this situation as follows. On your first day, you are likely to be asked to come in quite late (you won't have keys in any case). Don't interpret that time as your expected routine start time. Ask your peers, "So, when do people usually get here?" You'll want to be one of the first ones in the office (no matter what your commute) to make a good impression as the newest employee. So gradually advance your start time, by coming in earlier and earlier. You'll soon find out whether it's the group of ambitious juniors who are in first, or whether it's just you and the boss.

At the end of the day, you may find that people routinely work very late. In investment banking and at law firms, for example, many people work as late as 9 or 10 P.M., at least Monday through Thursday, and may also come in on the weekends too. This schedule can be very hard if you are not used to it. You may also find a cultural norm that everyone stays until, say, 6 P.M., whether they have productive work to do or not. Ideally, you'll be aware of the work routine before you accept a position. But in any case, you'll have to adapt to the firm's style, and this may mean changing family meal times and giving up some hobbies.

Here are some suggestions for how to handle long workdays. First, if it seems that people are staying at their desks, busy or not, just to create an impression, you should try to show some leadership: Make sure that your important tasks are finished, that you are prepared for the next day, and that your desk is cleared. Then choose one or two days to leave promptly at, say, 5 P.M. Announce "Well, I have a basketball game, and I'm out of here. I'll see you tomorrow." With luck, people who are just staying around to create an impression of hard work will get the idea and will no longer stay just to "look good."

If the norm for your group is to work very long hours, you can maintain your energy and balance your day by breaking it up. For example, in investment banking, there is a big rush of work early in the day. Then late in the afternoon, mid-level managers come out of meetings and assign new tasks to the juniors who are expected to stay late—very late—until the work is done in preparation for the next day. You'll find that many of your peers waste time in the middle of the day, gossiping or reading the paper. With luck you will also find one or two people who are amazingly productive but make use of "down time" in the middle of the day to go to the gym, to go walking, or to go shopping for daily necessities. You are likely to be much more efficient in your work if you've taken a break. Similarly, you'll see many people eat dinner at their desks and work—very inefficiently—for hours and hours. Perhaps it would be better to take a short meal break away from your desk and then feel re-energized to finish your work efficiently.

Even if everyone seems to come into the office on both days of every weekend, they are quite possibly being inefficient—doing some work, yes, but also e-mailing friends or taking personal phone calls. It's much better for your mental health and to avoid "burnout" to declare that at least one day each weekend has zero work, and make an effort to stick strictly to work when you are in the office. You'll find some people who seem to put in hours and hours but don't get a lot accomplished, and other people who do indeed get their work done in fewer hours. Follow their style. People will be impressed if you meet deadlines and get your work accomplished more than if they see you laboring long into the night, seven days a week.

14-3 Orientation

Your firm may well offer a formal **orientation** or even a training program that lasts for several weeks. However, many firms don't, and even when they do, they invariably present too much information at one time: You

TABLE **14-1** Topics Typically Covered in
New-Employee Orientation

Topic	Notes and details
Security and access	Company ID badge—must it be worn at all times? What keys and card-keys do you need? Do you have the right to be in the building after normal work hours?
Time and record-keeping	Do you have to keep track of how you spend your time ("billable hours")? How do you report sick days and schedule vacation days? Which public holidays does the firm observe?
Parking and transportation	Does the firm pay part of your commuting expenses? What are the rules for parking, and where do you get a pass?
Business dining	Are some meals with clients and associate firms reimbursable? What are the rules, and what are the limits?
Business travel	Must travel be approved in advance? Does the firm make arrangements, or do you seek reimbursement after the fact?
Using company resources	Is it acceptable to use company resources for occasional personal needs such as photocopying a few pages or e-mailing a friend during your lunch hour? Is this "discouraged" for "forbidden"?

are just trying to figure out where the bathrooms are, and you are stuck in a two-hour lecture from Human Resources about options for your pension plan at age 65. Ideally, firms should practice "continuous orientation" with information spread over several days or weeks and give you just the information that you need to know at the time you need it. However, as much as you can hope for from the usual "overload" orientation is to develop a personal index to the information (for example, "My company has both long-term and short-term disability insurance—that's not

Topic	Notes and details
Confidentiality	Is it permissible to mention the names of your firm's clients in discussions with other clients or with people outside the firm, or does your firm insist on very strict confidentiality including forbidding you to even mention the names of clients?
Insurance benefits	What decisions do you have to make to be enrolled in company-paid health insurance or life insurance? Are there additional benefits you need to know about? What do you have to do to enroll family members?
Pension benefits	You may have some early decisions to make about how you want your funds invested.
Club memberships	Does the firm provide a discount or pay part of your membership in athletic or dining clubs?
Educational benefits	If you take a class, will the firm pay for any education, education related to your job, or only education selected by the firm?

something I need to know right now.") Then try to map the topics to either the person who can give you more information or to the place where you could look it up (brochure or on-line through an "intranet") when you need it.

Table 14-1 outlines some topics that ought to be covered in an orientation. If you are not offered a formal orientation, you should use this table as a checklist to make sure that you understand company policy.

14-4 Time Management

You may start out with a few days when you wonder why you were hired, because there doesn't seem to be enough work for you to do. Treasure these moments. There's not a person working in America who doesn't have more to do than can possibly be accomplished in the workweek. So one of the most important skills to develop is time management.

A great deal has been written about this topic, and your firm may send you to a two- or three-day seminar about time management, but here is a brief outline of the important issues.

First, don't waste time. Many activities look "value-added" but nonetheless distract you from finishing projects on time. Opening mail is at the top of most people's list of time-wasters. Mail is interesting and distracting. Put it aside and go through it while you are waiting for a meeting to begin or if you are on hold on the phone. Just chatting to colleagues is probably the next biggest time-waster. You can manage this by engaging in pleasant social chitchat away from your work area. You can bring conversations to a natural and polite close by honestly saying, "Well, better be getting back to work." If you routinely hang around colleagues' desks chatting and allow them to do the same at your desk, you'll find time slipping away from you.

Most people have difficulty terminating phone calls. You can develop a personal style of short, efficient calls. If you have an associate who loves to chat, call him or her right before another event on your calendar; begin by announcing, "I have only a few moments before I have to leave to go to a meeting, but I did want to call you and. . . ." If someone calls you at your desk and seems to want to chat, you can say, "Well, I can answer a quick question, but I'm really in the middle of a project here." If your caller doesn't get the hint that you need to go, you can interrupt—if necessary with the words "I hate to interrupt, but I need to complete a presentation for later today. Can I just summarize where we are?"—and take control of the conversation.

At the beginning of each workday, take a moment to review your schedule and make a realistic assessment of the tasks you plan to complete this day. Your PDA (personal digital assistant), contact manager software, or e-mail program should have a "Tasks" or **"To Do" list.** This tool can be helpful for making a record of a task that you can put off for a while. If you find yourself overwhelmed, remember to make a difference in your mind between what is *urgent* and what is *important.* There are many important tasks in business that need to be done—but that don't have to be done right now. You should begin each day with a manageable list of at least three action items that you want to get accomplished. Then scan your e-mail for recent urgent messages and check your voice mail. Decide whether you have any action items that need urgent attention.

You should balance an approach of "**do it now**" (completing tasks immediately) versus constantly interrupting yourself with trivial tasks when you're working on a major project. For example, if a colleague comes over to your desk with a routine copy of a sales report, accept it and file it away in one motion (don't give yourself extra work by putting it in a pile to be re-examined and re-sorted later). That's the "do it now" approach. On the other hand, try to arrange that you don't get side-tracked with a stream of constant, unimportant interruptions so that no value-added work gets done. Many time management experts suggest a two-minute threshold—if you can do the task in two minutes or less, do it now.

If you are facing a large project, you can make it more manageable by breaking it down into stages and developing a timeline. If you complete small, preparatory steps, you won't feel overwhelmed, and you can see that not all the work needs to be done at once. One way to sustain your motivation is to tie little personal rewards to completion of tasks. For example, you may know that you plan to stop and have coffee mid-morning. Make it a miniature celebration and refuse to take a coffee break until you have accomplished one of the tasks on your "To Do" list.

At the end of your workday, a moment or two spent in tidying and planning can make the next day more efficient. For example, sticking little notes on documents on your desk—"Copy and discuss with Finance" or "Update budget"—can make your work get off to a fast start the next day.

Of course, you'll be punctual for meetings. In general, even if other people in your workgroup are less structured ("Oh, he always runs late!"), you'll get a reputation for being on time and may help other people work efficiently with you. If you join a workgroup in which meetings always start late and run over, you may have to address the issue directly. If the "house style" is that meetings tend to get started 15 minutes after the scheduled time, people soon interpret all meeting times as floating. The team may waste as much as half an hour just gathering people together. Although you may be reluctant to take the lead in bringing this issue up for discussion as the new member of the team, it's most likely that this has been a nagging problem, and people will appreciate your bringing an end to a long-standing problem.

If you have seemingly impossible conflicts between tasks, begin negotiations early with people who are expecting your work products. Some due dates are nominal ("Get it in by the first of the month"), but the material isn't actually needed until a specific date somewhat later. Or, perhaps you can find that someone needs only part of a larger project ("If you could just give me the personnel costs—I can wait for the rest of the figures"). Friendly forewarning is much more professional than begging an extension after you've missed a deadline. Similarly, when you accept projects, try to set realistic expectations: "I'd be happy to work on that, but I won't be able to start on it until I've finished the employee reviews next week."

If you are faced with schedule conflicts that you cannot resolve, you'll have to engage your supervisor. Management is all about allocating resources in the face of competing demands, and your boss is paid to make the tough decisions.

14-5 Managing Your Boss

Many books have been written on the subject of "how to manage your boss." The idea is that in addition to your supervisor directing your work to get the best out of you, you must adapt to your manager's style to make the best possible working relationship. It's important to start by under-standing that there are many different management styles, and no one, single best approach. You should be prepared to "diagnose" your boss's style and work with it as best you can.

Workgroups and their leaders have a preferred channel of communi-cation. In some teams, nothing is discussed unless it's face-to-face, but in other firms, everyone may communicate by e-mail, even if two workers are just a few feet apart. The same is true for managers: Some may prefer that every issue is presented as a formal memo on paper, whereas others may prefer phone calls and actually try to avoid in-person meetings. Observe how your co-workers interact with the boss and follow the same style.

When you are assigned work, it's good to paraphrase the instructions and repeat them back so you can be sure that you are not setting off in the wrong direction. Here's an example:

> "So, you'd like me to develop this year's capital budget, but you feel that last year's should *not* serve as a guide. And it's OK with you if I talk directly with people in the other departments?"

Your manager may prefer regular, semi-formal meetings (for exam-ple, once a week) or may encourage you to interrupt and drop in to his or her office at any time (see Figure 14-1).

Figure 14-1 Some bosses may encourage you to drop in, while others prefer regular, more structured meetings.

Photo: comstock.com

One cardinal rule of communication with supervisors is that no one likes surprises. So if you have bad news to deliver, you should foreshadow it with your manager. For example, you might say, "I'd like to talk with you about the cost estimates on the new project—we're having a lot of difficulty in meeting the targets." In general, you should keep your direct supervisor up-to-date on the status of projects that you've been assigned, without "grandstanding" (boasting of your own accomplishments). If you are having difficulty, it's usually best to seek help early, although you will need to be careful. You don't want to get the reputation of being unable to do anything without extra instructions.

When problems arise, some managers want only a statement of the situation. Others may want a problem definition and a range of options (for example, "So we can spend money from reserves now or delay implementation until the next fiscal year"). Still other managers will want a problem definition, range of options, and your proposed solution. You may find that your manager has a style of debating and challenging your ideas to test your reasoning or to refine her or his own thinking on the matter. You shouldn't take offense at this friendly sparring.

Try to learn how your manager handles successes. Some managers will give you immediate, detailed feedback, telling what they liked—and didn't like—about your work. Other managers may accept projects and reports with a mere "thank you," and some other managers may never say a word unless things are going wrong. Of course, you'll have some feelings about this. It's ideal if you can work for a manager who takes the role of being your "coach"—always encouraging improvement but continually acknowledging your efforts. Such managers are rare.

In business, there is always something that doesn't go according to plan. You'll learn your boss's personal style for dealing with adversity. Some managers have a tendency to panic and exaggerate difficulties. Other can accept imperfections with grace. When a team member makes a mistake, the manager's response can vary along a scale from suffering in silence, through annoyance and a mild rebuke, all the way to a screaming tantrum. There are quite a few bosses who would be described as follows: "He blows up pretty wild, but don't take it to heart—he's never personal about it. He's a bit of a screamer when things don't go right, but it's soon over." If you have a volcanic boss, it's helpful if your peers can warn you. Try not to take the outburst as personal criticism and never respond in kind. Your professionalism and calm demeanor will model appropriate behavior.

At the limit, you may find that you are working for what has been called a "toxic boss"—someone who seems to get joy from belittling people and who constantly criticizes those around him. If you are sure that is where you have landed, you'll want to look around for a better situation. Looking for a new position in the same firm is a risky proposition. If you haven't been able to develop a good working relationship with your boss, in the long run it may be the best for both you and the supervisor if you find another position. However, you should be aware that if you begin to mention that you are considering other situations, the news is likely to get back to your boss sooner than you intend, and you should be prepared for a confrontation. You should plan a euphemistic explanation:

> "Well, it's true. I do feel that I'd be better suited to a position that made more use of my background in computers, so I had mentioned my interest to other people."

14-6 Getting Ahead

No matter how much you like your colleagues and how pleasantly you get along with your boss, you should keep an eye on your own career and not stagnate. No one expects you to work for 15 years at the same position (even if it makes your manager's life easier to have one function covered with a solid reliable worker). It's perfectly appropriate to talk about your career path and to discuss new challenges with your supervisor. You don't want to take on ever-increasing responsibilities at the same salary, but you are more likely to be promoted if you can master new skills, functions, or areas of business.

Most large US firms have a formal review process—typically an "**annual review.**" As a new hire, you may also have a provisional review after three or six months. This review may be done in a number of ways. You may be asked to begin by writing a self-review, which your supervisor then critiques. You should define accomplishments and things that are different about this year than the past. Alternatively, your manager may complete a written evaluation without your input and present it to you for comment. Finally, you may be subject to an extensive review, called a "360-degree review," in which your firm seeks input from your colleagues and subordinates, people in other departments, and even customers. For many people criticism is hard to take. You should correct errors of fact but try not to be defensive by engaging in argument. Strive to hear negative comments in the context of an overall evaluation (that may be quite positive) and convert them into positive action steps for the future. When there has been a problem situation, address it in terms of "What I have learned from this and what I would do differently next time."

14-7 Time to Say "Goodbye"

Even when you feel you have a great job, there'll come a time when you want to move on. Perhaps you want to go to graduate school, move to another geographic location, or simply experience a different firm or industry. The general legal principle underlying your employment is called "employment at will." That is, just as your employer can fire you at any time and for any reason, your employer cannot demand that you continue to work at the same job (because that would be "indentured servitude") and, in general, cannot require long periods of notice. Unless you have signed an employment contract to stay with a firm for a specific time period (and very few firms ask for such a contract), even high-level executives usually give quite short notice, often as little as two weeks. (To "give notice" means to communicate to your employer that you plan to quit.)

If you are leaving because you really don't like the situation, it's best to leave on good terms. You never know when your old company will buy your new company and you'll be working with the same team, or when the one person whom you detested will be hired at your new firm as your co-worker. You may be asked to take part in an "**exit interview**" with your manager or with people from the Human Resources department of your firm. There's a great temptation to unload every frustration and to vent about every shortcoming of your experience with the firm. Unless you feel compelled to leave because of fraud or sexual harassment, it's best to leave as much as possible unsaid. Remember that one of the fundamental rules of business is "It's nice to be nice."

Put This Chapter into Practice

1. Interview a friend who has taken a new job in the last year or so and find out whether the firm used a formal orientation and whether it was too much information at once. How did your friend eventually "learn the ropes"?

2. Think about a supervisor you've had in the past. How would you "diagnose" her or his style according to the dimensions in section 14-5, "Managing Your Boss"?

Examples of Business Documents

Remember, your firm may have its own style

The appendices contain examples of common business documents. Consistent with the rest of the book, these examples are in "middle American style." That is, they would probably be seen as acceptable in most contexts. However, don't forget that your company may have a very specific style guide that determines how you should format your work.

As long as you don't violate the rules of typography (for example, by underlining something written in a proportional font or by having too many styles of type on one page), you could reasonably borrow elements from each of these samples. For example, two styles of letter headings are shown, and there might be some instances when each one would best suit your communications purpose.

Appendix 1: Resumes

Appendices 1a, 1b, and 1c are three versions of more or less the same resume. The first (1a) is a *standard chronological resume* (although remember the chronological order is backward with *most recent first*). This example shows how to handle two addresses and study abroad. If you have several degrees or a double major, you should make every effort to make your achievements stand out.

Under "Experience," the second job (Soccer Camp) shows how to handle increasing responsibilities and intermittent employment at the same firm. Work in student government (unpaid) comes under "Additional Experience."

Remember that the order of ideas is important and that as recruiters scan resumes quickly, they tend to focus on the first and last items—of the resume as a whole and also within sections. In this case, the last word in "Interests" is "Chess"—the writer wants to signal his analytic abilities. The effect of the resume would be different if it ended with the word "skiing."

You can choose from many possible formats for a resume, and some creativity will allow you to achieve a smart appearance that is readable and distinctive. In this example, the writer uses a *sans serif* font that holds up well under faxing and scanning. Three typographic effects are used in addition to the normal font: ALL CAPS for the subheadings, SMALL CAPS for the names of universities and firms, and *italic* for positions and dates.

The second example (1b) shows how the same resume might be presented to an employer who asked for submissions as "text only" within the body of an e-mail. Of course, you lose formatting, and you can anticipate that the firm will be analyzing applicants by computer. Note the addition of "Relevant Coursework" in case the scanning program is set up to search for certain words. ("Relevant Coursework" could appear on a well-formatted chronological resume under "Education," especially for a person whose degree is in a liberal arts subject such as History, where technical expertise wouldn't be obvious to the recruiter.) In the *text-only resume*, all the parts of the chronological resume would be included—although some are omitted here.

In this resume, the writer has chosen to end with "soccer" because he has read that teamwork is an important attribute of the job in question. The word order is less important when you think the resume is going to be analyzed by computer, but it's worth taking the order of ideas into account in case the resume passes the first screening and is then reviewed by a human.

The third resume (1c) is an attempt to tell a similar story in the *functional resume* style. You can see the writer has chosen a serif font (Garamond) and a different layout. The functional resume is recommended by some career counselors for candidates who have had interrupted education or careers, or whose work has largely been volunteer. Although this type of resume might earn you a first-round interview, you should anticipate that at some point in the process a recruiter is likely to ask for a chronological resume that clearly shows the starting and ending dates of positions and that shows which positions were volunteer and which were paid. Expect to be asked at an interview for additional information about any apparent gaps in your chronology.

Appendix 1a: Sample Chronological Resume

Benoit LeClaire
bleclaire@hotemail.com

College	*Permanent*
6933 Martin Luther King, Jr. Way	282 Blackhawk Drive
High Point, NC 27260-3930	Danville, CA 94720-1919
(704) 555-6775	(510) 555-1234

EDUCATION   HIGH POINT UNIVERSITY   High Point, NC

Jeremiah School of Accounting and Finance
BS Finance and Statistics (double major)   *Class of May 2003*
Trustees Scholar   GPA 3.27 GPA (Finance courses) 4.0

LONDON SCHOOL OF ECONOMICS   London, England

Study abroad, Fall 2002   Coursework in EU economic policy and corporate finance.

EXPERIENCE   PRECEDENT CHAIR COMPANY   High Point, NC
Summer   *Intern, Treasurer's office.* Responsible for reconciling inventory reports from
2002   eight cost centers. Prepared weekly reports. Staff member to internal
committee on $0.5 billion pension plan.

Summer   DAN JONES SOCCER CAMP   Danville, CA
2001   *Assistant Director* Interviewed and hired 12 coaches and 24 counselors for a
nationally known summer sports camp; assigned daily teaching schedules;
responsible for briefing parents on students' progress and managing minor
sports injuries.

Summer   *Coach* Developed daily lesson plans for groups of 18 teenage soccer players;
2000   counseled students on game strategy and personal training.

Summer   *Counselor-in-training* Under the direction of Coach, assisted in drill practice
1999   and class management for three different groups of 18 students. Provided first
aid for minor injuries.

ADDITIONAL   HIGH POINT UNIVERSITY   High Point, NC
EXPERIENCE   *Office of the President of the Student Body: Chief of staff* Organized calendar
Sept 2001-   for President and Exec. Committee. Supervised disbursement of funds from
continues $35K student government budget to 14 recognized student groups. Resolved
space allocation conflicts.

ACTIVITIES   HPU FINANCE CLUB *Active member 1999-continues, Treasurer, 2000-2001* With 5
colleagues, refounded undergraduate association; raised $600 budget; brought 6
speakers to campus and oversaw development of website with links to recruiting firms.

MILTON DANIEL HALL, *Security Chair, 2001,* Committee member responsible for safety in
120-student residence. Developed new system for handling lockouts and lost keys.

SKILLS   MS-Excel (expert), MS-Word (intermediate), PowerPoint (novice)
French (fluent business written and spoken), German (conversational)

INTERESTS   Traveling, community service (tutoring), skiing, soccer (intramural), and chess.

Appendix 1b: Sample Chronological Resume as "Text-Only" Submission

Benoit Leclaire
bleclaire@hotemail.com

College address:
6933 Martin Luther King, Jr. Way
High Point, NC 27260-3930

College phone:
(704) 555-6775

Permanent address:
282 Blackhawk Drive
Danville, CA 94720-1919

Permanent phone:
(510) 555-1234

EDUCATION

High Point University, High Point, NC
BS Finance and Statistics (double major)
Class of May 2003
Cumulative GPA 3.27
GPA in Finance Courses 4.0

Relevant Coursework:
Multivariate analysis, Capital Markets, Corporate Finance

EXPERIENCE

Summer 2002
Precedent Chair Company, High Point, NC
Intern, Treasurer's office
Reconciled inventory reports using Excel. Wrote weekly
reports in MS-Word. Staff member for pension committee with
$0.5 billion assets.

Summer 2001
Dan Jones Soccer Camp, Danville, CA
Assistant Director
Recruited and hired summer employees. Trained and
supervised 36 temporary workers. Conducted weekly staff
meetings and made reports to parents.

Etc., down to ...

INTERESTS

Traveling, community service, skiing, soccer.

Appendix 1c: Sample Functional Resume

Benoit LeClaire
bleclaire@hotemail.com

College	*Permanent*
6933 Martin Luther King, Jr. Way	282 Blackhawk Drive
High Point, NC 27260-3930	Danville, CA 94720-1919
(704) 555-6775	(510) 555-1234

Objective

Position in junior management that will permit me opportunities to apply my analytical and organizational skills.

Profile

A highly motivated recent college graduate with excellent computer skills and substantial experience leading teams of co-workers to achieve superior results.

Skills

Analysis Consolidating and summarizing operating and accounting results, data verification, graphing of quantitative information, mastery of multiple computer systems. Proficient in MS-Excel and MS-Word. Expert chess player.

Organization Schedule management for workgroup, recruiting and hiring, implementing training programs, staffing committees, preparing timely written reports.

Team Leadership Clarify team objectives, motivate team members, respect deadlines. Captain of intramural soccer team.

Employment

Textbooks Direct, Territory High Point and Winston-Salem, NC. Campus representative. July 2001 – present

Precedent Chair Company, High Point, NC. Intern, Treasurer's Office. July – August 2000

Dan Jones Soccer Camps, Danville, CA. Assistant Director, June – August 1999, Counselor, May – July 1998

Education

University of Western North Carolina, Cullowee, NC. Certificate in Entrepreneurial Management, August 2001

High Point University, High Point, NC. BS in Business Administration, May 2001

Wake Technical College , Raleigh, NC. Associate in Arts degree, General Studies, June 1999

Appendix 2: Cover Letter

Appendix 2 shows a standard form for a cover letter, with three sections, as described in Chapter 12. Note that the writer uses a smart personal letterhead with current contact information. He has looked up a specific person to address and doesn't address "Human Resources" impersonally.

The font is Bookman Old Style, a particularly clear serif font. The writer sets the specific job title in **bold.** While many people feel that using bold type makes the appearance of the letter itself a little choppy, it will help the letter to be directed to the right recruiter for summer jobs. This example does not have an "Enclosure" line for the resume that is mentioned in the second paragraph. Using such a line wouldn't be wrong, but it doesn't add value here and takes up space.

The writer ends with a clear action step.

Appendix 2: Sample Cover Letter

Benoit LeClaire

6933 Martin Luther king, Jr. Way, High Point, NC   27260-3930
bleclair@hotemail.com   (704) 555-6775

January 3, 2003

Leslie K. Travis, *Head Recruiter*
College Relations
Investment Company of America
749 Broad Street
Newark, NJ 07102-3777

Dear Ms. Travis:

I'm applying with enthusiasm for the **summer internship in risk management** in the New Jersey office of Investment Company. I'm a Junior at High Point University, double majoring in finance and statistics.

As you'll see from my resume, last summer I worked in the treasury department of a large furniture manufacturer. I showed my initiative by developing an Excel macro to automate consolidation of weekly reports from the firm's eight divisions. I'm expert in Excel, and I am working diligently on improving my PowerPoint and presentation skills. This semester, I've been studying derivatives and I have a particular interest in learning more about how a major investment firm manages its risk. At HPU, I've worked on reviving the Undergraduate Finance Club, which had nearly become extinct. We now have 25 active members and a strong program. I have demonstrated my responsibility and hard work in two volunteer positions on campus, as security chair for my dorm and as chief of staff for the president of the student government.

I know that Investment Company does not schedule on-campus recruiting for internship positions. I'm most willing to come to Newark for interview, if it could be on a Friday or Monday, as I'll make a weekend visit to my godparents who live in Princeton. I'll call you next week to ask for an appointment.

Sincerely,
Benoit LeClaire

Appendix 3: Reference List

Most firms don't do much with the Reference List that you give them, but this is one case where "the medium is the message." Merely having a well-prepared Reference List will show that you are a serious candidate for a job and that you have good work habits. When the recruiting process slows down, handing over a detailed list of your references is a way to encourage a company to make a decision about you.

Of course, you should always ask for permission to use someone's name, and it's reasonable to review what you hope others will be able to say about you. Ask the people providing references how they like to be contacted—some people prefer to be called at home, and others want to deal with these matters only at work. Giving an e-mail address would be more common than giving a street address, as almost no company would take the time to write by US mail to take up a reference.

Appendix 3: Sample Reference List

Reference List for Benoit LeClaire
bleclaire@hotemail.com
(704) 555-6775

Referees, contact information	How they know me	What they can say
Dan Jones (o) (510) 111-1234 dsmith@sportsecamp.org	Was my supervisor for three summers at sports camp	General employee reliability, work habits, good team member.
Sheila Patel, Ph.D. (o) (704) 222-1234 (h) (704) 333-1234 finguru@hpu.edu	Professor for my Finance 21 class	I ranked 2 / 132 in this class and prof. offered me the TA's job next semester. Can talk about my study habits, math abilities and computer skills.
Father Maurice Bonilla (cell) (415) 555-1234 padremau@heaven.net	Family friend, has known me for 20 years	Can confirm I'm honest and trustworthy.

Appendix 4: Sample Letters

The letters shown in Appendices 4a through 4g are by no means exhaustive of all business situations, and you should take a look at models that already exist at your firm. You may be expected to follow a particular wording that covers certain legal requirements. These letters are all quite short, and you may find that your business correspondence runs a little longer. All are carefully addressed to the recipient and are centered on the page. Some use a subject line, and most have instructions on how to contact someone specifically for additional information.

In the Letter of Acknowledgment (4a), an employee is merely documenting the receipt of a form. The letter uses the American style of subject line ("Re:") above the salutation and refers the customer to a general customer service line for any further questions.

In the second example, the Letter of Transmittal (4b), an Account Executive adds a few words to lead the reader into the enclosure. He uses a bullet point format because the two choices for the customer could come in any order, and both are described in the brochure. He doesn't use an "Enclosure" line because he's stuffing the envelope himself, but he includes a personal phone number as he's hoping to win new business directly.

A simple Letter of Thanks (4c) is the third example. Although it's fairly short, it includes some conventional elements:

- Specific description of what the writer is grateful for
- Mention of other people who were present
- A detail that shows the writer is not reciting generic thanks
- An expressed hope to work together in the future

Although a great deal of information and explanation is done by phone calls, e-mail, and referring customers to websites, there might be an occasion to write a letter giving clarification in a business situation, and this is shown in the Informative Letter (4d).

The writer begins by defining (and repeating back to the customer) the specific inquiry and then goes on to give the information. This is definitely a place where the writer would want to give a direct phone number—he'll hope that any further questions come by phone and won't need a long letter!

Certain letters—usually those addressing employment and buying and selling things—can have the force of a contract when both sides of a transaction agree to them. You should be sensitive to which letters in your line of business have the force of contracts and learn the protocol associated with them. In many cases, you'll send out two identical copies of a letter, asking the other person to sign the second copy and return one to your firm—that will be your record that he or she agreed to the terms you've proposed. In this example of a Contractual Letter (4e), an employee is defining the terms of some legal work to be done by a group of attorneys that are not members of the firm. Because the letter will be processed and mailed by an assistant, the writer has specified the two enclosures.

The Good News Letter (4f) uses a European style of subject line—bold and centered *after* the salutation. This style is quite common for letters that are promoting a product or service. In this case, the firm is announcing a fee reduction to present customers. If you have an occasion to announce "good news," you should think through what you would like to have happen as a result. Here, the writer is asking the existing customer to refer colleagues for new business.

Bad News Letters (example 4g) have a conventional structure. In this sample, the writer has chosen a standard subject line, with the word "Subject" instead of "Re"—either one is acceptable. The letter observes the usual order of ideas for bad news:

- A "soft lead" gently leading into the problem
- A clear "no"
- An attempt at amelioration or to show the bright side of things

Here, a customer has asked for a discount on last year's fees, in light of a fee reduction. Note that the writer doesn't offer any explanation such as "to do so would bankrupt the company." And the letter does not contain excessive apologies. It was a "nice try" by the customer who likely expected a negative response. The letter ends with a pleasant regret and appeals to the recipient's reasonableness by using the word "prudent."

Appendix 4a: Sample Letter of Acknowledgment

Bigco Investments
88 First Avenue, Memphis TN 38109-1801
(901) 555-6000

November 23, 1998

Menxi Ma
2789 Dawkins Court
Kansas City, KS 66103-2031

Re: Change of Beneficiary: Account 219034

Dear Ms. Ma:

We have received your change of beneficiary form for your 401(k) account. The change will be made in our records at the end of the month, and you'll see the new beneficiary shown on your quarterly statement at the end of December.

Please call our Customer Service line (800) 555-6000 if you need any additional transactions on this account.

Sincerely,

Sammy Choo

Account Executive

Appendix 4b: Sample Letter of Transmittal

Bigco Investments
88 First Avenue, Memphis TN 38109-1801
(901) 555-6000

November 23, 1998

Daniel Franklin
64 Summit Street
Kansas City, KS 66103-2031

Dear Mr. Franklin:

Thank you for writing to ask about our rollover 401(k) plans. I am enclosing a brochure that describes the two options:

- Self-directed Account (where you choose the investments)
- Model Portfolio Account (where Bigco chooses the investments)

The form at the back of the brochure has complete instructions. If you have any questions, please call me directly at (901) 555-1122.

Sincerely,

Derek Lemori

Account Executive

Appendix 4c: Sample Letter of Thanks

Bigco Investments

88 First Avenue, Memphis TN 38109-1801
(901) 555-6000

November 23, 1998

Natasha Petrova
3341 Steiner Street
San Francisco, CA 93123-2706

Dear Natasha,

On behalf of the 401(k) team at Bigco, I want to thank you for your presentation on Time Management last week. I've heard many positive comments from the team members—they particularly liked your focus on specific action steps.

For myself, I appreciated the tip to turn off your e-mail when you're trying to get work done. It's already helped me get more important projects completed.

I hope we have the opportunity to hear you at Bigco in the future.

Again, my sincere thanks.

Best regards,

Sacha Yevelev

Manager, Training and Education

Appendix 4d: Sample Informative Letter

Bigco Investments
88 First Avenue, Memphis TN 38109-1801
(901) 555-6000

November 23, 1998

David Mershon
4258 Piedmont Avenue
Seattle, WA 98108-1226

Dear Mr. Mershon:

Thank you for writing to ask for clarification of our two different 401(k) products, the Self-directed and the Model Portfolio accounts.

In the Self-directed account, your balance will begin in money market funds. You can then instruct us to move money into any one of the seven investments outlined on page 16 of the brochure. You can change your allocation at any time, and can direct any new contributions into any one of the investment choices.

In the Model Portfolio account, Bigco fund managers make those decisions for you, on your behalf. We use a time-tested risk preference model, which takes into account both your expected retirement date and the current volatility of the stock market. In the last few years, this has meant that the accounts have been from 15 to 85 percent invested in common stocks, with never less than 10 percent in money market funds, and the remainder in short-term bond funds.

The rules for withdrawing money from either account are decided by the IRS, not by Bigco. There's a summary of the current rules on page 24 of the brochure. You can see the effect of various withdrawal options by visiting our website (www.bigco/whatif) and putting a few numbers into our financial engine. It will show you how long your money would last, and how much you can withdraw each month, under various assumptions.

If you have any further questions about which product is best suited to your personal situation, do not hesitate to phone me at (901) 555-6613.

Sincerely,
Ella Miskie   emiskie@bigco.com

New Accounts Executive

Appendix 4e: Sample Contractual Letter

Bigco Investments
88 First Avenue, Memphis TN 38109-1801
(901) 555-6000

November 23, 1998

Ryan Lessler, JD
LESSLER & SONS, LLP
4258 Piedmont Avenue
Oakland, CA 94611-4741

Dear Mr. Lessler:

This letter is to confirm the arrangements we made by phone today for you to review the status of our 401(k) plans for compliance with current Federal law and IRS regulations. Your fee will be $5,000, which we will pay when you have issued us an opinion letter. You've agreed to complete the review by 28 February 1999.

We understand that you will not be able to comment on Bigco's compliance with any state laws, except for California. We will provide you with our current by-laws and regulations, copies of our filings with the IRS, and our marketing brochures.

Our agreement is that you will be able to do this work without additional travel, and Bigco will not reimburse Lessler & Sons for any travel or other incidental expenses on this assignment.

If these terms are acceptable to you, please sign the enclosed copy of this letter and return to me in the envelope I am enclosing.

I look forward to working with you on this project. If you have any questions, you can reach me directly at (901) 555-6599.

Yours truly,

Ravi Ranganath
Treasurer

Enclosures: Copy of letter
               Return envelope

Appendix 4f: Sample Good News Letter

Bigco Investments

88 First Avenue, Memphis TN 38109-1801
(901) 555-6000

November 23, 1998

George Sinclair
28 Prescott Avenue
White Plains, NY 10605-1239

Dear Mr. Sinclair:

Reduced Fees for Accounts over $100,000

I'm very pleased to be able to tell you that Bigco is changing the fee structure for our 401(k) Self-directed accounts. Beginning January 1, 1999, the fee will be a simple $25 per year, and no longer a percentage of the assets under management. You'll notice a one-time charge on your March 1999 statement, and then no further fee deductions for the rest of the calendar year.

At Bigco, we've been working hard to improve the efficiency of our operations, and we are happy to share the savings with our loyal account holders, such as you. We now have one of the best fee structures in the industry and hope that you will mention the firm to professional colleagues who are looking for a firm to manage their rollover 401(k) funds.

Sincerely,

Simi Dubay
Vice President of Marketing

Appendix 4g: Sample Bad News Letter

Bigco Investments

88 First Avenue, Memphis TN 38109-1801
(901) 555-6000

November 23, 1998

Cheryl Tai
2020 Thomas Olney Common
Providence, RI 02912-0001

Subject: Request for retroactive fee change, Account: 109176

Dear Ms. Tai:

Thank you for writing to me about your account, and I'm glad you like the new fee structure for our Self-directed 401(k) accounts. But I'm afraid it's not possible to retroactively reduce the fees for the 1998 calendar year.

I reviewed your account this morning, and the new fee structure should save you more than $800 in fees between now and your planned retirement date. We hope you agree that we have a good record of passing on our savings from more efficient operations, as soon as it is possible to do so. The new fee structure will save our loyal account holders with big balances more than $1 million in fees next year.

As a company founded by prudent investors like yourself, we want to continue to earn your trust. I'm sorry we weren't able to grant your request on this occasion.

Yours sincerely,

David K. Mew

Vice President, Customer Service

Appendix 5: Sample e-mails

The first e-mail (5a) is a routine request to a colleague for information. The subject line nicely summarizes the text of the message. Note the attempt to lay out the paragraphs in an interesting way. The salutation (without "Dear") and the simple closing "With thanks" are typical for inter-office e-mails. The writer is using a signature block intended for people within the company, so this example shows the physical location of his office, rather than a street address.

In the second example (5b) the writer is addressing someone outside the firm. He begins by saying who he is up front, in much the same way one would do in a phone call. The request is specific and the e-mail provides additional information. The writer ends with his full name in its familiar form, followed by a signature block that gives the formal version of his name, his street address, and contact information. Including one's own e-mail address here is worthwhile, in case it has been lost in the header if the message is forwarded from one server to another.

The third example (5c) is a very routine inter-office announcement that a regular meeting has a location change. Again, note that the substance of the e-mail is all contained in the subject line, which is helpful if someone wants to check it later without re-opening the e-mail.

Appendix 5a: Sample e-mail to a Colleague

```
To:       Lindsay O'Brien
From:     Tommy Chang
Subject:  MSFT Contract: Can you send me a copy?

Lindsay,

Could you send me a hard copy of the Microsoft contract
through office mail? I need it for the quarterly review
meeting on Thursday.

With thanks, Tommy

-------------------------------
Tommy Chang, Assistant Counsel
Legal Affairs, Mail Stop 223
H 630 Ordway Building
<tchang@bigco.com>
(415) 555-6932
-------------------------------
```

Appendix 5b: Sample e-mail to Someone Who Doesn't Know You

```
To:       Declan Shaughnessy
From:     Tommy Chang
Subject:  Invitation to speak: Future Financial
Professionals: February 2001


Mr. Shaughnessy,

I'm Tommy Chang, a law-school classmate of your sister
Elizabeth at Emory. I'm hoping you can help me with a
speaking engagement.

I'm serving as the events chair for the Future Financial
Professionals of America, Peninsular Branch, and I'd like
to invite you to address the group about the bond market.
Something on duration risk would be particularly helpful.

The FFPA is made up of community college students from
several local schools. We meet at the Foster City Diner at
8 a.m. on Thursdays and our speakers usually talk for half
an hour, followed by some time for Q&A. About three dozen
students usually attend.

Could you let me know if you could do this for us? Sometime
in late February or early March would be best for us, but
of course, we can be flexible on dates to accommodate your
schedule.

In advance, my thanks,

Tommy Chang


-----------------------------
Thomas W. Chang, Assistant Counsel
Bigco Investments of America
Bigco Plaza
225 Produce Avenue
South San Francisco, CA 94080-6512
<tchang@bigco.com>
(415) 555-6932
-----------------------------
```

Appendix 5c: Sample e-mail to a Workgroup

```
To:       Legal Affairs
From:     Tommy Chang
Subject:  Team Meeting will be in WEST Conference Room


The team meeting on Thursday afternoon will be in the

    WEST Conference Room

    2:00 - 4:00 p.m. Thursday 1 March

as our usual East Conference room is being used for staff
ID photographs this week.

See you there as usual, Tom
```

Appendix 6: Memo Format

Memos don't have a place for a signature and are typically bunched at the top of the page. Although most memos have been superseded by e-mail, you might use a memo when it's helpful to have a paper copy of a decision, as is the case in Appendix 6. There's been a change in supplier at a firm, and employees might want to keep this announcement around for quite a period of time to refer to in the future.

Most firms have a preferred format—the example shown here uses a template from MS Word in which the sender's and recipient's names are shown in ALL CAPITAL letters. This is just one possible format, and not a general rule for memos. Be sure to look around your workplace for good examples of your "house style" to follow.

Appendix 6: Sample Routine Memo, Change of Supplier

INTEROFFICE MEMORANDUM

TO: DEVELOPMENT WORKGROUP

FROM: JAMIE CHARLES

SUBJECT: CHANGE IN SUPPLIERS: USE STAPLES OFFICE PRODUCTS

DATE: 2/23/05

CC: STACEY PRAHALADAD, PURCHASING

Effective 1 March, we are changing our main supplier for office products from Office Max to Staples. You can order on-line from our firm's own intranet.

If we all use Staples, there'll be substantial cost savings for us. If there is any item that you are used to purchasing from Office Max that you can't find at Staples, please contact Stacey Prahaladad in Purchasing to get approval to purchase from any other vendor.

360-degree review   See *Annual review.* Ch. 14.

401(k) plan   A federal government program that allows employees to save money in tax-deferred accounts for retirement. A firm may or may not offer a 401(k) and if the employer doesn't offer it, an employee cannot participate in this program on his or her own. Ch. 13.

A

Academic major   In American universities a "major" is the chief subject of specialization, which corresponds to "honours in {subject}" in universities based on the British model. See also *Academic minor.*

Academic minor   In American universities a minor is the second specialization, less important than the first subject, and with fewer courses taken. See also *Academic major.*

Active voice   The active voice is the form of speech or writing that puts emphasis on the subject, rather than the object of a sentence. "The boy hit the ball" is active voice; "The ball was hit by the boy" is passive. It is the preferred voice in *Plain English.* See also *Passive voice.*

Airport Test   A colloquial set phrase in certain industries referring to whether a job candidate would be pleasant company during a three-hour or longer layover at an airport. A euphemism for "personality" in recruiting circumstances. Ch. 13.

Alias   Literally, an alias is an alternative name, such as a pen name or stage name. In e-mail, it can refer to a non-personal name, such as roomreservations@bigco.com, or to a distribution list of several people, such as teamA@bigco.com. Ch. 4

Annual review   A routine but formal review of an employee's work, usually conducted once a year by the worker's direct supervisor. A "360-degree review" asks for input from the employee's co-workers and subordinates, and possibly also from customers. Ch. 14.

Attachment   Something sent with a letter or e-mail. When postal mail is used, the attachment usually isn't physically attached but is just enclosed. For e-mail, it's a way to send a file along with a message. Ch. 5.   **259**

Audience heterogeneity   The concept that audiences are made up of individual members who may have greater or lesser expertise and familiarity with the subject matter of a presentation and greater or lesser interest in the topic at hand. Ch. 6.

B

Boilerplate   Routine recitals (that is, wording which is always the same); usually inserted for legal reasons to cover all possibilities. Ch. 5.

Brainstorm   A group process in which team members are asked to contribute all possible ideas on a topic, and they are listed without comment or critique. Often parts of two infeasible ideas will give the best solution to a problem. Ch. 7.

Broadcloth   Ordinary fabric for shirts that is not "Oxford cloth." Ch. 11

Brunch   A late-morning meal (a combination of breakfast and lunch), which is common for social gatherings at weekends. Food is often served "buffet style," where you serve yourself.

Business attire   Formal clothes to wear to an office, such as a dark business suit, shirt and tie, and polished leather shoes. Ch. 11.

Business casual   Clothes worn to the office, but not the same as "formal." Typically, shirt with collar (but no tie) and slacks but not jeans. But there are many variations in acceptable "casual" attire. Ch. 11.

Business context   Each communication falls on a continuum from social or everyday purpose to non-routine, or contractual. The context of a communication determines the appropriate level of formality. Ch. 2.

Butterfly format   In public speaking, when several people share a presentation, the format in which they stand with members who are closest to the screen (or middle of the group) farther away from the audience, and the outermost members a few steps closer. Ch. 7.

C

Calling in   In US business terminology, a general term which implies that a staff member is ill and unavailable for work. "He's not here—he called in" means "This employee is on sick leave. He telephoned to say that he would not be in to work today." Ch. 10.

Catastrophizing   A tendency to take small mistakes (especially during public speaking) and to treat them as if they were great problems or catastrophes. Ch. 6.

Channel of communication   The medium that a person chooses to communicate with another. For example, a message could be written in an e-mail or delivered by a phone call. In this case, "e-mail" and "phone" are two different channels of communication.

Chronological resume   The most usual format for the summary of a person's education and experience. Within each section, the most recent work is presented first. Ch. 12 and Appendices.

Comp day   A day off in place of a day that an employee has worked. For example, a supervisor might say, "If you come in on Saturday, I'll give you next Friday as a comp day." Short for "in compensation for." Executives who are paid monthly usually do not file for overtime pay if they work additional days. They may—or may not—be granted comp days. Ch. 9.

Conference call   A phone call with more than two people able to hear at the same time. Ch. 3.

Costume jewelry   Jewelry that is not made of precious metals. Ch. 11.

Cover letter   Part of the formal process of applying to a firm for employment. The letter that goes on top of (covers) your resume. Ch. 12.

Cultural norms   Patterns of behavior that are shared by members of one country, society, social class, or group. Cultural norms determine what is considered appropriate behavior and what is considered rude or unsophisticated. Ch. 1.

D

Distribution list   In e-mail, a way to send out a message to many people at once. Choose the smallest distribution list that works (for example, salesteam@bigco.com rather than hqstaff@bigco.com). Some firms have defined distribution lists for paper media such as memos. Ch. 4.

"Do it now" approach   A part of time management. The approach involves completing tasks at once, immediately, rather than setting them aside and going back to them later. Ch. 14.

Drilling   In public speaking when one audience member asks successive questions on the same topic. Ch. 7.

E

Employee Assistance Program (EAP)   A scheme at most large firms to provide counseling about personal difficulties for staff members. EAPs will refer people who are in trouble to appropriate community resources. Such programs save managers from getting involved in the personal problems of their colleagues. Ch. 9.

Employment application   A form asking for specific information in a specific order, unique to each firm, for job candidates. Firms are restricted from asking about certain topics, but applicants must answer all questions truthfully and fully. Lying on an employment application can be grounds for instant dismissal. Ch. 13.

Enclosure   See *Attachment.* Ch. 5.

Endnote   A comment or citation (note on the source of data) placed at the end of a chapter or report. Ch. 5.

Ethnic food   Also called "international cuisine." At a restaurant, food from a country other than the United States. Most American food is derived from other countries (French fries are from France), but many styles such as Italian food and steaks have become "mainstream." "Ethnic dining" implies somewhat exotic food that will be interesting—but might not be to everyone's taste. Ch. 8.

Euphemism   Literally, "beautiful speech." A way to talk about something unpleasant without resorting to unpleasant, graphic terms. For example, "Harold passed away last year" is a euphemism for "Harold is no longer with the firm. He died last year." Ch. 10.

Exit interview   When an employee leaves a firm, he or she may be interviewed either by a supervisor or by someone from Human Resources, most often to find out the reasons for his or her departure so that organizational problems can be identified and addressed. Ch. 14.

F

Fired, "Let go"   Typical turns of phrase for ending employment other than when the employee chooses to resign. "Fired" often implies that the employee was terminated "for cause," that is, that he or she did something wrong. "Let go" implies that all employees are straining to leave their companies all the time, which is silly, but it saves the embarrassment of using the word "fired." See also *Reduction in force.* Ch. 13.

Flame   A colloquial term that means an e-mail of hostile tone. Don't send or forward flames. Ch. 4.

Footnote   A comment or citation (note on the source of data) placed at the foot (bottom) of the page it refers to. Most word-processing programs manage footnotes automatically. Ch. 5.

Functional resume   A type of summary of a person's abilities that emphasizes skills rather than positions held. Ch. 12 and Appendices.

G

Gender-neutral   Writing or speaking in a way that is inclusive of both men and women. It avoids using "he" when the person referred to could be male or female. Ch. 2.

Group interview   A style of interview in which several candidates are in the same room with one or more interviewers. Ch. 13.

H

Headhunter   A colloquial term for an "executive recruiter"; a firm that tries to develop candidates for open positions, usually by phoning people with similar positions at competitor companies. Ch. 13.

Heterogeneity   See *Audience heterogeneity.* Ch. 6.

Honorific   A title that "gives honor" to the recipient of mail, such as "Mr.," "Ms.," or "Dr." Ch. 5.

I

Inform, persuade, or remind   Three possible purposes of a speech. You can effectively accomplish only one at a time. Ch. 6.

J

Job description   An exact statement of the duties of a position and the skills required to perform it successfully. Ch.'s 13,14.

L

Let go   See *Fired.* Ch. 13.

Letter of transmittal   A simple letter describing something such as a brochure or contract that is being sent (transmitted) from one person to another. Ch. 5.

Level of formality   In both written and spoken language, a dimension concerning the type of language used. Informal language has contractions and colloquialisms and simple structure. Most formal language avoids these in favor of strict grammar and style. Ch. 2.

M

Mail code   A notation (such as "Mail Code: 1550") that helps postal mail get to the right desk in a large company. The Mail Code is invariably assigned to a department, not a building, so that if the offices are rearranged, the Mail Code remains the same. Some firms use the term "Mail Drop." Ch. 5.

Major   See *Academic major.* Ch. 12.

Medium (singular), media (plural)   The channel of communication a business person chooses to communicate with the intended recipient of a message. For example, a decision could be announced by a phone call, letter, or e-mail—these are three different media. Ch. 2.

Minor   See *Academic minor.* Ch. 12.

Mitbringen   A small gift for a host and hostess brought with (*mitbringen* in German) a guest to express thanks. Ch. 9.

Mute button   On a business phone, a button that silences the microphone at your end so you can avoid the person at the other end hearing coughs or paper-shuffling. Ch. 3.

N

Networking   Developing acquaintances with the hope of possible mutually beneficial business relationships later. The process of networking involves developing contacts (people you know well enough to phone) at many companies.

Nickname   A familiar name that is other than a diminutive of a person's forename. Example: "Tug" Wilson. Ch. 1.

Non-verbal communication   Interactions between people other than words. Often called "body language." Might include stance (how you stand), inter-personal distance, facial expression, and hand gestures. Ch. 1.

O

Offer letter   The formal communication from a firm to a successful candidate specifying the terms of employment proposed. Ch. 13.

On-campus recruiting   The process of formally announcing hiring for a firm using the Career Center of a college or university. Large firms like on-campus recruiting because they can interview a large pool of candidates on one or two days. Ch. 13.

Orientation   The process of educating a new employee about a firm. It can be a formal, structured program, or a process that a new hire must manage for himself or herself. Ch. 14.

Outline   The skeleton of a communication; some notes that allow you to set out your ideas in the correct order, before beginning to write. Ch. 5.

Outplacement   Job counseling offered to employees whose work has been terminated. It's almost always paid for by the firm. Ch. 13

Oxford cloth   A type of textile for shirts in which strands of thread are doubled so that the weave is visible and the fabric is quite thick. The opposite is "broadcloth." Ch. 11.

P

Passive voice   The passive voice is a literary form of speech or writing in which the object of an action becomes the subject of a sentence. "The boy hit the ball" is active voice; "The ball was hit by the boy" is passive. Avoid this form in *Plain English.* (The passive voice form of that sentence would be "This form should be avoided in Plain English.") See also *Active voice.* Ch. 2.

Placeholder   In speaking, non-word sounds such as "um" and "err." Ch. 6.

Plain English   An approach to business writing that avoids bureaucratic language and forms. The key elements are short, direct sentences, using the most-common word that expresses meaning and avoiding the passive voice. Ch. 2.

Politically correct (PC)   The concept that certain turns of phrase are unacceptable in American public discourse. It is considered offensive to make disparaging generalized comments of any social group (national origin, gender, ethnicity, sexual orientation) even if that is your personal opinion. Visitors to the US consider this a minefield, but you can be politically correct by avoiding any sentence of the form "All {*name of group*} are {*something critical*}." In addition, carefully choose forms of address which show respect—for example, "women," not "girls" for adult females. See also *Significant other.* Ch. 9.

Portfolio   A folder made of leather or imitation leather, about 12 inches by 9 inches; useful for keeping documents clean and flat and for carrying a notepad. Ch. 13.

Prop   An object used to express a point or get attention in a presentation. Ch. 6.

Q

Q&A (Questions and Answers)   An expected part of almost all speeches and presentations in which members of the audience are invited to ask questions of the speaker. Ch. 6.

Quid pro quo   Literally "this for that." In labor law, an issue in sexual harassment if an employee feels pressured for sexual or personal favors in return for promotion or even just not being fired. Ch. 9.

R

Rate of speech   How fast a presenter speaks (that is, number of words per minute). Ch. 6.

Recipient   The person who will receive a communication. Ch. 5.

Reduction in force, "riffed"   When firms "downsize" (reduce the overall size of their workforce), some employees remain in employment, and the rest have their employment terminated. They are "riffed." Ch. 13

Reference   See ***Taking up references.***

Regrets   A shorthand for saying that a person cannot attend an event. A contraction of the form "I regret I am unable to accept your kind invitation." Ch. 8.

RSVP   An abbreviation for a courtly French phrase, "Repondez, s'il vous plait," literally, "Reply if it pleases you." In American usage, it means "Please let us know whether you are going to attend or not." The phrase "Please RSVP" is a tautology and shows that you don't know what the phrase means, so it's better to say, "RSVP," or in Plain English, "Please reply." Ch. 8.

S

Shadow an employee   The process when a job candidate follows an existing employee around (like a shadow) for all or part of a workday to learn about the job. Ch. 13

Sick leave   Part of all employment agreements that allows a worker to stay at home while ill, and yet still be paid. There are limits on sick leave, and if a person is ill for a long time, his or her salary will be covered (probably at less than 100 percent) by a separate arrangement, "disability." Ch. 10.

Significant other   A politically correct term to refer to the spouse, partner, or live-in boyfriend or girlfriend of someone else. For example, if two unmarried people have been living together, but no one in an office is sure whether they are married, an invitation might read "and please bring your significant other." Ch. 9.

Spam   An e-mail term meaning a message that is sent to a very broad group of people, such as a company-wide message. "Spam" is usually used in the disparaging sense to indicate that the message was sent to many more people than cared to know about the subject. Ch. 4.

Splitting the bill   The process of two or more diners agreeing to divide payment for a bill at the end of a meal. Although people sometimes pay more or less depending on the cost of the items they themselves consumed, it's more usual for people to make a simple mathematical calculation: "$42— that's $14 each" (among three people). Ch. 8.

Stance   In public speaking, where and how the speaker stands. Ch. 6.

Suffix   For a personal name, an addition after the family name to indicate the difference between family members who share the same forename. Example: Lee Jacobsen, Senior and Lee Jacobsen, Junior. Pronounced "Senior" and "Junior" but abbreviated "Sr." and "Jr." in the written form. Ch. 1.

T

Tab or tabulator   Spacing over five or six spaces so that text on successive lines comes in a left-justified block. A holdover term from typewriters. Ch. 5.

Taking up references   The process by which a firm interested in hiring someone calls an associate, former employer, or teacher of a candidate and asks for input on the suitability of the person for a specific position. Ch. 13.

Tchotchke   A small gift of little monetary value, often a souvenir from another country. Ch. 9.

"Thank you" notes   A routine part of polite social behavior. A short letter expressing thanks for hospitality or any other kindness. Ch. 9.

Time management   A set phrase describing the process of being well-organized and prioritizing tasks. Ch. 14.

"To Do" list   A list of action items, probably in order of priority or due date. Part of effective time management. Many computer programs (such as MS Outlook) provide ways to manage To Do lists. Ch. 14.

Tone   The third dimension of written or spoken language. In general, it stretches from warm and friendly to cold and officious. It is independent of level of formality (that is, you can have a formal but friendly letter). Ch. 2.

Twin set   For women, a matching fully-fashioned thin sweater and over-cardigan suitable for business attire. Ch. 11.

Two-martini lunch   A joking term for a business mid-day meal in which strong liquor is consumed, thus diminishing effectiveness in the afternoon. Ch. 8.

U

Universal terms of reference   In polite conversation, a way to refer to someone else without using personal names. For example (to a waiter), "My colleague asked for more dressing," rather than "Helen needs more dressing." Ch. 8.

V

Vesting   The processes by which employees are considered eligible for a benefit (such as pension) that accumulates over time. In the first years of employment, an employee may be paying into a pension plan but would lose all contributions if they were not "vested." Benefit packages will explain how many years of service are required for vesting. Ch. 13.

Video conferencing   A way to arrange meetings without being present in person. A video conference is a phone call with video images of the participants. Ch. 3.

Visual aid   A prop, flip chart, overhead, slides, or projected media accompanying a presentation. Ch. 6.

Index

Tables are indicated by *t*; figures and illustrations are indicated by locators in italics; footnotes are indicated by *n*.

35 mm slides as visual aids, 86*t*, 88
360-degree review, 233

A

Academic honors on resume, 187, 189
Academic major, resume, 187
Access, in new-employee orientation, 226*t*
Account name, e-mail, 47–48
Acknowledgment as business letter type, 71
Action items and daily time management, 229
Action step in voice mail messages, 34–35, 36–37
Active voice
    Plain English preference for, 15–16
    in resumes, 184
Activities section in resume, 189, *195*
ADA (Americans with Disabilities Act), 212–213
Address, parts of business letter, 63, 64
Adobe electronic format for resume, 182
Adversity, dealing with, 223–230, 231–232
Aftershave, 170
Aggregation technique in persuasive presentation, 95
Airport Test, 203–204
Alcohol
    brought to co-worker social function, 136
    consumption and business dining, 125–126, 134
    wine as gift, 137–138
Aliases, e-mail, 52–54
America
    dining experience, 118–119
    informal names, 6–7
    introductions in, 3–5
    long hours worked, 151, 224–225
    nonverbal communication during
        introductions, 4–5
    recruiting in, 178–180

spitting phlegm, 156
    wardrobe size, 164
Americans with Disabilities Act (ADA), 212–213
Annual bonus in offer negotiations, 210*t*
Annual review, 233
Answering business phone, 30–31
Apartment communities' gift, 141
Appearance, professional, video conferencing, 42
Application for employment, 209–210
Archiving old e-mail messages, 55
Arrival time, workday, 224
Asia
    gift opening, 142
    gifts of money, 139–140
    introducing others, 9
    nonverbal communication during introductions, 5
    tea lady duties, 223
"Athletic attire" as business attire, *169*
Athletic club benefits
    in new-employee orientation, 226*t*
    offer negotiations, 211*t*
Attachment to written message, 60, 61, 77
Attending business conferences, trade shows and
        conventions, 143–144
Attention
    attention span during presentations, 83
    in business letter addresses, 63, 64
    of server at restaurant, 129–130, *130*
Attire. *See* Business attire and grooming
Audience heterogeneity, 89–90
Audience in presentations
    knowledge of, 89–90
    size of, 82, 84–85
Awards and honors section in resume, 189–190, *195*